Paul Gleye

Behind the Wall

An American in East Germany, 1988–89

Southern Illinois University Press
Carbondale and Edwardsville

Library of Congress Cataloging-in-Publication Data
Gleye, Paul.
Behind the wall : an American in East Germany, 1988–89 / Paul Gleye.
p. cm.
ISBN 0-8093-1743-5
1. Germany (East)—Politics and government. 2. Germany (East)—
Social life and customs. 3. Gleye, Paul—Homes and haunts—
Germany (East) I. Title.
DD289.G58   1991
943.1087′8—dc20   90-28575
CIP

The paper used in this publication meets the minimum requirements of
American National Standard for Information Sciences—Permanence of
Paper for Printed Library Materials, ANSI Z39.48-1984. ∞

To
Maggie Valentine

Contents

Preface

I N LATE 1989 hundreds of thousands of East German street demonstrators brought down a government that had ruled the country for exactly forty years in fortified isolation from Western society. On November 9, 1989, the "antifascist protection wall" through the center of Berlin, constructed in 1961 to stem the increasing outward migration of East German citizens to the West, was torn apart with hammers and chisels. It was not destroyed by NATO forces from Western Europe, but largely by East German citizens themselves, as masses surged through its new openings to glimpse the bright lights of a world that had been forbidden to them for twenty-eight years. The East Germans climbing over and passing through the Iron Curtain on that November day were not doing so illegally. That very day, in fact, the East German leadership had issued an order allowing all citizens to travel freely to the West for the first time in the country's history.

West Berliners themselves swarmed to the Wall to greet their long-unseen brethren with hugs and invitations to dinner, free rides around the city, and mountains of gifts. Some East Germans went to stay, but many more went merely to see what the West was really like and how it differed from the television images they had viewed for so long. Many more went to shop. Armed with the 100 deutsche mark "welcome money" handed out by West German banks, they bought portable oil-filled electric radiators and stuffed animals, chocolate and books. Most of all, it seems, they bought bananas, a fruit seldom found in East German stores and for many a symbol of their deprivation.

In the chaotic months to follow, East Germany, the country that had been the German Democratic Republic, would be engulfed by West Germany and united with it, but even a month before the fateful November 9, 1989, opening of the Wall this event would have been beyond any anticipation. As East Germany approached its fortieth anniversary on October 7, 1989, the country's communist party, the Socialist Unity party, was still in control, though the momentum for change had reached serious proportions. Thousands of East Germans had already streamed through Hungary's newly opened borders with Austria, and others had taken refuge in the West German embassy in Prague, desperately attempting to reach the West. Unable to convince them to return, the East German government provided trains that would carry them nonstop through East Germany to the West German border city of Hof.

The East German government did not anticipate the response to the refugee trains as they passed through Dresden, in southern East Germany, on their way west. Demonstrators stormed the railroad station, many attempting to climb aboard the trains, others smashing the station windows and milling around the open square shouting their frustrations at the police attempting to disperse them. For the first time since the worker uprising of 1953, East Germans were carrying their political ambitions to the streets, and this time there was no Soviet Army to respond. East Germany suddenly became enmeshed in a "peaceful revolution," as demonstration banners proclaimed, driven not by violence but by the persistent presence of people—many, many people—demanding to be heard. Massive, joyous crowds choked the streets of Leipzig every Monday night, and demonstrators in other cities encircled police buildings with lighted candles, singing songs of peace and freedom. By the end of 1989 the old communist leaders had been forced out in disgrace, charged with corruption and failure.

This drama has been, and will continue to be, the subject of much analysis. The book before you addresses part of this great upheaval—a part that was largely inaccessible to many of those who will probe the transformation of East Germany from a communist society to a liberal democratic one. In order to understand the tenor of this "peaceful revolution" and the attitudes of many East Germans who risked much to bring it about, it is necessary to understand the conditions of life in the country during 1988 and 1989, while the Wall still stood and before anyone could predict *die Wende,* the "turning point," that brought the people to the streets. That is what this book is about.

For ten months, the academic year 1988–89, I lived in the provinces of East Germany as a visiting university professor under the Fulbright academic exchange program. It was only the second year that American Fulbright scholars had been allowed into East Germany, and the first year they could actually teach at a university. Neither a political scientist nor a Marxist, but a city planner interested in issues of urban identity and historic preservation, I lived during my Fulbright tenure as a participant observer in the city of Weimar, where I taught courses at the *Hochschule für Architektur und Bauwesen,* the Higher School of Architecture and Construction. In addition to my scholarly purpose of teaching American architecture and studying East German urban design and preservation issues, I spent much time listening, watching, and traveling in an attempt to figure out how life functioned in the provinces of the German Democratic Republic. I wanted to know what it was like to live under communism and how it affected the people who had grown up there. I wished not only to understand the dissatisfaction that dominated nearly every conversation, but also to discover what was good about the country.

The discussion in this book is the result of my voluminous daily notes, recording images and events that seemed to define East German life. Beyond my own observations, much of what is reported was related to me by East German acquaintances, and I attempted to obtain independent verification of stories I could not vouch for myself. This narrative varies from my notes in two respects. First, some vignettes are actually composites of events and conversations, partly to forge coherent statements without altering the content of assembled notes, and partly to veil my sources from recognition. Second, I renamed places and situations sufficiently to conceal their sources, while keeping the integrity of the statements intact.

The information in Chapter 6 on May Day and Labor Day is taken from Philip S. Foner, *History of the Labor Movement in the United States,* vol. II (New York: International Publishers, 1955), and the Rosa Luxemburg quotation about freedom is from her *The Russian Revolution and Leninism or Marxism?* (Ann Arbor: University of Michigan Press, 1961).

I should like to express my gratitude to the academic exchange program inspired by Senator J. William Fulbright in 1946, immediately after the devastation of the Second World War. It has enabled many of us who have chosen the academic profession to live and work in other cultures, from which we can learn to improve our own. I hope this volume can help encourage the United States Congress to maintain the Fulbright program in good health for years to come.

Much of the manuscript was written after my return, during an extended stay in Ron and Judy Hess' Torch and Toes Bed and Breakfast in Bozeman, Montana, where discussions with the guests who came and went helped me sort through my ideas. Specifically I wish to thank Marilyn White and Pamela Bancroft, both of Montana State University, for commenting on earlier drafts of the manuscript, and especially Patricia Deeg. Her thoughtful command of the English language returned me to clarity where I had strayed from it. Attempting to forge a coherent narrative from a file of notes reminds one of the seemingly effortless dancing of Fred Astaire, who spent grueling hours perfecting his technique so that it would look spontaneous.

The book is dedicated to Maggie Valentine, who assisted me greatly to understand what I had witnessed. She is an unceasing fount of insights into the human condition. Many of my stories began as letters to her from Weimar.

During the ten months covered in this narrative I made numerous friends and visited historic artifacts of Western culture that few Americans had seen for over two generations. I endured late trains slicing through the night air laden with brown coal smoke and lived as the East Germans did—without bananas, but with plenty of red cabbage. I broke bread with communists who believed in Marx as Patrick Henry believed in America and with people who saw themselves wandering through life with a bear trap on their legs and a mousetrap on their lips.

Unfortunately I cannot name those whose lives are revealed in these pages but hope History will be as good to them as they were to me.

Behind the Wall

1

Meeting the Mayor

THE VILLAGE of four hundred residents had an old church, modest in scale yet imposing in its neatly joined masonry and wooden altar. It was falling apart. A large, carefully fitted stone at the upper corner supporting the roof frame had worked its way loose, and villagers had propped it in place with an old telephone pole braced to the ground. A few villagers in their spare time had attempted to keep the church from further deterioration, but water was seeping into the walls and mildew was destroying the mortar. The mayor gave us a tour and explained the problem, but he saw no solution to the falling-down church. There was no money forthcoming from the state, especially since the country's budget for preserving historic buildings was cut by 40 percent that year, 1989. Even if there were funds, it would be difficult to find the workers necessary for restoration. There were plenty of jobs in East Germany, many more jobs than workers, and few people wanted to come to the village when they could find permanent work in the city. The stabilization had been carried out by a free-time brigade, called a *Feierabendbrigade,* but there were many other things to be done in one's free time such as repairing one's own house. Even that could be difficult because materials were in such short supply.

The villagers had discussed among themselves what should be done, but nobody had made much effort to do anything because the church did not actually belong to anybody. After the war village churches such as this

1

were taken over by the state, since religion had been declared a vestige of the old capitalist order, and the people were discouraged from entering. Early on one would have "received disadvantage" from the local Socialist Unity (communist) party leaders for entering the church. In East Germany, one tried to avoid doing things that suggested antisocialist attitudes because they brought disadvantage from the Party. The Party distributed many things necessary to live comfortably, and people with disadvantage seemed not to receive them. It was better merely to mind one's own business, because other people knew one's beliefs only when one said something. It was much safer to wait until the Party made a decision, and then there would be no disadvantage in agreeing.

Since the early 1950s when East Germany—the German Democratic Republic—was being forged from the former Zone of Soviet Occupation as the "first workers' and farmers' state on German territory," many of the old churches had been returned to the custody of the Evangelical or Roman Catholic church administration. With the help of contributions by West German churches, some had been restored where enough parishioners had returned to the fold. Officially, however, this church still belonged to the state. That meant it belonged to the people of the village, but only a few of them cared about architecture or religion. So occasionally, about every ten years or so, the district historic preservation committee would come around to assess its condition and mark down on a card what had happened to the church since the last visit. The card said there had been a pair of eighteenth-century candlesticks behind the altar, but they were not to be found on this visit of the preservation committee, who had invited me to come along. On the card went the entry, "Expropriation of people's property: two candlesticks, eighteenth century."

Also in the village were many old farmsteads, typically composed of a house in front along the street, with a gate to the farmyard between the house and the large, half-timber barn complex behind. Most of the barns had stood empty and useless for years in this village, as in many villages. Many had been empty since those early postwar years when agricultural land was removed from private landowners and turned over to the LPGs, the *Landwirtschaftliche Produktionsgenossenschaften,* or agricultural cooperatives. Large tractor stations, storage and processing facilities were built outside the villages, taking the old uses from the barns. Only the houses had continued to be lived in, and ever fewer of these were cared for as generational change had brought fewer people to the villages to replace those who passed on.

The mayor's house was a typical half-timber farmhouse dating from the eighteenth century. Its street facade had been restored because the house was a historic landmark and part of an ensemble of half-timber houses so designated in the village. A small baked-enamel plaque on the front of the house announced its landmark status. Though the view from the street suggested a romantic eighteenth-century German farming village, the house inside was a ruin. It had been uncared for during forty years' time, since World War II in fact, and no state funds were available for renovation. The mayor, who had purchased it for a thousand marks a few years previously as part of the country's "citizens' initiative" (*Bürgerinitiative*) program, had been trying to repair it. He could have the materials to do so, since one of his jobs was to allocate things such as building materials to the villagers, at least to those who had not received disadvantage—*"Nachteil kriegen,"* as the East Germans said—but he felt that the villagers' needs should come first. The mayors' houses in some villages had new concrete driveways and interiors embellished with new wood trim, but this mayor wished not to appear as one who took advantage of his position. Yes, he said, there was a timber industry in East Germany, but much of the lumber was exported to West Germany for hard currency.

Heating the mayor's house was accomplished by the usual tile furnaces in each room fueled by brown coal. Every fall a truck brought a load of coal and dumped it into the street in front of his house. Since he was mayor, he could have had the coal shoveled directly into his basement, but he chose to shovel it himself, just as other villagers had to do. Brown coal was a problem because it was so sulfur-laden that during cold winter nights the smoke from every house's several chimneys billowed down into the street and made breathing difficult, but brown coal was the only source of heating fuel in East Germany. It came from huge strip mines near Leipzig and was shipped by train all over the country.

The mayor's house had hot and cold water and indoor plumbing because he, on his own initiative, had installed it. But there were so few materials with which to undertake rehabilitation work that, beyond the basic necessities, the house was just hanging together. To the rear, the cavernous barns were caving in. Roofs were falling as the half timbering rotted from fungi that attacked the wood in the moist climate. The mayor would have liked to restore his barns as an example for the villagers, but the people needed the materials more than did his barns. In West Germany, he told me, such village farmsteads would be purchased by "yuppies," or people with collections of antique automobiles who could use the storage spaces, or perhaps bought by developers to turn into rustic condominium units. In East Germany, however, there were no such people and no such condominiums. He could buy his house because it was just big enough for one family, but there were houses in the village too large for a single family. These had to be rehabilitated by a state-enterprise housing cooperative, and the housing cooperatives could provide dwellings faster and cheaper by building large prefabricated concrete panel housing complexes. Luckily there were none of these in this village, said the mayor, because the village was too small to warrant their construction.

In West Germany, he also knew, people could buy an old house like his, fix it up, then sell it for a profit that would enable them to buy another house and fix it in turn. He could, of course, sell his house, the mayor told me, but not for a profit. The price was set by the state and maintained at a very low level precisely to assure that nobody would make a profit from selling a house. Under socialism, where one earned money from one's labor, it was inappropriate to engage in exploitation (*Ausbeutung*) by making such unearned income. The mayor liked his house, though, and over the course of several years he would finish repairing it to have a cozy place when he retired and room for his three children to visit. He was not concerned about losing his job as mayor, because as long as he was loyal to the Party he would be reelected, though he was concerned about how long the Party might last since everyone knew by then that the country would have to change. Nobody knew how it would change, or when. The upper levels of the Party had to do something, but everybody also knew that the upper levels had no idea what to do. The mayor had some suggestions, but he could only speak to the functionaries at the district level, and he had to be careful what he said in order not to receive disadvantage himself.

So it was in East Germany during the spring of 1989, half a year before the Berlin Wall would come down and the Communist party would reluctantly abdicate its role as the sole guardian of the socialist future. As I sat in the mayor's living room, I was still trying to understand this Party and how it had seemed to organize all thought and action in what was still a tightly controlled country.

"Why did you join the Party?" I asked him. He looked around the group sitting in his living room. They were his friends, these historic preservation people, and the evening was getting late. We had been drinking plenty of beer from heavy glass returnable bottles that came from the VEB

Brewery "Pilsator," and by this time I was his friend too. "VEB" were the initials for *"volkseigener Betrieb,"* the "People's Own Enterprise," proclaiming the way industries were organized in socialist East Germany. The other guests had been listening intently to his stories and had made sure I, an American visitor, was understanding. *"Kapierst Du?"* they asked me over and over. "Do you get what he's saying? That's the way it is here in The Zone!"

Yes, I understood. Thuringian German accents are not the farthest removed from High German, as German accents go. That honor might go to *Schwäbisch*, from a region in southern West Germany, to say nothing of *Schwytzerdütsch*, the Swiss reorganization of the language. But I had spent a long time learning German, first as a teenage "army brat" while my father was stationed in West Germany, then majoring in German at the University of Wyoming, then writing my Ph.D. dissertation on the postwar reconstruction of Münster in West Germany, once I decided my real interest lay in planning to preserve historic buildings. Thuringian German is something else again, since the people pronounce their *o*'s like *u*'s and their *l*'s so high in their mouth they sound like *i*'s, but I was getting the hang of it, and I had been there a while.

For ten months, the academic year 1988–89, I had the opportunity to live in the provinces of East Germany as a visiting university professor. I had taken a leave from my teaching position in the School of Architecture at Montana State University to live and work in Weimar, the city of Goethe and Schiller, and the first home of the famous Bauhaus that all architects know about. It was an opportunity few Americans had had for nearly sixty years, to live an everyday life deep in East Germany. Nobody could then foresee the shattering political changes in store for the country by the end of that year, though many hoped or feared that the threshold was near, and nobody knew how those changes might affect their lives. It was a year full of intense frustration, intellectual speculation, and growing resentment.

Weimar was quite a different place from East Berlin, or rather "Berlin, Capital of the German Democratic Republic," as it was invariably called. Four hours away by train from the capital, it was far from the Wall, far from "Radio in the American Sector," far from capital-city gossip, from the embassies and foreign diplomats, and from the opportunity—for me, anyway—to stop by West Berlin for an afternoon to read the *International Herald Tribune* and have a salad with real lettuce for lunch. Out in the provinces one was in the heartland of that staid communist state, one of the last orthodox Marxist-Leninist holdouts.

During my tenure, East Germany was still a very secretive place, much unlike the West Germany of Heidelberg and Neuschwanstein that Americans know and love, but it was nevertheless Germany, a country strongly influencing North American culture, a place from which many of our ancestors came, part of the industrialized world, with the same history until 1945 as that of West Germany. Yet for Americans East Germany had long had a forbidding sense, partly because they could hardly go there. One could peek behind the Wall in East Berlin for a day, or take a short package tour to trace the wanderings of Martin Luther or Johann Sebastian Bach. Business people had traveled to the Leipzig trade fairs. But these brief encounters gave little insight into what East Germany was *like;* what it was *really* like to live there within that system that still seemed so hostile and impenetrable. One could talk about the police state, about scarce consumer goods, about the Wall—but though these were all part of the picture, they alone did not convey the reality of living within that system against which the NATO troops in Western Europe were defending us.

I went to East Germany with as open a mind as I could muster. To be sure I wanted to learn how socialist cities were planned, how they preserved their historic buildings; but I had more fundamental questions as well. Was life in East Germany really like that portrayed in films such as Alfred Hitchcock's *Torn Curtain?* Were there positive attributes of the system that had governed East Germany for forty years, and was there something to be said for East Germany that Americans had missed? Why indeed were so many people trying to leave, but also why did so many others wish to stay, despite their unhappiness? With these and other questions in mind I packed my suitcase full of slides showing American architecture, flew from Montana to Frankfurt, and hopped on the daily train linking the two Germanies, plying between the West German metropolis, Frankfurt am Main, and the East German city called Frankfurt an der Oder, lying far *hinten,* "in the back," as the East Germans said, on the Polish border. Enroute it stopped in Weimar.

At the architecture school in Weimar I taught my classes in American architecture, showing students things they had never seen, such as slides of everyday towns and American life. For their assignment, I had them redesign the Main Street of a typical American small town. I wanted to see what students with a socialist upbringing would recommend for revitalizing American towns. Since my teaching load was light and I was thankfully excluded from faculty meetings, not being a Party member, I had plenty of time to travel. In my ten months I visited about a hundred cities and towns, traveled with students to their homes on weekends to be shown the sights and meet friends and family, met with city architects, toured housing developments, gave lectures about American life, answered a thousand questions about America, and drank plenty of People's Own Enterprise Pilsator.

So there I was in the village during the spring of 1989, with the mayor and his friends from the historic preservation committee, and I asked, "Why did you join the Party?"

He stared thoughtfully into his Pilsator for a moment. "Ah, it was an earlier age," he slowly replied. "It was a time when there was much idealism, when socialism could be made to work, when the way to participate in the great future was to join the Party, become an *Insider,* as East Germans say. Once I was in there was no way out, since one cannot merely leave the Party. So why am I living in this little village? It's my way of being a dropout, an *Aussteiger.* There are a lot of dropouts here, you know. People hide away in the cities, doing whatever, not participating, or maybe they become active in the church groups. Others hide in the country, living in villages with their animals, doing whatever. You don't need money here, so if you want to you can fade away. Except that I can't fade away because I'm in the Party, so this is about the closest I can come to it. There are good people here. The village Party cadre is composed of four old men in their nineties, and I meet with them occasionally, but other than that I can try to make life a little better here and raise my family."

The hour was late, the Pilsator finally gone, and the mayor gave us each a room for the night in his rambling house, every room with an old couch or something else soft on which to sleep. We said we had to get up early because we had more inspections to make in the morning.

"Yes, and I have to go report myself."

"Report yourself?"

"As mayor I am not allowed contact with Western foreigners. So I must go the Party office and report that I had contact with you. But what could I do? You arrived with the inspection committee. I didn't know you were coming, although I really did of course, so I must say this was an event beyond my control and part of my mayoral duties to be hospitable. I must concoct some conversation we had, to demonstrate that I told you about the wonderful life here in the German Democratic Republic. But it's no big deal. It will look good on paper and nobody will question it."

As we left the next morning he took me by the arm, "Just remember what Lenin said: 'There can never be a revolution in Germany because you aren't allowed to walk on the grass.'"

2

Little Superman:
An American behind the Iron Curtain

AN AMERICAN in East Germany, unlike an American in Paris, was an uncommon sight in 1989. While many Americans roamed the streets of Munich or Cologne, once one crossed the border into "the other German state," or "The Zone," as the locals had wryly nicknamed their former Soviet zone of occupation, foreigners were noticeably less present and took on a different character. Most visible, of course, were the Russian soldiers in their handsome, well tailored uniforms with bright red epaulettes sporting the Cyrillic initials "SA," for "Soviet Army." One often encountered African "factory apprentices" eating in the inexpensive and handy railroad station restaurants. There were also occasional Russian and Czech tourists who traveled about in tight groups, politely listening to the sing-song voice of a local tour guide describing the significance of a historic monument.

Then there were the Poles. Almost daily the benches along the pedestrian streets in the center of many East German cities were commandeered by Poles who brought things to sell—brightly colored plastic belts, denim jackets, sweaters, jewelry. These individual entrepreneurs provided inexpensive goods unavailable in East Germany and, with their profits, bought East German goods to take to Poland. "We leave them pretty much alone, since they don't hurt anything," one Party member said to me, although the police would pick them up regularly and ship them back to Poland by train. Polish traders had engendered some strong resentment among East

Germans because they tended to buy large quantities of low-priced, state-subsidized goods such as baby clothes, leaving an insufficient supply for East German mothers.

In addition, a steady stream of West Germans passed through East Germany, many coming to Weimar as tourists. Locally called the *"Bundis,"* after *Bundesrepublik Deutschland*—translating something like the "Feds," after "Federal Republic of Germany"—the West Germans made the rounds of Friedrich Schiller's and Wolfgang von Goethe's houses, both refurbished as museums displaying artifacts of the great authors' lives; Goethe's and Schiller's sarcophagi lying side by side in the basement of a building constructed to house their remains; and Buchenwald concentration camp, lying a few kilometers north of Weimar. Easily identified by their brightly colored clothes and jaunty manner, the *Bundis* tended to be less regimented than the other foreigners, since they were completely at home with the language and German culture, which despite the socialist veneer had not changed all that much in the forty years of a divided country.

Most tourists in East Germany, however, were the East Germans themselves. Outside the major tourist cities of Weimar, Leipzig, and Dresden, and East Berlin of course, foreign tourists were hardly to be seen at all. In East Berlin, American as well as French and British soldiers roamed around under the four-power agreement, making East Berlin a very different place from the rest of the country. With stringent visa requirements and expensive Interhotel bookings that one had to make before entering East Germany proper, Americans as well as most other NSW, or "non-socialist economic state" (*nichtsozialistisches Wirtschaftsland*) foreigners were usually limited to a short stay in controlled surroundings. It was difficult to get off the beaten path to cities like Bitterfeld or Zeitz, or to meet the locals.

The nearly total lack of foreign tourism in East Germany created some situations that, along with the brown coal smoke hanging in the winter air, seemed to transport one back to prewar Europe. I visited Quedlinburg, a small town with a historic center almost entirely composed of intact half-timber houses, the medieval building form of massive wooden frameworks filled in with masonry. Its narrow, cobblestone streets wandered up to a massive church set on the side of a hill. Quedlinburg was a storybook place, one that revealed as almost no other the charm and wonder of Old Europe, and the entire was listed as a historic monument of international significance on UNESCO's World Heritage List. If the town were in West Germany it would vie with Rothenburg ob der Tauber as an enchanting tourist stop for Americans. On a weekend there might be four hundred tourist buses parked in the market place. Every tiny half-timber house would have been renovated as a boutique, ice cream stand, or expensive restaurant. The throngs in the streets would be so great in August that one would hardly expect to see the buildings.

In Quedlinburg, DDR, or *Deutsche Demokratische Republik,* as the German Democratic Republic was called in German, there were four tourist buses in the parking lot when I visited one Saturday afternoon in May. The town's three restaurants were crowded at lunch, but one expected a twenty-minute wait before being seated in a restaurant in almost any city at lunchtime. There were a few camera-laden East Germans wandering the streets, and one of the old houses at the entrance to the church grounds had been turned into a shop selling postcards. The town's oldest half-timber house had been restored as a museum of half-timber architecture, mainly containing large photographs of other buildings in the town. Other than that Quedlinburg had remained a real town, absent almost any pretentiousness. It was wonderful to be there, to enjoy a beautiful place and be nearly alone, with nobody selling dark glasses or plastic eye visors.

The scarcity of foreigners not only affected one's response to the country but also affected the people's response to foreigners and to the cultures they represented. Because contacts with Americans were so limited, because so few East Germans could leave to see the United States for themselves, or visit nearly any other place for that matter, and because rock music, movies, and other cultural influences readily penetrated the Iron Curtain from America, I found that East Germans, sometimes called the "*Ostis*" (*Ost* means East), tended to be fascinated by the United States. This fascination was fueled by the extremes in which America was made visible to them. At one extreme were the articles in the daily paper *Neues Deutschland* ("New Germany"), published by the SED, the country's communist party, officially the "Socialist Unity Party of Germany" (*Sozialistische Einheitspartei Deutschlands*). *Neues Deutschland* reported a fairly constant stream of bad news about the States. The militaristic stance of the Bush administration was a frequent topic when I was there, as were oil spills, train wrecks, and swindles. The newspaper reported extensively on the *Exxon Valdez* disaster and the Boeing aircraft problems in early 1989, and information was presented to suggest that the cause for such malfunctions was capitalist rapaciousness, the placing of profit over human welfare. Other articles reported various ceremonial events that were of no consequence. A complete list of articles referring to the United States that appeared in *Neues Deutschland* during the first two weeks of May 1989 sets the tone:

- U.S. refuses to withdraw troops from Europe.
- Bush continues Reagan's militaristic policy.
- U.S. refuses to negotiate short-range missiles.
- U.S. government will continue to refuse entry to "undesirable foreigners" on ideological grounds.
- U.S. construction workers' real income fell by 3.3 percent in 1988.
- Jimmy Carter wants Bush to negotiate short-range missiles.
- U.S. warplane drops bomb in Georgia.
- U.S. interferes in Panamanian elections.
- U.S. sends Battleship *Iowa* back into service without repairing the exploded gun turret.
- U.S. hit by disastrous tornadoes.
- U.S. police arrest peace protesters.
- Thirty-seven million Americans without health insurance.
- One million U.S. citizens in prison.
- Two hundredth anniversary of George Washington's inauguration.
- Five hundred thousand mice killed in fire in animal laboratory in Maine.

At the other extreme were the American films constantly offered in theaters and on television. DDR television showed occasional American films, though it preferred Russian films, but West German television offered a steady diet of American films to those East Germans living outside the "Valley of the Ignorant," the area around Dresden where Western television did not reach. It also regularly aired "Dallas" and "Dynasty," the latter renamed as "The Denver Clan." Whenever I brought out my map of the United States to show people the country, the first question often was, "Well, show me where Dallas and Denver are." The students seemed to be more interested in hearing about Montana State University when I told them it was about 850 kilometers northwest of Denver than when I described its setting in a picturesque Alpine valley in the Rocky Mountains.

"Is life in America really like we see in 'Denver' and 'Dallas'?" was part of the litany of questions I came to expect. I assumed at first that people were kidding me, but I came to be less sure as I gauged the response to my answers. I told them to remember that these programs were actually made for American audiences. "Would you watch a program about the everyday life of some factory manager in the DDR? Why not? Because it's too boring, eh? Well, Americans wouldn't watch a program about anybody's everyday life either. You Germans have a better expression for the appeal of these shows than we do: *'Schadenfreude'*, the joy at others' misfortunes, especially if they are rich, beautiful, and powerful. This is pure fantasy, based not on capitalism but on human nature: lust, intrigue, getting even, loving to hate the bad guy. Americans like 'Dallas' for the same reasons you do."

At the same time, the two programs did provide spellbinding images of capitalist life for those peering in the window. When one coupled them with Western movies (East German television showed *Shane*) wherein moral tensions are played out in the magnificent empty landscape of the western states, and with films like Neil Diamond's *The Jazz Singer,* where incredible dreams come true and hard-boiled capitalists have soft hearts, one begins to imagine the extremes with which the United States was viewed by a people who had never seen it.

The extremes were intensified by the tendency of West German television to search out the bizarre in America and gleefully report it. One bimonthly West German television program, entitled "Pictures from America," reported on such American goings-on as elderly, homespun, normally reserved housewives vaulting up onto the stage and dancing around ecstatically as Bob Barker yelled out "A New CAR!" on "The Price Is Right." To many East Germans, who perceived glimpses of America only through television, the American world seemed partly characterized by lunacy. The general media repertoire accessible to the East Germans suggested that America was a gigantic, sunny land of lanky cowboys and tanned women living totally spontaneously and ordering pizzas on the telephone while eating squishy white bread and mindlessly buying detergent they saw on television. Electronic wizardry freed these Americans from normal work so they could spend their time plotting to disenfranchise the working class and exploit the Third World, unless they were busy killing people, robbing banks, and driving their cars off cliffs.

So when word spread through the School of Architecture in Weimar that an American was coming, the image was that of some heroic figure who would guffaw a lot, chew gum, and pat everybody on the back. Only after I had been there for several months was the true response to my arrival divulged to me. On the one hand, there was incredulity that it was not, in fact, John Wayne who appeared, but a modestly human, bearded, five-feet, seven-inch man. The prevailing attitude toward this apparition was probably best summed up by someone after of one my lectures on American architecture: "This Gleye can't be a *real* American. In the first place he speaks German, and in the second place he isn't tall. Americans are tall." On the other hand my unassuming demeanor probably helped me make friends, as people realized they did not have to contend with John Wayne but with someone closer to a normal mortal. My ancestry also won me some friends and opened doors. It did not take long before my associates knew that in the 1850s my paternal great-grandparents had come from the cities of Dresden and Stendal, both in what would become East Germany. This fact was made a standard part of introductions and dispelled a lot of curiosity about why an American would voluntarily live in the Zone for a year.

I quickly learned never to anticipate attitudes about the United States. One day not long after I arrived, one of the secretaries told me she had a book about the United States she wanted me to see. The book, entitled *American Images,* was written by a Dane, Jakob Holt, who had traveled around the States for five years in the early 1970s. He searched for and lived with the poorest of the poor, the least able to cope, the residents of drug-wasted ghettos and those who had fallen hardest between the cracks of American society. His text rampaged against capitalists and warmongers who sold out their own people for private profit, and described the gory details of wasted lives and disease-infested bodies. His pictures, hundreds of them, showed close-ups of skin lesions caused by malnutrition, squalid living conditions, rotting alleys. One double-page spread contained many photos of people taking the same pose: undernourished, sickly, dirty people sitting at a table with empty beer bottles in front of them, heads in hands, staring blankly into space.

The book, which originally appeared in Danish but of which a German version was published in the DDR, carried a preface stating that the dream images of America were well known, but here was the reality of capitalist exploitation. "The book gives the citizens of socialist states new confidence in their own system," continued the preface, "and also reminds one that compassion is needed for the true plight of many Americans." That no American publisher would accept the book was evidence that the United States was not the free society its propaganda claimed.

"What did you think of the book?" asked the secretary. I stammered something unintelligible. "Well, of course those things exist," I finally said, "but you must understand that we are a huge nation of 250 million people, and we do have some problems, but the author has really found the extremes. I don't wish to hide realities, but if you were to go there I'm sure you would not find this to be representative of American life. . . ."

"This is our *Feindbild* of America," she interrupted, obviously not interested in my answer. "Our 'image of the enemy.' " German has many handy words that English lacks. "Of course that's why it was published here. But do you know what? He spent FIVE years hitchhiking around the States to do this book. Can you imagine, FIVE YEARS? *Au, Mann,* it would be great to hitchhike for FIVE years around the States. That would be impossible to do here. We are so crammed into this little country and can't go anywhere. You know, there's this joke:

'On our vacation we drove all the way around East Germany.'

'Yeah, but what did you do in the afternoon?'"

This fascination for America became evident when the architecture students invited me to give a lecture on "Everyday Life in the United States" at the local student club one cold January night. I put together my slides and on the evening of the lecture arrived at the club early to prepare the projector, but when I arrived I found that many students had preceded me. Already, nearly an hour early, they began filling the room, and the air was electric. The hall filled to its capacity of sixty, and they kept coming, bringing stools and pillows, up to a hundred people, soon crowding on the floor, perching on the windowsills. Like deprived soldiers in town for the weekend, they charged the air with anticipation of the naughty revelations to come. "This is the biggest crowd in years," said the organizer. "We can't get them here for talks on socialist countries; they've had it up to here. A few weeks ago we had a lecture on 'New Developments in Socialist Architecture' and packed in twelve."

I cleared a small patch of floor at the front on which to stand, and began. My modest opening statement, that I had flown back from Weimar to Los Angeles for Christmas and had taken these slides, or rather their response to my statement, set the evening's tone. It brought forth a burst of laughter and cheers as if I had just committed some outrageous act, which in their terms I suppose I had. The late December days had been clear in Los Angeles, and my slides revealed the Southern California paradise that the reality so often hides. The clear blue skies heightened the sense of forbidden delight the students had come to see, making the gray, brown-coaled haze of Central European midwinter days seem even more gloomy.

"American society can be characterized as rather loose," I said, "and Los Angeles is even looser." Echoes of something like "All right!" and "Yeah, man!" from the audience. I showed slides of idiosyncratic houses with crenellated towers and phony Spanish facades. The students laughed. I showed modest homes and spoke of the American dream, "a single-family home with grass around it, two cars, and a dog." They roared. "This is my house," I noted offhandedly, showing the huge Moorish Revival pile of an ex-resort hotel in Pasadena where I had my apartment. It looked like something only a drug king would live in. Cheers and laughter brought down the walls. Of course I explained it was not *only* my house, that there were fifty apartments in this old hotel, and spoke of the unending rush to California in search of the Mediterranean paradise on the Pacific. Titters. "This is how we eat," flashing a McDonald's, then an interior photo with people waiting to order. "Even Americans stand in line." I had hit home, since lines seemed to be everywhere in East Germany. Hands slapped knees and grabbed stomachs, and the hall rocked with laughter.

"This is where we buy food," showing the interior of a supermarket, especially the vegetable department. Rapt silence until I pointed to a section of shelf with red bottles from top to bottom. "This is all ketchup." Peals anew, and cries of "Can you BELIEVE it?!" Ketchup was popular in East Germany; it went with their french fries as well as with ours. The problem was that there wasn't any. There weren't any tomatoes, actually, which made it hard to make ketchup. I showed a shopping mall, with the weather-protected indoor pedestrian street, and then a laundromat. "If you really want to get to know America, go to the laundromat." Murmurs of doubt in the audience. Don't all Americans have washing machines? Every East German family wants one. Then a crafty subterfuge. A slide of the interior of a photocopy store, with the "Open 24 hours" sign in plain view. "You can copy recipes at two in the morning," was met with a general "Mmnh," in Weimar where the most popular copy machine was still a sheet of carbon paper. "Here is how we celebrate," with pictures of the Tournament of Roses parade. Among the slides of flower-bedecked floats, which seemed to the East German students like an unconscionable waste, I showed an inflated Superman looking like he was flying between the buildings. "Superman!" exclaimed the audience. "People camp out on the streets beginning the day before the parade and stay up all night having a huge party," I noted. In East Germany, of course, people would not camp out on the streets, and if they did it would not be for a party.

For my finale I had taken slides of Chinatown and a Hispanic district in Los Angeles and had bought Chinese and Spanish tape cassettes so I could synchronize the slides to music. My Spanish song was a typically poignant piece about a macho man's suffering from lost love, as only the Norteño music, the country music of northern Mexico, could express it, and the slides of low riders, taco stands, Mexicatessens, and "credito facil" signs flipped images before their eyes that they never had imagined as the United States. "We say we're a melting pot, but we're really more of a salad." I ended with a sign, in front of a particularly junky garage, hand painted with "Tires New Used Retreads Llantas Nuevas Usadas," and decorated with red, white, and green painted tires—the national colors of Mexico. My audience was becoming exhausted from laughter. Then photos of the entirely different atmosphere of Chinatown, with pagoda restaurants and people sitting in the plazas reading Chinese and Vietnamese newspapers. "Acupuncture, where East meets West," reads the sign. "You won't believe it, but this is American music," I said as I played a Chinese-language disco cut. The room was drunk with glee. With my last slide, a skywritten happy face in the blue California sky with the airplane ducking out of the corner, I ended with "Greetings from America!"

Never in my life had a lecture of mine been greeted by such spontaneous, thunderous applause. It was certainly not just applause for the lecturer from Los Angeles and Montana; it was applause for a whole vision of life that represented blue skies and freedom, spontaneity and extravagance, a vision where the embers of fantasy glowed ever brighter so long as the people were forbidden from testing the reality.

Once something approaching sanity returned to the lecture hall, the questions began coming. Is is true that when you say, "How are you?" the response is always "Fine," even when things are not fine? Is it true that anybody can to go a university who wants to? Are all American children really as sassy and witty as they are in the American television shows? What do you eat for breakfast? Is American beer as bad as we hear? And the inevitable, that I was asked so many times, "Why would an American want to come to East Germany anyway?" The more pointed questions came from the smaller group gathered around afterward. What about the blacks and the Indians? Why does your armaments industry control your politics? Are people really homeless? For days afterward I heard students talking about this lecture, two people from other universities invited me to give it to their student clubs, and the organizer said to me, "You know, you are really the little Superman, coming here from America and showing all your slides."

It was difficult to tell what people actually knew or did not know about the United States, but several points emerged often enough to suggest that many East Germans did not know, for example, that the United States had a volunteer army (all East German men had to serve for two years, and there was pressure to serve for three), or that American citizens carried no national ID card or "personal identification number" (Every East German had such a number, which included one's date of birth). "How do the police know where you are?" they asked. They did not know that the United States indeed had pension plans and health insurance, or that the American government had adopted fairly stringent auto safety and occupational health regulations. These were not normal topics on "Dallas" and were not part of the information their government provided them about America.

I spent a weekend in a village as far out in the middle of nowhere as one could get in East Germany, with a group who had been devoting their spare time to rescuing an old windmill. Such things were accomplished by groups called "interest associations" (*Interessengemeinschaften*), formed by people who would take an interest in something and decide to devote their spare time to pursuing it. There was not all that much to do in one's free time, except perhaps attend an activity at the local house of culture, and a rule of human nature seems to be that when people have nothing to do they will find something to do. So people tended to band together, decide on a program, have it approved by an official organization such as the League of Culture (*Kulturbund*), and set about their task.

It was a very socialist notion, this *Interessengemeinschaft,* of people devoting their spare time to improving some aspect of society. A number of old windmills still stood in the East German countryside, no longer in use and ravaged by neglect, and windmill interest associations had sprung up around the country to save them. Some members even hoped eventually to make bread the old-fashioned way, from flour they would grind themselves at the mill. The particular association I visited at the village included local people whose ancestors had lived there for generations, plus professionals from the cities who had never seen a windmill in operation but who sought an opportunity to get out into the country and restore old wood with their bare hands. Architecture students from Weimar had drawn up restoration plans, and some of the students were there too.

The windmill in question had finally been rendered watertight with a temporary roof of tin sheets laid over the top, and it was time to celebrate. As we assembled in the village bar where the group had reserved the back room, word went around that an *Ami,* an American, was among them. I was certainly the first American most of the villagers had ever seen. As I wandered through the front room where the regulars drank beer I noticed first a few stares, then finger points and nods. Then, "Hey man, come over here a minute. Listen, you're not really an American, are you? Actually from the United States? Naw, show us your passport. By golly, look at that. Wow, that's sure a surprise. Well, tell us, how do you like it here in the Zone? You know, you work your butt off around here and can't get ahead. You always need connections. It must be a lot better in America, where everything works and everything is easy." We drank and toasted, bought more beers all around, and I promised to send them a postcard from the States. "Yes, one showing those skyscrapers. Is is true that sunlight never hits the streets between them?"

Children often seemed fascinated by the American as well. On one of my trips I traveled the three-hundred-mile length of East Germany north to Rostock on the Baltic Sea, in my view the country's most beautiful city. As I sauntered down a street and stopped to photograph a fountain with bronze statues of revolutionary high-seas fishermen, three eight-year-old girls playing in the fountain approached me with the question I often received from children, "Oh, mister, would you take our picture?" I obliged with several pictures, first together, then each girl separately because each insisted on striking her own silly pose by the bronze fishermen. As we chatted they noticed my accent and asked where I was from. "Oh, America! Is everything beautiful in America?" Suddenly they were asking me to send them things from America, mainly brands of chocolate they had seen advertised on West German television. These questions were interspersed by ones like, "Do you have drugs?" obviously not knowing what a drug was, except for something terrible-wonderful that happened only in the West. And then, "Hey, can we come to America too?" No, but I promised them a postcard.

One evening in Stralsund, a Baltic Sea city with a large naval base, I was eating dinner at a table by myself in the *Ratskeller*. One of the great German traditions is the restaurant in the basement of the town hall, usually a building several centuries old, where vaulted rooms and traditional German cooking make for a truly Gothic experience. One often shared tables with strangers in East German restaurants since they were usually crowded, and two Poles came and sat at my table. Soon we were joined by an East German sailor in his crisply ironed white uniform. He would not have sat there had he known my nationality, since a sailor could receive disadvantage for talking to an American, but he stayed and we chatted. The two Poles, who spoke no German and a little English, were the East German equivalent of "guest workers," though officially there were no guest workers as there were in West Germany. They were working under contract at a nearby agricultural cooperative, where Poles could earn more than they could in similar positions in Poland. Having just been paid, they were out for a night on the town, buying me brandy I did not want, questioning my manhood when I did not drink it, and busy doing black market money exchanges for West German marks with an African "apprentice" who apparently had some direct line to West German financial sources. They bought cigarettes all around, filled the table with empty beer bottles and piled the ash trays with cigarette butts.

The East German sailor, part of a helicopter squadron, and also out on the town, was a clean-cut, naïve, wide-eyed youth, and after the "Oh, wow, an American. That's something for me, boy, but I really shouldn't be talking to you," we got to talking. "The navy? Well, in the navy we learn how West Germany is ready to attack us, but I have friends in West Germany and, although I have never been there, I can't really believe they are our enemy. Being in the navy isn't so bad for my military service, since I get plenty of time off to come to town. The poor guys in the army get only one weekend every three months, and the border troops have it roughest of all. They hardly ever get time off. They have to be on standby for national holidays like May Day and be on guard when dignitaries come to Berlin. Hey, thanks for your address. I'll send you a postcard in Montana. . . ." In the meantime the two Poles had left us, leaving the table entirely heaped with cigarette butts and beer bottles. The waitress came by, obviously assuming I was a German myself since I was chatting away with the sailor, and leaned over to whisper in our ears, "What were they, anyway, Polacks or Russians?"

Everywhere I went, it appeared, people were enthusiastic that an American had come to visit—except when I had to do with Party officials—and many people thought America must be a great place. People told me of their cousin in Milwaukee or said, "Boy, everything must function better in the States, *wah*?" "*Wah*" was the regional locution corresponding to something like "eh?" When I searched the parish records of a church in Stendal in search of my great-great grandfather's wedding entry, the pastor, a woman, told me her parents were just then in Baltimore under a scientific exchange program. I would have imagined, despite downtown Baltimore's joyous rebirth, that it would be difficult to cope there for a pair straight from East Germany. I erred. "They are really enthusiastic," she said. "*Begeistert*." "Everyone there is so proud of their country."

Taxi drivers seemed glad to have me as a fare. Since Weimar's only taxi stand was at the railroad station, I would usually take a taxi home after one of my train trips around the country. Taxis, like nearly everything else, suffered from overdemand. Drivers would pull up to the eagerly waiting line of people, ask everyone where they were going, assemble a carload of passengers headed generally in the same direction, then whisk them home and hurry back for the next batch. Since I was a regular passenger I struck up fleeting acquaintances with some of the drivers who would tell me about their uncle in Pittsburgh or ask what life was like in the States, or tell me they had some great music in their tape deck and shove a pirated Janis Joplin cassette into the slot. One driver told me why he was a taxi driver. By profession he was actually a plumber, but since conditions were so bad in the country he had applied for a permanent exit visa (*Ausreisegenehmigung*) to leave for West Germany. After he did so he was fired from his factory job and had to drive a taxi to make ends meet. Another driver liked to practice his English which amounted to "Alright, Man," and a few things he had picked up from rock songs. To others the word got around that an *Ami* was in town, and I would jump in a cab and the driver would say, "Hey, you're the American, *wah?*"

In fact the friendliness toward me as an American was one of the memorable aspects of my year in East Germany. In Salzwedel, a town of twenty-three thousand people nestled in a corner of East Germany near the West German border, and a true relic of prewar Germany neither destroyed by bombs nor by new industrialized housing, I made the mistake of standing on the street taking some pictures of the handsomely maintained half-timber houses. A man on a bicycle came up to me.

"Have you seen the ruin of the castle? It's probably the most beautiful building in town."

"Yes, I was just there. Say, this town of yours is very handsome."

"Where are you from? . . . Really? Listen, there are some old photographs of Salzwedel in a storefront around the corner. Let me show you what the town used to be like. . . ."

It took me an hour to pry myself loose. I learned not only about the town's architecture, but how it used to be on the main railroad line between Berlin and Hamburg until Germany was divided, when Salzwedel became a dead end because the tracks were torn up at the border. I learned how the town used to be a major market center, hence its high-quality nineteenth-century buildings, but most of its market area ended up on the other side of the Iron Curtain so the town had become a backwater, and what's it like in America, anyway?

People wanted to show me their church, describing every triptych scene as if it were a soccer game. Museum directors—there were thousands of museums, it seems—dragged me through their museums to describe each exhibit in much more detail than I ever cared to hear. As this kept happening, a certain image worked ever stronger in my mind about what I was experiencing. I kept imagining that I was opening the door to a basement full of friendly dogs who had been locked up for a long time. When I opened the door they could not wait to rush out, tails wagging, jumping all over the guest, hardly able to get enough attention.

My presence occasionally set up a somewhat incongruous situation. One day I was asked to give a lecture to the monthly in-house training session for the support staff of the architecture school. My talk was about Bozeman, the picturesque mountain town of thirty thousand people where Montana State University is situated. I showed slides of pridefully maintained bungalow neighborhoods, the city's historic main street, the tree-lined campus with mountains rising in the background, the grain-elevator industrial district. The attendees were eager to see images of a typical small American town, but they made particular merry over my presence before them because the training sessions, called the "School of Socialist Work," were usually characterized by cliché-laden exhortations about building socialist society. The support staff supervisors were not quite prepared for my slides showing how a garage sale functioned.

It was a most pleasant experience, exploring places like Eisenhüttenstadt, a Stalin-era new town on the Polish border that few Westerners had ever had an opportunity to see, and being met with curious smiles and friendly questions. One time, however, while exercising my newfound feeling of being welcomed everywhere, I thought I was in deep trouble. An acquaintance and I were driving around looking at some things he liked near his town, when over a hill loomed a castlelike tower. I asked what it was; he did not know himself, so he said we should find out. We found the gate to the grounds of what turned out to be a large nineteenth-century mansion with a fanciful tower reminiscent of medieval castles. A sign on the gate said "Access to the Home is for authorized persons only." The gate was open, the guardhouse empty, so my acquaintance suggested we walk in and find out what it was. We strolled up the hill through the grassy lawns to inspect the mansion, when we suddenly found ourselves amid several platoons of teenagers in military uniforms marching around. The inscription on a sign suddenly told us what we had happened upon: "*Jugendwerkheim.*"

Literally "youth work home," a *Jugendwerkheim* was a residence for problem youths, not intended so much for antisocial children themselves as for children of antisocial parents; parents who vehemently refused to cooperate with the government, were openly antisocialist, sometimes violent. Children of the *Asis,* the antisocials, were removed to the homes and given a disciplined upbringing.

As we stood before the mansion, a comrade on the staff walked by and asked us about our business. (All staff members were Party members, I was sure, but he was wearing his *Parteiabzeichen,* his Party lapel pin.) My companion explained that we were interested in historic buildings.

"Well," he growled, "the building is not open to the public," and he paced off. Since he did not specifically order us to leave, we continued to examine the handsome mansion when a second staff member, an athletic coach at the home, approached us with the same question.

"I'm a city planner interested in historic buildings," I said. "We saw this building on the horizon and wanted to see what it was."

"Yes, it's beautiful," said the coach. "Say, you aren't from the DDR, are you?"

Well, I thought, it was probably jail now. Things like youth work homes were certainly off limits to the probing eyes of Western foreigners. "No, I'm an American."

"An American? Well, come on in, I'll show you around." He took us into the lobby and public rooms, describing the history of the house and the restoration work that had been accomplished to give the young people as elegant a living environment as possible. Wall murals painted over by postwar communist zealots who attempted to obliterate traces of the "old order" had been beautifully restored. He showed us the dining room where students were setting the tablecloth-covered tables for the evening meal, and he let me photograph it. Then to the gardens at the rear. "I'm an amateur photographer myself," he proclaimed proudly. "You can get the best picture of the mansion if you just stand right over there. . . ."

One day I met a man on a train who said to me, "I was a prisoner of war in Oklahoma in 1944 and 1945. A whole group of us worked on a farm. Yes, I remember those years; they were probably the best two years of my life. For forty years since then I've been a prisoner in East Germany."

3

Life in "The Zone"

STUDENT: Is it true that Karl Marx was a doctor?
TEACHER: Yes, he was.
STUDENT: Then why didn't he try his experiments on mice first?

A STUDENT from a technical university in another city heard my lecture on everyday life in the United States and invited me to present it at his school. He would arrange everything. A few weeks later he told me, as he rescinded the invitation, that he had run into a snag. The director of student affairs had hit the roof. "What are you doing inviting an American here? It's my job to invite people, not yours. What's he going to do here anyway, make politics?" The lecture was off until the director of student affairs realized that he had offended a foreigner, and since he did not know who this foreigner was, apparently he suspected he may have made a mistake that would bring him disadvantage. When I finally met the man, who was of course a comrade, I realized that his being a Party member probably constituted his principal qualification for the job. The student himself was a Party member, but at a lower and less responsible level, and had acted beyond his authority. At any rate, it was finally arranged through more official channels that I should be invited to give the lecture.

"Oh, how pleased we are to have you here," chirped the director of student affairs as I was introduced on the arranged lecture day. "We have looked forward to your distinguished lecture for such a long time. I'm sure

24

many of the students will be interested, since they are very worldly of course, even though they are training for excellent jobs with industry here in the German Democratic Republic, and just out of curiosity, what kinds of things might you be saying in your lecture? I shall be honored to attend myself, you know." During my talk he sat himself right up in the front of the room and took feverish notes of everything I said. I am sure the East German Ministry for State Security soon gained a file containing a detailed description of how one orders a hamburger at McDonald's.

One night I went to a lecture at the Weimar *Kulturbund*, the local branch of the League of Culture, given by a retired professor from Weimar who had toured the United States in search of information on émigré German architects. Since the crowd had been enthusiastic, I went to the office a few days later and offered my lecture on everyday life in the United States. The director said that of course they would be interested but that the regional administration would have to approve the request. I assumed the response was akin to that of "Your resume is most impressive but unfortunately we are unable to offer you a job at this time," since I quickly learned that to make things happen in East Germany, people had to make decisions on their own initiative, especially regarding things Western. To send things through channels was to kill them.

At the same time, I had offered my more technical lecture on American city-center revitalization to the architecture school in Weimar. As it turned out, the head of the lectures committee at the Weimar League of Culture was also on the architecture faculty. He had recently been sent down from the Ministry of Construction in East Berlin, apparently to keep an eye on things at the school. He called me to say that he would be pleased to have me present a lecture at the League of Culture, but not the one on everyday life because the people really would not be interested. I could give my talk on American city-center revitalization. It would, of course, not be publicized and would be open by invitation only, given its specialized nature. Selected guests, namely certain persons in town involved with historic preservation, would be invited. I suspected a less than forthright agenda in the affair and spoke to some of my confidants at school. Yes, your talk on everyday life in the United States was surely seen by this Ministry-professor as too inflammatory for the League of Culture, and he shunted you to a safe topic before a trusted audience. You should have expected it, they said. That is the way life is here in East Germany.

Besides giving my lectures I wanted to get to know as many East German cities as possible. I eventually visited, explored, and photographed about a hundred cities and villages, and in many I wanted to meet the city architect to discuss what was happening in town. It was difficult, however, for an American merely to call and request a meeting; such an approach was outside the normal procedure of East German professional life and was generally greeted with mistrust. Indeed, the presence of an American in these towns to begin with was outside normal procedure. Such things had to be "arranged." In this, the departmental secretary at the architecture school was a person of long experience, a gifted arranger. She would call the city architect, announce that an American guest professor wished to visit the city and ask if a tour could be arranged. Yes, of course, was the universal response. And by the way, continued the secretary, the American guest could give a lecture on the United States. This also engendered interest, for two reasons. First, any guest lecturer could be put to good use in one of their continuing education programs for the School of Socialist Work and provide the attendees with another entry in their societal engagement file. East Germans were all expected to participate in activities that helped build "advanced socialist society," as the intended future state was called, and their participation was logged in some way. Who kept track, and how, were not clear, but people assumed the Ministry for State Security included such information in everyone's political file. To be involved in such activities was to be "societally engaged" (*gesell-schaftlich engagiert*), a good thing to be if one wanted to ward off disadvantage. The windmill interest groups were one means of engagement, as was membership in organizations such as the League of Culture, and certainly participation in the School of Socialist Work. Second, many people seemed sincerely eager to hear about the United States, given the general fascination with America.

With these supplemental lectures and various meetings with professionals about their activities, I had plenty of opportunity to get to know the country. During much of my ten-month sojourn I traveled extensively, gave my lectures, met with the architects. This I did by train, on the *Deutsche Reichsbahn*. The term *Reich* stems from proprietary ownership of the traditional name of the German railroads, referring not to the Third Reich but to the Second, to the late nineteenth century when the German railroads were built. The *Reichsbahn* headquarters was in the Soviet zone of Berlin, which became the capital of East Germany, so the East Germans kept the name.

The problem in traveling by train was that I lived on the southern edge of Weimar and the railroad station was on the north edge of the old urban center. A bus ran to the station from my part of town only every hour and a half, and never on Sunday. So I studied the shortcuts through the city and honed my walking time from door to track down to an exact thirty-two minutes. From Weimar one could, in a single day, travel to and from nearly any point in the country except Baltic Sea cities in the far north, such as Rostock. Sometimes it made for a long day, but hotels were scarce and usually required reservations a month or so in advance. I made some overnight trips, but for the most part day trips were the answer. To travel in this way, however, I had to know the country's train schedules, since I often had to make connections at obscure places. One could inquire at the information counter at most railroad stations, but the lines were always long and the information people sometimes curt. The answer was the *Kursbuch*.

Every May the *Deutsche Reichsbahn* published its *Kursbuch,* the timetable of the entire railroad system. Someone gave me a copy when I arrived, but the new edition was issued while I was still traveling, and I needed one. Though most schedules changed little from year to year, the *Kursbuch* was quite detailed and some of the explanations took a while to decipher. "Train travels only until June 19 and after September 4, and only on Sundays; also on March 27 and May 16, but not on December 25, March 26 or May 14."

Though the *Kursbuch* was published, one could not necessarily obtain copies. They would suddenly appear each year and were gone before one knew it, unless one had what was called "Vitamin B," the most helpful *Beziehungen,* or "connections," of which I had none in this regard, or unless one was well placed in a People's Own Enterprise or an administrative agency where many were circulated, since so much of East German society was organized around the workplace. Otherwise one had to buy a copy at the railroad station on the day they came out. I asked several people when the new timetables would appear (sometime in May, but nobody knew exactly when), and how to get one (you have to be lucky; they'll probably be available for a half day). Can I slip somebody some West German marks? (no, that isn't done here). I began asking at the railroad ticket counter but received hostile answers from ticket agents tired of the question and having no idea when to expect the new schedules.

Then the rumor went around. Next Tuesday there will be timetables. Tuesday, the day after the Whitmonday holiday. Why the day after Pentecost was an official holiday in Marxist East Germany appeared to be a contradiction that nobody could explain, but nobody much cared since a holiday was a holiday. As it turned out, I had to go to Leipzig that day to give a lecture at the East German Institute of Geography; I would snatch a copy at the station. At 6:30 in the morning I showed up at the Weimar train station after my half-hour walk, early enough to devote some line-standing time before my train left. Sure enough a long line stood at the information counter waiting for timetables. A twenty-minute wait got me to the counter but sorry, no national timetables. We only have the regional timetable for the Erfurt district. I picked up two copies (fifty pfennigs each) as better than nothing, thinking perhaps I could trade one, and caught the train to Leipzig.

Leipzig, East Germany's second largest city, has perhaps Europe's most magnificent railroad station. Its twenty-six tracks converge into a gigantic vaulted hall filled with the clicks of echoing footsteps and the powerful hum of electric locomotives. When I arrived at nine there was quite a throng in the concourse standing around a baggage cart, upon which were sitting piles of the telltale green national timetables. "No, do not touch them, they will go on sale at four this afternoon, not before," said the woman who was unloading them into the information office. I gave my lecture, returned about 3:30, and hustled to the end of what had become a line snaking two hundred feet through the station. Exactly at four they began to dispense the timetables, and after a half hour I picked up two. The cost was two marks each, another of East Germany's many subsidized products. Clutching my prized timetables, I walked around Leipzig taking pictures while waiting for my train, and when I returned two hours later the line was gone, along with the timetables, for another year.

Later, in Weimar, I told my associates I should have bought a handful since I could have sold them all at ten or a hundred times the purchase price and made some good spare change. Nobody thought it was funny. "Do all Americans try to take advantage of other people like that?"

The speed of trains varied considerably. The best express trains, called "City Rapid Traffic," (*Städteschnellverkehr*), were fairly fast and normally punctual. One had to pay a surcharge to ride them. The daily train from Berlin to Meiningen, which traveled its first 274 kilometers with only one intermediate stop, covered the entire 377 kilometers at an average speed of 87 kilometers per hour. Another train, a *D-Zug* also classified as "fast" and also requiring a surcharge, traveled from Dresden to Meiningen, a distance of 345 kilometers, at an average speed of 45 kilometers per hour. Part of the problem on this route was the need to negotiate two stretches of single track, which—it was pointed out to me several times—had been double-track stretches until 1945 when the Russians took half the track. In fact the Soviet Army removed the track, but in popular expression it was always "the Russians." The slow speed was also due to inexplicably long dwelling times in stations. I boarded this train in Weimar during its scheduled fourteen-minute stop. When the stationmaster announced the departure of the "express" train from Dresden, continuing to Meiningen, the passengers hooted with derision.

I contemplated the nature of trains while I was there, partly since powerful railroads had often been portrayed in Russian movies as symbolic of working-class command over the socialist state. The international trains in East Germany, those carrying pensioners, functionaries, and occasional businesspeople into West Germany, were immaculate. Local trains, the ones serving the primary transportation needs of many East Germans, were filthy. Excrement was frequently splattered on train toilets and windows were caked with grime. East Berlin's main station, from which the trans-European trains (mainly trans-East European trains) departed, was a splendid showpiece with polished granite floors and an electronic schedule board. Small train stations in the provinces were layered with years of filth, having faded destination boards sometimes dimly lit by a flickering fluorescent light. The men's lavatories were usually dungeon-like affairs with the urinals consisting of a tile-covered wall with a gutter at the bottom, a lingering tradition of Old Germany. Most had probably not been cleaned since Old Germany either; one did not loiter in the men's room. If I were to organize a true socialist state, I thought, I would do it backward. I would make sure the local trains and small-town stations that served the workers and farmers in whose name the state had been constituted would be immaculate. The functionaries and expense-account higher-ups who rode the international trains should suffer a lack of attentive care, if there had to be one.

The condition of the trains reflected the status of East Germany under "actually existing socialism" (*real existierender Sozialismus*), by which the Party officially characterized its political system. The term was coined some years ago in response to charges from the idealist Left that, in reality, the so-called socialist countries were hardly socialist at all but merely dictatorships. The establishment response was that undemocratic socialism as it "actually existed" would have to do until the threat posed by capitalist societies had been overcome.

I would often take my work to the dining car, if there was one, and if it was not crowded (as, for example, when there was nothing to eat) order coffee and work at a table for most of the trip. In the West the working businessman is a common sight when traveling, and I thought nothing of it until one day in the dining car of the Halle-Erfurt express I realized that not a single time in East Germany had I ever seen someone working while riding the train. Trains during the week were full of business travelers, with functionaries, managers, and army officers riding in the first-class compartments, but I never saw anyone spend this time working. Soldiers were often well into the beer, sometimes aiming the empty bottles out the windows past the "Do not throw things out the window" signs to see what target they could hit along the tracks. Students, who traveled en masse on Friday evenings and Monday mornings, did not study on trains. Women seemed to spend a lot of time knitting on trains, but they knitted a lot in class, too.

The "connections" to which I referred, the society's "Vitamin B," were a nonmarket mechanism that facilitated the accomplishment of one's affairs since they helped solve the problem of how to distribute goods and services for which demand exceeded supply. With connections one could obtain something not available to all, and one's use of connections was often quite crafty. For example, many East Germans from the provinces made the journey to East Berlin to shop, since goods manufactured throughout the country were often distributed first in Berlin as part of the competition between the two halves of the divided city. Carrying the goods home to the provinces could pose a problem, however. Once at the Berlin-Lichtenberg railroad station I observed a man who had purchased a washing machine in East Berlin. He was from Zittau, a town in southern East Germany, and wanted to take it home. Since there was no baggage car on the train he wanted to ride, a large object like a washing machine would not be allowed on the train. The man pondered what to do, and finally asked the train dispatcher on the platform, "This train here, where is the conductor from?"

"Oh, you want to take that big box," said the dispatcher. "Well, I think he's from Zittau."

"Excellent," said the man. "I work in a garage there, and if he lets me put this on, I can be useful to him."

I visited a ceramicist who had relocated to a small village where he could make a pottery studio out of an abandoned barn and have enough space to store and process materials. The problem was that his electric kiln doubled the amount of electricity consumed by the village, and electricity itself was a rather scarce commodity generated by brown-coal-fired heating plants. Nevertheless, he was able to obtain the necessary electrical connections from the district authorities, plus the materials to build his studio, without delay. An open-air museum in a neighboring village, which I also visited, required many of the same materials in order to restore its historic farmhouses for public education. However, the authorities were less forthcoming in allocating the materials to the museum than to the ceramicist. I discovered the reason: It was difficult to buy interesting gifts in East Germany. Every store of a certain type sold the same items, and even the booths at events such as the Christmas fairs were stocked with identical goods that could be found in the stores.

My mother went to the big Christmas fair in Nuremberg, West Germany, where she saw piles of little wooden Christmas villages made in the East German *Erzgebirge* region near Dresden, all being sold for hefty prices. She refrained from buying any because she was coming to visit me in Weimar and expected to see the same piles in East German Christmas fairs, only less expensive. When she arrived she found no Christmas villages at all in the fair in Weimar, only cheap plastic toys one could buy any time in any store. All the *Erzgebirge* toys had been shipped to Nuremberg where they would earn West German marks. East Germans were out of luck if they wanted some, unless, of course, they had connections.

At any rate, a handcraftsman such as the ceramicist in the village, unlike an open-air museum, produced the very type of unique gifts coveted by all East German gift-givers, including the local Party authorities. So the potter would appear before the responsible officials and obtain what he needed to run his kilns because at Christmastime the officials were among his best customers, receiving special discounts. The importance of connections brought forth a joke:

"What is the stiffest sentence in East Germany?"

"Ten years without connections."

Sometimes even connections could not deliver the goods, however, and one had to wait for time to take its toll. This typewritten note was tacked to the bulletin board in my apartment lobby one day:

From: People's Own Enterprise Community Dwelling
       Administration, Weimar, Warm Water Division

To: All users of the Humboldtstraße heating plant

Notice:

> Due to urgent repair work and laying the remaining water lines by the principal contractor, People's Own Enterprise Dwelling Construction Conglomerate of Sömmerda; the investment contractor, People's Own Enterprise Dwelling Provision of Gotha; and the People's Own Enterprise Technical Water Lines Conglomerate, we must institute a standstill time, and thereby the total stoppage of warm water, including that for direct use, from May 22nd until June 6th. This two-week standstill time is in accordance with the provisions of the Energy Regulation Law of January 9, 1988. We ask for your understanding and hope in this way to guarantee the provision of warm water through the following winter.

> (Signed) Diploma-Engineer Smuda
> Chief Engineer, Warm Water

My apartment had been without warm water for a short time previously, when a note had been tacked to the bulletin board saying "For technical reasons warm water has been temporarily suspended." I had then wondered what other reasons there could have been, but eventually I learned that any stoppage in the provision of goods and services was always attributed to "technical reasons." This time it was to be a whole two weeks without warm water, which seemed a catastrophe until I spoke with a resident of another new housing area in Weimar who said that happened *every* year. Though for the next two weeks I gazed daily out my window to the central heating plant across the street, its brown-coal boilers silent, I saw no activity. I discussed the matter with the *Hausmeister* of my building, but the hot water was not his department and he knew no more than I. Then on the day hot water was to be restored, a new note was placed on the bulletin board:

> Esteemed Renter:

> Due to technical problems which have arisen in the completion of the work on the heating plant by the People's Own Enterprise Dwelling Construction Conglomerate of Sömmerda, warm water cannot be assured until an indeterminate future date.

> We are making all efforts to provide service at the nearest possible date and ask for your understanding.

Two weeks later, a total of four weeks after hot water was shut off, two trucks arrived at the heating plant, and that afternoon water was restored. Luckily I had a WM 600 washing machine in my bathroom. For four weeks I had heated water in the washing machine, placed the discharge hose in the bathtub and unloaded the hot water into the tub in order to take a bath.

The architecture school had kindly provided me with a furnished apartment, complete with the WM 600 washing machine—"WM" stood for *Waschmaschine*. The device was about the size of a large kitchen garbage can and manufactured by the People's Own Washing Machine Works in Schwarzenberg. Instructions for using a WM 600 were quite straightforward. Initially, one filled the basin with cold water from a hose handily attached to the sink faucet. When the machine was full, one turned the knob to "heat" and waited about an hour and a half until the water had reached the desired temperature. Then one added the clothing and detergent and turned the knob to "wash," whereupon the agitator would spin rapidly in a clockwise direction, pulling all clothes into a tight knot in the center of the basin. Once the knot had swirled around for the desired period of time one turned the knob to "drain," which pumped the water out through another hose leading into the bathroom sink. When the WM 600 had been emptied of its water, one reinserted the hose from the first step into the machine and began the process again for the rinse cycle.

The picture I have presented in these vignettes suggests the overall pace and quality of everyday life in East Germany during the last year of communism. It was not characterized by strife, since nearly everything one needed for a reasonably comfortable life was available. The problem was that these items were not necessarily available when one needed them. American society is often characterized by the word "hustle," but life in East Germany was a hustle as well. Leaving aside differences in political systems, both societies could be described by this same term, with one difference. Socialist society assured the long-term well-being of its citizens, as I shall discuss in chapter 18, but meeting everyday needs was continually characterized by the kinds of frustrations I described above. In American society, the needs of daily life are met easily by most—not all—people, given credit cards and all-night supermarkets, but long-term needs such as assuring adequate health care or putting a child through college are the ones for which people must hustle. In East Germany, one encountered a fundamentally different perspective.

Although the following joke vanished with Erich Honecker, the country's leader deposed in 1989, people had told it with relish:

Lenin, Stalin, Gorbachev, and Honecker are riding on a train, when suddenly the track ends. They get off the train and discuss what to do.

Lenin says, "Let's all help to lay the track so we can reach our destination together."

Stalin says, "Shoot the engineer."

Gorbachev says, "We should each take initiative to analyze the situation and recommend action."

Honecker says, "No, have a couple of people get out and rock the train, so everyone will think we're making progress."

In short, everyday life in East Germany was not unpleasant, but it was an endless challenge, and my associates felt generally helpless to make things better. Here is reflected part of the nagging frustration with "actually existing socialism." The coffee break at the architecture school, every morning at nine (since the work day began at 7:30), never lapsed into silence for want of a topic, and more often than not the discussion focused on yesterday's "technical reasons." Not stated but obviously underlying the conversation lay the generator of most of those technical reasons, the country's communist party, the Socialist Unity, and its *modus operandi*, called "democratic centralism."

4

The Core of the Poodle:
Democracy versus
Democratic Centralism

EAST GERMANY was officially called the German Democratic Republic. In fact, the term "democratic" played a prominent role in the society under communist rule. Article 47 of the DDR constitution stated directly that "The sovereignty of the working population, realized on the basis of democratic centralism, is the guiding principle of building the State."

Contrary to my anticipation, I found East Germany literally drenched in democracy, full of public discussions about bettering socialist society. Every place of employment, from factories to universities, had multiple workers' councils with elected heads, vestiges of the original "workers' soviets," that discussed nearly every problem and made recommendations for action. The secretaries at the architecture school in Weimar, for example, were represented by, and indeed could be members of, the support staff council, composed of men and women in clerical positions; the women's council, composed of women from all ranks, custodians to professors; the council of the academic department of the university, representing all employees; as well as the local council of the Free German Trade Union, or FDGB (*Freier Deutscher Gewerkschaftsbund*) which served as a gigantic trade union for nearly all workers in the country. Students went through the university as part of a seminar group, sort of a homeroom of about fifteen people, which met frequently to discuss issues and make decisions expressing the group's recommendations for societal action. Beyond the workplace there were housing district councils, neighborhood councils; the list went on. Every place of employment had a Party cadre as well, which discussed issues. The East Germans also called it "The Party," by the way: *Die Partei*, the "Socialist Unity Party of Germany."

Each of these organizations, in every workplace and neighborhood, would meet to discuss issues of importance to socialist society, ranging from Third-World liberation movements to improving working conditions, and each regularly made recommendations that were forwarded to higher levels where central decisions were made. Even beyond such formal meetings, plenty of open discussion took place. Nearly all organizations prided themselves in the lectures and discussions about issues affecting the workplace held in the "School of Socialist Work" programs. Mass organizations such as the League of Culture, to which millions belonged, regularly sponsored events where the state of the world was discussed.

One day I happened by a big anniversary celebration of the daily newspaper in Dresden. The event resembled an American community fair held in the city park. It offered rides and games, agricultural extension agents' demonstrating vegetable-washing techniques, the fire department's showing off its new fire engines. There was also a small stage where representatives from the paper were answering questions from the audience. "Why is the Turkish minority in Bulgaria acting up? Why is there nothing in our press about this? Why are things about East Germany reported in the Western press that we never see in ours?" The questions seemed uninhibited and challenging, sincere in their formulation, and the answers seemed respectable: "Because the Bulgarians are trying to eradicate the Turkish language and culture. Because we don't involve ourselves in the internal affairs of other countries. Because they are trying to foment unrest in the German Democratic Republic."

With so much discussion about issues, with democracy directly stated in the constitution, I was curious to find the point where open discussion and free decision-making veered from the path Rousseau would have recognized as democracy and transformed itself into totalitarianism. Scholars of communism have explained the phenomenon, of course, but here I was suddenly a consumer of the system and wished to comprehend from within how it happened, when it happened, whether it actually happened.

Early on, as I began to participate in public discussions, I perceived a curious difference between my expectations of a discussion and what seemed regularly to transpire. Soon after my arrival I was invited to attend the annual meeting of people active in preserving historic buildings in the Weimar district. On the podium were representatives of city and district government, along with other authorities having decision-making and budgeting responsibility for historic buildings. Each made a presentation of last year's accomplishments and next year's goals for his agency. Then came time for the discussion, when members of the audience, about fifty people, could participate. Those who wished to speak were recognized by the chair, stood up, and made one of two kinds of statements. Either they said, "I worked on the program of which Comrade Schmidt just spoke, and I wish to add to his comments that . . ." followed by a positive statement about the program and ending with something like, "We can be proud of this program in helping build our socialist fatherland." Or they stated their situation: Here is what my preservation association accomplished last year in working to preserve the windmill (country estate, salt mine, whatever). We found that we had a shortage of bricks (wood, tools, workers), and in order to accomplish next year's goals we need additional paint (tin roofing, use of a bulldozer). Then they sat down. From the podium came silence.

Discussions at this meeting, and indeed in all such situations, appeared to consist entirely of people expressing their own supportive views of what they saw and heard, or merely stating what they needed, while never directly challenging one of the authorities on the podium, never actually asking a question. I recalled, in fact, that this part of the program was called "discussion," not "questions from the audience." When I would give a talk, people seemed to have no hesitation about asking me pointed questions about the United States, but normally in their own forums no real questions were asked and no real responses given to a statement anybody would make. So I thought I would speak up.

In chapter 2, I noted that Weimar was for Germans quite a Mecca. Not only was it the home of Goethe and Schiller, but it had been a great center of culture for a long period before and after their lifetimes in the eighteenth and nineteenth centuries. It was one of the cities where Johann Sebastian Bach had lived, and Franz Liszt lived there during what was perhaps the most renowned period of his career. The city flowered with neoclassical art and architecture during this time, in the movement called Weimar Classicism, resulting in one of the great cultural constellations of German history. For many years tourists from German-speaking lands had been visiting Weimar by the thousands to immerse themselves in the relics and aura of this earlier culture. Had the American Army, which arrived there before the Soviet Army in 1945, remained in Weimar after the war and made it part of West Germany, it would certainly have become one of the country's foremost tourist attractions. It would be, in its own way, another Heidelberg, an architectural and cultural jewel.

As it turned out, of course, Weimar ended up in East Germany, not West, and like most East German cities many of its buildings had reached a point of serious deterioration by the late 1980s. The city was shabby and ill-maintained, with especially few restaurants. The East Germans brought tourists through by the busload but without offering them very much beyond a view of Goethe's and Schiller's sarcophagi and museums. What a missed opportunity to revitalize the city through tourism, I thought, so at the historic preservation meeting I asked a real question.

One of the people on the podium was the Weimar city director for culture, who oversaw historic building preservation among other responsibilities. He was a true politician, with neatly coiffed gray hair above a wizened but hardened face. To him I directed my query. "In my country a city like Weimar would be a preeminent tourist attraction, and I could well imagine that tourism could be developed here as an important vehicle for urban revitalization. In Weimar I see the tourists but not the revitalization, so my question is, what do you see as the role of tourism in Weimar?"

I sat down. A kind of stunned silence captured the room. Whispers. "Yes, that's the American." Presently the moderator made his way to the microphone. "Well, let's move on to the next discussant, since our purpose here is not to engage in one-on-one conversations. Next comment, please. . . ."

"Yes," someone spoke up, "my name is Uwe Rettig with the preservation committee of the agricultural cooperative 'New Future,' and I wish to report on our success in preserving our old barn. . . ." And so on. A while later, I noted that the city director for culture passed a note to an underling from his office who was sitting in the audience. After several more people had given their testimonials, the underling stood up to say, "I would like to try to answer Professor Gleye's question." He rambled a bit, something about tourism being important and trying to do what they could with limited resources, and "Yes, we recognize that Weimar is a special place." He was actually an excellent preservation professional; I came to know him later. At that meeting I do not remember exactly what he said, but it had little substance and addressed no real issues, and the

The Core of the Poodle / 39

person in charge merely continued to sit on the podium responding not at all.

This nonengagement was the case in discussion sessions after lectures at the architecture school as well. Not only were the speakers never challenged, but if someone from the audience spoke, nobody else ever took that person to task. There was never, to my knowledge, a situation where insight was gained or real problems addressed. So I began making it a point to ask a direct question of the speaker when I attended a lecture. "What do you think of X," or "How would you apply to the DDR what you saw in Bulgaria?" I must say I enjoyed these chances to set the speakers a bit on their toes as the rest of the audience sat there in polite embarrassment. My questions were not caustic. I merely asked questions that probed what they had said or attempted to connect their comments to something else. It came to be a matter of pride with me that people in audiences would say to each other afterward, "Oh, that's the American, didn't you know?" Sort of like, "Who was that masked man, anyway?"

Beyond the discussion councils in the workplace, East Germany was also formally democratic because the citizens regularly elected representatives to local, regional, and national *Volksvertretungen,* or elected bodies. Indeed, one even had the right to express one's opinion to the responsible elected officials regarding a public issue. This opinion was normally transmitted through a letter called an *Eingabe,* or "petition," which tended to have a specific form. Americans petition their elected officials as well, of course. A typical letter from a constituent in the United States might read, "On the basis of A, B, and C, House Bill X will have disastrous effects. I urge you to vote no on Bill X." In East Germany a petition was somewhat different. First, it could only be sent *after* a decision was made, since one did not know what was being discussed by the elected body, or by the Party's central committee, until the decision was announced, usually in the following day's *Neues Deutschland.* Second, one usually did not disagree with the decision. One nearly always agreed with the decision, but one may have had questions about it that prompted the petition to be written. If, for example, the next year's budget for some activity such as support for cultural activities were drastically reduced, as happened in 1989, a concerned citizen had the right to petition the legislator representing the cultural community, to enquire what the future might bring. A typical petition to a nationally elected representative, which is actually a composite of several I read so that the writers may remain anonymous, looked something like this:

Honored Friend of the State, Dr. Z:

First allow me the opportunity to thank you for your outstanding support for the betterment of socialist society.

After much hesitation I write you as representative of the artists in my district, after having read with great interest your comments, and the comments of the other legislators, on the most recent budget decisions. I am of course in wholehearted agreement with all that was said.

One question arises from this discussion that I and other artists in my association cannot answer. I refer to Section XX of the law, in which it appears that support for artists has been reduced by 50 percent. If my reading is correct, this line-item reduction is more than double the reduction of any other related expenditure.

The concrete result of this decision will be that the artists in my collective will be substantially less able to provide works of art that support the call to socialist achievement by the working class. We will in fact be able to meet only 20 percent of our goals in the five year plan.

I am fully aware of the difficult financial situation and the need to render our socialist work more efficient, and it is clear that priority must be placed on the development of technology and the productive sector, but the reduction in this small area will result in a lesser position for socialist art in the eyes of the world.

Minister Y, in his decision implementing the ordainments of the 11th Party Congress of the Socialist Unity Party, stated that socialist art is essential to the welfare of the working class, as noted by the following citations:

(lengthy quotations)

My question is thus, Honored Friend of the State Dr. Z: Do you see a hope for next year and in the upcoming five year plan, that this underestimation of the importance of our work might be corrected?

With deep respect,

One could also expect an answer to such a petition, which might read something like this:

Dear Friend of the State A:

Thank you greatly for your letter. It touched me deeply, and I feel the great sense of responsibility which led you to write.

The problem is painful, and I and other elected officials have expressed our feelings in this regard.

In your reading you may have noticed that support for other endeavors has been reduced as well, because the economic situation is

truly difficult. We have at least endeavored to assure that art for important public buildings shall go forward.

You can be sure that this matter stands near to my heart, and I share
your hope that in the next five year plan we can place more resources in
this direction. However, you must remember that the difficulties we
face do not promise to become easier.

Let us, together, continue to work responsibly, critically, and con-
structively in this important realm.

Yours sincerely,

In such a petition, both parties were quite careful not to engage the other.
There is little question about what was being said—here the writer obviously opposed the cuts and the legislator said that was too bad—but such
exchanges never called anyone to task for not responding to a need perceived by a constituent.

Another popular medium for discussing issues of general concern was
the newspaper *Neues Deutschland,* where one often found letters to the
editor. Most letters were uniform in format; either they expressed support
for a policy announced in the paper, or they criticized some aspect of life
in the West, or they asked a question.

A reader asked *Neues Deutschland* in March 1989 how one defined
"standard of living," since it had been noted by a Party official in a previous article that the standard of living in East Germany was higher than that
in West Germany. The comment had generated some discussion among
my colleagues at coffee breaks, who regularly watched West German television and were convinced that their own standard of living was far below
that of their Western brethren on almost any scale of physical prosperity
one could concoct. "Is that really true?" the letter asked, prompting further
explanation.

Yes indeed, replied the newspaper. In some Western lands, standard
of living is simply taken to be the average gross income, disregarding the
qualitative aspects of life. Income is only a reasonable measure when one
takes into account the prices of groceries, consumer goods, services,
rents, taxes, costs of medical services, education, and cultural offerings.
In the DDR, the paper continued, one must consider the significant state
subsidies for stable prices of basic foodstuffs and rents, and the free health
care and education for all citizens. One must take into account the "right
to work" in the DDR, where every citizen has a right to a job, and one
must consider free child care and support payments for mothers and chil-

dren. One cannot calculate living standards with a computer, continued the response. The essential values for the lives of working members of society must be weighed. If one does this, it is clear that the living standards for the working class are higher in the DDR than in West Germany.

One might conclude that the response did not actually address the question. It merely repeated what everyone knew, that basic necessities of life were provided for all in East Germany. On the other hand, one might indeed conclude that the newspaper had expressed a valid statement of standard of living based on traditional socialist values rather than on quantity of possessions. Yet it had remained on a level of platitudes unconvincing to much of its audience, at least those of my acquaintance, who watched West German commercials about vacations in Italy and were less interested in theoretical statements or reminders of state subsidies for bread.

These examples have suggested the tenor of public discussion I found in East Germany in early 1989: a polite, almost tender caring for the speaker, writer, or person of authority. This gentle realm of public debate, however, was not the only type I observed. There arose during my stay some less polite expressions of opinion on public issues that fell outside of this normal procedure. One such event occurred when the government banned the sale of the Soviet magazine *Sputnik*.

Several German-language Soviet publications were offered for sale in East Germany. The Soviet Union in fact published numerous magazines in various languages for distribution around the world. *Sowjetfrau,* the English version of which was called *Soviet Woman,* was readily found on East German newsstands, as was *Sowjetunion,* corresponding to the English *Soviet Life*. Another was called *Sputnik,* the "Digest of the Soviet Press." It was handsomely designed with many color pictures and printed on slick paper in Finland. Until the arrival of perestroika these magazines had not been read with particular gusto in East Germany, but in recent years people had begun to take increasing interest in them, especially *Sputnik*. Its pages often contained articles on new attitudes in the Soviet Union as well as critical articles about the country's past. Many East Germans began following the magazine like a hawk following its prey. It was not merely a window on the Soviet Union; it became a huge picture window that shed bountiful light on events to the East. Subscription lists for *Sputnik* began to soar, and as each issue arrived it would generate lively discussions. Not only could one read about Soviet artists, newly emerging private entrepreneurs making and selling consumer products, beautiful

Soviet tourist resorts, or Arnold Schwarzenegger in *The Terminator,* one could also read about problems the country had suffered under Khrushchev. In particular, in the November 1988 issue, one could read about Hitler and Stalin. "Would Hitler have been possible without Stalin?" *Sputnik* asked.

The East German government, which had always tread softly on its Stalinist roots, did not like the question, let alone the implied answer. "The publication no longer contributes to the furthering of German-Soviet friendship," said the government, and promptly banned *Sputnik* from the country forever.

Reaction among East Germans is difficult to describe. It may be compared to Americans' reaction if the United States government suddenly banned *Time* magazine. There was universal outrage. Coffee breaks sizzled with disgust at the action, it was the talk in all the corridors of the architecture school, in the local bars. As I rode the train during the next few weeks or sat in restaurants around the country, I would overhear "Sputnik, Sputnik" laced into the conversations. Some of the students in Weimar sitting around the Wieland Cafe, a favorite hangout they had lovingly dubbed the "W.C.," suggested renaming it the "Sputnik Cafe."

Some of the other students were particularly zealous in their response, and a couple of them made a mistake. They printed up a few flyers on the school's blueprint machine that said, "*Sputnik* lives!" signed "MfS," and plastered them around the walls where people waited for elevators in the dorm. "MfS" were the initials of the Ministry for State Security, the *Stasi.*

By eight o'clock the next morning, every dorm room was being given a thorough fire inspection by plain-clothed inspectors. Students found this odd, since two weeks previously an inspection had been undertaken by uniformed fire inspectors who checked the general cleanliness of the rooms and all the fire extinguishers. The plain-clothed inspectors did not check the fire extinguishers, but they did search everyone's closets and dresser drawers.

Simultaneously, some other students had exercised their democratic rights by writing a petition to the Party central committee expressing their disagreement over the decision to ban *Sputnik.* They also made a mistake. Rather than merely sending the letter, they made 180 copies on the school's photocopy machine and distributed them around school. The students were arrested.

By noon of the following day, an urgent tenseness had gripped the entire architecture school. The corridors were alive with gossip about these audacious deeds. Who saw them first? Where were you when it happened? I hear they're in the interrogation unit right now. Did the police find anything? Sitting around coffee break that morning was like waiting for the hurricane to hit. The question on everybody's mind, of course, was how would the Party respond?

Respond the Party did, and quickly. The dark blue Volvo limousines of the high officials converged on the school and stood parked outside the school building for days as the functionaries held apparently heated, and secret, sessions with the local Party cadre about expunging antisocialist behavior. Decisions were handed down.

First, security measures for all photocopy and blueprint machines would be strengthened. Heretofore they had been kept in locked rooms, and now they would be housed in locked cabinets within locked rooms, with specific control mechanisms for the keys to assure that no unauthorized persons could gain access.

Second, each instructor was required to discuss the unfortunate events with the students and state in no uncertain terms that such behavior was unacceptable. Following the meeting in which this order was handed down to the faculty, I spoke to several faculty members who were more depressed than I had ever seen them before about the state of the country. They themselves disagreed with the decision to ban *Sputnik* and were placed in a position of having to represent themselves to their students in a way that ran counter to their beliefs, and the entire issue was severely increasing the tensions already felt between the students and the government. However, the penalty for refusing to cooperate was probably dismissal, and no faculty member to my knowledge balked at the order.

Third, the rector of the architecture school was censured for failing to maintain a correct political posture among the students. For the rector to be censured meant that the entire faculty serving under him would share in this censure. I gathered that the responsibility chain was not unlike that of the U.S. Navy's tradition of the ship's captain being accountable for everything that happens on the ship, whether or not he knew about it or could have prevented it.

Fourth, all the architecture students were required to meet in their Free German Youth groups, into which they were organized, and to sign a petition stating that they disagreed with such antisocialist actions and denounced the perpetrators. Several students discussed this requirement with me. They universally disagreed with what they had to sign, and would have to lie about their beliefs in order to show solidarity with the Party.

Shortly after the affair, the school's Free German Youth cadre held another meeting. They needed to make a recommendation to higher levels about what should be done regarding the dissatisfaction over the *Sputnik* banning, and members were told to express their opinions openly. The organization's secretary, studying to be a teacher, and who sincerely believed in socialist goals for the country, spoke up. He said he disagreed with the decision to ban *Sputnik,* apparently using the word "Stalinist" to describe his views of the action. A couple of weeks later the student was expelled from architecture school because of his negative attitude inappropriate for a future teacher. Needless to say, every student in the school was soon talking about the case, and one could feel the level of tension rise for days after the expulsion.

"Why don't you speak up?" I asked some of the students. "If a hundred of you were out on the streets tomorrow, there would be a thousand the next day, and ten thousand the following day." The *Sputnik* affair caused only a few minor demonstrations. Less than a year later, hundreds of thousands in the streets would bring down the old order, but at that time such a demonstration was hardly imaginable. Students expressed two reasons that seemed to hold things in check. First, with such severe repression for even mild actions, they believed the penalty to be paid by the first wave of demonstrators would be so great that nobody was willing to make the sacrifice. Second, they believed that nobody in the world outside of East Germany would support them. The world would fear that an uprising in East Germany might lead to a reunited Germany, of which many people were afraid, and that an uprising would suggest the specter of the Nazis' rising again, as they did in street riots during the 1930s. To be sure, in late 1989 these concerns, if they were universal, would not stop the demonstrations, but even a few months previously, the thought of going into the streets to express popular political power was still out of the question.

Several days after the *Sputnik* activities it was announced that the perpetrator of the posters in the dorms had voluntarily admitted his guilt and had expressed regret for his untoward actions. What the students knew, of course, was that he had indeed admitted his guilt, but only after a long interrogation session by Ministry for State Security agents, with whatever may have been attendant to it. The sentence (or, rather, penalty, since there was no trial) handed out to those guilty of these antisocialist acts was not incarceration but merely a reprimand regarding their activity placed in the file that recorded each citizen's social and political commitment. Such a reprimand, however, carried rather severe penalties. It meant that one could no longer participate in building socialist society. It meant no position on a waiting list for a dwelling or automobile and no foreign travel. To a Westerner such things might seem to be superficial concerns, but they were central to socialist life where money could not buy them. Position on lists was the only means by which they became available. The students were expelled from the architecture school and would be unable to pursue that profession or any other, and would be unable to attain any position of responsibility as adults. Those actions suggest what the term "disadvantage" really meant.

The *Sputnik* affair apparently became well known all over the country. For the rest of my stay, as I traveled to new cities in East Germany, people often mentioned it to me when they found out I had been in Weimar for the events. The real interest was not in the affair, however, but in the banning.

Expression outside the normal channel of petitions was not the only time when a point of view made public could bring disadvantage. The response to a petition itself could not always be anticipated. An acquaintance and a group of his co-workers sent a petition to the Party Central Committee to say that *Sputnik* should not be banned on the basis of one article, when nearly all articles in the magazine did, in fact, serve the interest of German-Soviet friendship. For this action their superior was called on the carpet by his superior in turn and accused of harboring employees with antisocialist attitudes. Censure soon reached down to those who had submitted the petition.

An architect acquaintance concerned about inadequately constructed new housing in his city wrote a petition to the minister for construction suggesting improvements that could enhance housing quality. In response, he was removed from his volunteer position as a poll monitor for the local elections, and the housing construction enterprise he questioned imposed an information blackout on its work and refused to answer further inquiries. The suggestions were not implemented.

East Germans often used one of those expressions most languages seem to have, which enters popular speech from great literary works. It was "the core of the poodle" (*des Pudels Kern*), corresponding to "the crux of the matter." Toward the beginning of the Goethe's great dramatic poem *Faust*, Faust encounters a poodle, which follows him into his study.

Once inside, the poodle explodes into the person of Mephistopheles. "So this was the poodle's core!" exclaims Faust. I discovered that the poodle's core of socialist democracy in East Germany was a quite straightforward reformulation of the traditional notion of "democracy" to make it a form of pyramid, called "democratic centralism." Issues of whatever nature were discussed in the thousands of organizations such as the support staff group at the university, as well as in each Party cadre. When the discussion resulted in a recommendation, this recommendation was communicated upward to the next higher level of authority, which held its own discussion and forwarded a recommendation in turn to district, then to regional, and eventually to the central committee in Berlin. At each level, one was expected to engage in a full discussion airing all views freely and coming to some agreement. Final decisions of importance were made in the capital, Berlin, by the Party's Politburo, the inner circle of highest decision-makers. That was the democratic part, to be followed by the centralism part.

Once a decision was made, whether regarding the accepted point of view toward an event, the adopted procedure to be followed, or who had authority over what, all persons at every lower level were required to abide by that decision without further question or criticism. People were deferential in public discussions partly because decisions were actually made at higher levels that may not even have been aware of the content of discussions at lower levels, and one did not know what the acceptable response was until one learned of the final decision from on high. After a decision was made, in practice those who expressed another point of view during the discussion phase could be singled out for disadvantage from any higher level, given the ship's captain attitude that each responsible person had nearly total control not only over the actions to be taken by subordinates but over the subordinates themselves. Public discussion thus had little actual effect on what would finally be decided and carried with it the risk of later censure from above. Only the visiting American assumed that he could speak out without finding disadvantage lying in wait for him somewhere along the line.

Indeed, the phenomenon of downward-flowing censure was inherent in democratic centralism because the Party itself was in a position to station its own members at key points in all organizations and production enterprises, and could carry out its orders from above. In this way the Party further tightened its widely resented knot that bound together East German political power.

Democratic centralism had evolved, as did many practices of "actually existing socialism," from a fairly respectable lineage. It was formulated by Lenin after the turn of the century when the Russian revolutionary parties had to operate clandestinely to escape the Czarist police. Absolute obedience assured some measure of confidence that revolutionary cadres would not be compromised by the actions of others in the movement. As with other practices, however, it had become mechanistic and manipulative by the time Stalin completed his purges of the 1930s.

Thus my East German associates generally took it for granted that the Ministry for State Security, also under Party control, placed one person as an informant in each organizational unit such as a seminar group or office, to monitor all discussions. One never knew which person served as the informer, and people with whom I spoke disagreed as to what was reported and what resulted from the reports. One opinion held that the attitudes of individuals were entered into the political records maintained on each person. A more benign opinion held that only general information was recorded, without individual names, so the government could make appropriate decisions in guiding the society. It seemed to me that the latter kind of information did not require an informant.

Like a steel reinforcing bar in a concrete slab, Party representation was independent of yet inextricably built into every organization; one might even say it held the organization together. Irrespective of the unit in society, final decisions and their implementation, plus the assurance that they would be carried out, was in the hands of a centrally directed Socialist Unity party. "Democratic centralism" turned out to be an interesting term. It may be likened to its constituent word "democratic" as the term "dog catcher" is to the word "dog," where the latter element in the phrase is intended to eliminate the former. The repression felt under democratic centralism helps explain why so many East Germans would not be satisfied with a "reformed" communist party once its hold was broken, but abandoned it.

Thus a joke circulated:

"How many social strata will remain in the advanced stages of socialism?"

"Two. The lower stratum will be the Communist Party, and the upper stratum will be six feet of dirt."

5

Good Is the Party:
Actually Existing Socialism

In capitalism people exploit other people.
In communism it is the other way around.

WHEN I WENT TO East Germany I decided to leave my preconceptions behind and pose, among others, a simple but fundamental question. What had been the attraction of communism? Historically one could appreciate the clarity with which Marx analyzed mid-nineteenth-century English industrialism, but I wanted to understand, from the point of view of a participant observer of the system, the appeal of the Soviet model, the glue that had held a state together for forty years under tight control and in relative isolation. Though an academic by profession, I am a city planner, not a political scientist, and therefore could unabashedly ask naïve questions.

Subsequent events made it clear that the attraction was a fairly thin veneer, but during my ten months I came to see an aspect of East German communism that one would not often have gleaned from the Western press, given the concentration on stories about the Wall and attempted escapes. These stories were true, to be sure, and many East Germans readily expressed profound dissatisfaction to me, but behind all of this I came to appreciate another dimension of this movement that captured half the world for several generations. East German communism was in fact rooted in a vision of an ideal, prosperous, humane, stable society. Whatever had happened to the country during the forty years since its founding, and however much the leaders abused their trust, the deeply felt idealism of its founders and their fervor in pursuing those ideals largely shaped what was ultimately created.

People still holding some of the highest managerial positions in 1989 grew up in the 1930s when the conditions in Germany were wildly unstable as a result of the First World War. The disastrous inflation that saw the German mark fall to one trillionth of its former value in 1923, the rampaging excesses of cartel capitalism, the inability of government to manage the society, the violent wrenching of the Nazi rise to power and the feeble voices of leftist opposition that were systematically quelled became the foundation for a life's work. In short, the experience of many Germans with pre-1945 society, basically a free enterprise, pluralist society, was devastating.

In the formative years of this older generation no goal loomed larger than that of a stable society, the hallmarks of that society being a safe and warm dwelling for all in the postwar period when many people were living in remnants of bombed-out houses, a secure job where nobody would face the demeaning threat of unemployment in a period when any job was difficult to obtain, and plentiful food in a period when fathers would trudge far out into the countryside searching for a few eggs with which to nourish their families. These visions of devastation and postwar hardship had remained with this generation, just as the Great Depression had remained with many Americans who coped with their own humiliation and despair during those painful years. There was little place for the wasteful bickering of democracy or the destructive "freedoms" that allowed people to exploit each other, when the deepest needs were to alleviate hunger and provide shelter.

In establishing a socialist state after World War II, this generation set out with one paramount goal: The future Germany must not re-create the conditions of the past. A state must be forged where exploitation no longer existed, where nobody was rich and nobody poor, where everyone was assured a dwelling and a job, where society was stable, peaceful, and productive. The vehicle, of course, came from the Soviet socialist model.

It is difficult, given the system's subsequent collapse, to discern the relative influence of this idealism in imposing the socialist order, but in the end I came to believe that, whatever the role of the Soviet Army in establishing the German Democratic Republic, there were plenty of Germans who fervently believed in Marxist state socialism as the most equitable, humane model for postwar German society.

The long-standing belief in those ideals and the suffering endured by East Germany's leaders in order to realize them is evident in their brief biographies. Erich Honecker, state and Party chief from 1973 through the DDR's fortieth anniversary in 1989 after which he was deposed, was born the son of a coal miner in the Saar region in 1912 and witnessed as a child the grueling conditions of life in the German coal mines. He joined the Communist Youth organization at the age of fourteen and worked until 1933 for causes to realize class equality. Honecker was arrested by the Nazis in 1935 and served ten years in Nazi prisons until the end of the war. Politburo member Hermann Axen was the son of a Jewish communist party official executed by the Nazis, and he himself was imprisoned in Auschwitz and Buchenwald. A number of others who were instrumental in founding East Germany, including Wilhelm Pieck, East Germany's first president, escaped Germany during the Nazi period and lived in exile until war's end. Many of those participating in the founding of East Germany had experienced similar strife in their country and in their own lives during the first half of the twentieth century.

The founders in fact accomplished their goal. By early 1989 East Germany was nothing if not stable, at least outwardly, and nearly everybody lived within a fairly narrow band of prosperity. Unfortunately, two problems marred the dream. The first was a fundamental mistake, one inherited from Lenin. The idealists believed so fervently in the righteousness of their cause that they branded any opposition as counterrevolutionary, class-enemy revanchism that directly threatened the cherished goals and could thus not be tolerated. The cost of achieving their goal was the police state, a cost that proved unacceptably high by 1989.

Opposition to the new order was viewed as an attempt to reinstitute an exploitative capitalism to set the cycle of human destruction again in motion. However, the less enlightened masses knew nothing more than the old system and would not appreciate the ideal society until reeducated. They would have to be forced to live the new life for a time, even against their will, but the ends justified the means of social control until an enlightened socialist citizenry would emerge. In fact, there would be hardship and a stringent set of requirements placed on the people, but the outcome would absolve those who were seen as unrelenting. That the effort had never met with success was well expressed in a joke, furtively whispered to me by a waiter in a Stendal restaurant:

"Why is East German toilet paper so bad?"

"So that every last asshole will become Red."

However well founded it may be, idealism in practice needs criticism to help it maintain its course, to test its principles, to hone the values that drive it, and to keep its visionaries from succumbing to temptation. Unfortunately there is no particular contradiction between idealistic ends and repressive means. No humanly developed utopian ideal, at least to date, has been able to accommodate all the vagaries of human nature that make up society, and those vagaries can threaten any ideal state. This fatal flaw was a hallmark of East German communist idealism. It was the flaw that would bring out not much of the best in human nature in the public affairs of the country during its forty-year history, but certainly much of the worst.

The second fundamental problem resulting from the founders' original vision was perhaps due to its success. The stable society sought by the idealists was essentially achieved by the mid-1950s. None of those who were born after 1946 began their lives at "Zero Hour," as VE-Day was called by the losing side. They did not begin their lives in misery and destitution, but entered as children of this society already enjoying modest but stable security. This younger generation began by taking for granted the physical stability of state socialism, with enough potatoes for all, something to wear, and a place to sleep—those very attributes of society for which the struggle of the founders had been so intense. In taking the stable socialist state for granted, younger generations began to look beyond it for some deeper meaning in life than the struggle for necessities.

One did not particularly look to the East, for despite the propaganda Russian society actually had little to offer Germans in the way of models. Many in the younger generation looked rather to the West for meaning, to the place where the action was, where creative thinking was possible and encouraged, where effort was rewarded, where prosperity defined a thousand different ways was seemingly at hand. The younger generation said to the older, "You just don't understand the world any more," as one elderly believer in the socialist ideal explained a comment by his son to me, shaking his head in disbelief over how his son could so cavalierly dismiss all that had been achieved. If Americans have from time to time complained of a generation gap, I think it may have existed in the United States only in the 1960s to the degree that it wrenched East German society in the 1980s.

There were not many people in their forties in East Germany during the late 1980s, since relatively few children had been born between 1940 and 1949. Thus the demarcation between the older and younger generations was easy to see in the makeup of the population. The societal effect of this age gap was evident in the ease with which I related to the younger versus the older generation, separated by that ten-year space of which I found myself in the middle. After a few social encounters with most people under forty, we easily slipped into the familiar *Du* form of address, historically represented in English by the archaic "thou." Most of the over-fifty generation remained steadfast with the formal *Sie* (you) and were often embarrassed by my offer to use the familiar form. This generational demarcation in personal address prevailed despite an egalitarian, or perhaps elitist, policy by the Party that all members addressed each other with *Du*, at least in Party society. Student Party members would call the college dean *Du* at Party affairs but had to remember to use the formal *Sie* in public. Occasionally they would forget, and such lapses in handling circumspectly one's privileged position was acerbically noted by students not in the Party.

As I observed the Socialist Unity party as one affected by its actions during early 1989, I came to understand that the Party had exerted its authority over the country by means not so remote from the American consciousness as they may seem. Stripped of its ideological clichés, the Party's control over East Germany was in fact not too far removed from the old machine politics in American cities. One may cite the example of an East German village or small town, of which there were about seventy-five hundred in the country. The mayor, a full-time position in even the smallest villages, was in nearly all cases a comrade proposed for unopposed election by the Party, thereby being practically a Party appointee. The mayor controlled the distribution of many things needed for subsistence. When one needed some wood for building a hen house, for example, one went to the mayor. Although lumber was produced by a People's Own Enterprise somewhere in the country, it remained a scarce commodity. The Party secretary of the enterprise largely determined the distribution of its output and could distribute some to villages through the Party structure that eventually filtered down to the mayor. The mayor thus held great and nonappealable discretion as to who received any number of goods distributed through the centralized apparatus of the Party. In addition to allocating portions of a lumber delivery, the mayor would determine who received piglets for supplemental meat, or street-repair work in front of one's house. When a resident requested some commodity or service controlled by the mayor, the answer could either be, "Of course, we just happen to have some," or "I'm so sorry, we had some but you came just a little too late."

Personal relationships were thus important to nurture, and especially in a small town one tended to know who supported the governing authority and who did not. An Evangelical minister who presided over a circle of village churches told me that persons he knew to be dissenters in the villages were angered when he published figures showing vote fraud in East Germany's local elections of May 1989. By specifying the true number of persons voting against the Party, he had effectively identified the dissenters in the villages, who would be certain to receive disadvantage. They were the ones who always seemed to show up one day too late for a piglet. In American cities it was a bucket of coal or a job.

During my many hours on the train I had time to study the countenance of fellow riders, and after a while I began to notice a certain type of person who seemed to be frequently on the trains. Although the East Germans had developed wonderful terms for things in their country that they did not like, in this case they had no equivalent for the American term "party hack." Just as party hacks had been hallmarks of American political machines, so too were they found in abundance in the Socialist Unity party. One often noticed them in positions that had to do with control of people or brokering of power: in offices as administrative assistants or doormen who decided whether or not to allow one to enter a public building, functionaries controlling the movement of paper and knowledge. In particular, however, they could be seen riding the trains on their way to or from some Party activity.

The composite person I describe could be recognized as a man in his fifties or sixties, his age placing him on the older side of that wide generation gap. This composite party hack bore a kind of crusty, self-satisfied expression on his face as he would sit in the train's dining car in a cheap, ill-fitting suit and polyester tie with his Party pin in his lapel. He would gaze with self-satisfaction out the window surveying the land his Party administered. The look seemed consciously practiced, in fact, for much of what he saw out the train window in 1989 was fairly drab and unkempt.

The look was that of one who saw his life's charge as having great responsibility over a system that he did not well understand, that he did not control but was controlled by, and that indeed had placed him in a position of responsibility that exceeded his ability to master. He could not see a way clear to do anything but continue to do what he was doing until orders came from above, with which he might not be able to cope. He also knew, as revealed by his countenance, that the system for which he had sacrificed his life was generally regarded as a failure, and that if pressed to provide real solutions he would have absolutely no idea what to do. This person, with exactly this expression, was multiplied a thousand times among the riders on East German trains.

Party hacks were not the only discernible category of Party member in East Germany. Hacks tended to fill the functionary roles since the jobs were uncreative, but Party membership did seem to cut across the spectrum of society. Most Party members had certainly joined merely out of necessity if they sought responsible careers, but from my associations I identified three other types of Party joiners who appeared to have other motives. If party hacks were group number one, group number two were certainly the idealists. Some idealists deeply believed in theoretical socialism and hoped to further it, irrespective of the current state of the movement. One person whose insight I came to trust, and who had grown up during the ravaged pre-1945 period, said to me, for example, "It is no wonder that capitalism is further developed than socialism. It has a thousand-year history. Given what we have achieved in a hundred years, imagine where we'll be in another nine hundred." Other idealists may not necessarily have believed in socialism, but they sought Party membership in order to have a say in charting the country's course. Both types of idealists appeared particularly frustrated by the effect of democratic centralism, since it had thwarted creative movement in either direction, either toward or away from a true socialist future.

Third were the opportunists, always present in any movement. Members of this group were obvious in their attraction to the power that came with Party membership, irrespective of whatever the Party goals might be. Of all the types, these were the most despised by many people outside the Party, since it was believed that they would bend with any breeze to retain their power positions. The German term for them was *Wendehals,* a species of European woodpecker called "wryneck" in English, that twists its head around on its neck when alarmed.

In addition to the pure power players, there appeared to be three subgroups of opportunists. I can describe group 3A only by using a rather crude term. In the United States such a person would be described as a "nerd." It is a person who may be intelligent but lacks social graces, certainly lacks confidence, and views a power-oriented organization such as the Socialist Unity party as a personality extension that lends a sense of authority over people he feels would not otherwise readily accept him. This was the only group that appeared to be solely male; I observed both men and women as members of the others, except for group 3B which was entirely female.

A member of Party-joiner group 3B was a pretty, somewhat empty-headed woman who thrived on attention and the superficial trappings of prestige in being associated with powerful men. I presume members of this group were recruited because they made the otherwise long and boring Party meetings more pleasant, could be expected to do as they were told, and did not get in the way of the more power-oriented members. I suspect also that members of group 3A found here their only opportunity to woo the 3B group.

Every society seems to include people who are driven primarily by hostility. A member of group 3C was this openly hostile person, eager to wreak vengeance on others for whatever reason, who found the power associated with Party membership a handy vehicle for this outlet, and for which he or she would later not be called to account.

The fourth group comprised the aggressive career advancers, perhaps best described as the East German equivalent of "yuppies." Since the Party was the only vehicle of advancement for most people with ambition, most responsible positions being Party appointments, one had to join the Party to have a chance at attaining a position in society, irrespective of the enterprise in which the position was housed. Managers, department heads, and university faculty members were all appointed through the Party, and in fact primarily through a Party functionary assigned to each productive unit. This person, perhaps the backbone of East German society, was called the Party secretary. Unfortunately for East Germany, the person was usually a member of group number one, the party hacks.

Every organization was provided with a Party secretary. This Party secretary was a full-time representative of the Socialist Unity party lodged within the decision-making structure of the organization. In a university, for example, the Party secretary had little to do with research or teaching; he had much to do with decisions regarding people. Promotions and placements were largely his decision. (There may have been some female Party secretaries, but given its position as central to power brokering, the job appeared usually to be filled by a man.) In fact, the power of the position was enhanced by the secretary's role not exactly being made public, so that it was not necessarily known what decisions he made, and there was no established appeals process should one be denied promotion or other benefit. Given the loyalty of the secretary to the Party, to which he was beholden for the position, rather than to the organization in which he was lodged, decisions stemming from this man tended to be based on Party interests rather than the organization's interest. The Party secretary's presence in an organization, especially given the uncertain knowledge of the limits of his authority, was perhaps the single strongest incentive to guard one's comments in the democratic discussion forums within organizations.

Joining the Party was somewhat like getting married in the nineteenth century; one made an open commitment for the rest of one's life, and divorce was out of the question. Once in the Party, one could participate in predecision discussions as part of democratic centralism, and therefore could have some opportunity to persuade functionaries of the next higher Party level, but the Party decided where a member would work, how fast one would advance in his or her profession, and to a large measure what one could say. I often asked the question, "What do you see as the future of the DDR?" There were many answers, generally dominated by extreme doubt that a clear prediction could be made. Yet when the response to my question was absolute silence, not one word spoken, perhaps a slow shaking of the head, I knew I was speaking with a Party member, especially one of the opportunist group.

"The Party always knows best," was the saying, and the Party knew best about nearly everything having to do with its members' lives, including whether one should be allowed to resign. While I was in Weimar a student Party member decided he wanted to do this, and in making his application he was requested to write a statement of his reasons. The lowest level Party cadre at the school, composed largely of other students and faculty, decided that if he wanted out of the Party, that was his right. After all, the Party should be a voluntary organization of those committed to its ideals. They voted approval. When higher Party authority received their decision, however, they promptly overruled it and demanded that, first, the student prepare a strong, self-censuring statement that would bring him severe disadvantage by being placed in his file and, second, that the cadre dismiss the student from school. The cadre members considered themselves friends of the dissident member and held lengthy discussions about their possible courses of action. In the end they had no choice but to carry out the mandate of the higher authority, voting against their interest in humanizing the Party by reaffirming its nonvoluntary nature. One of the participants told me that the decision was clearly intended to intimidate other members potentially wishing to withdraw from the Party.

The inability to resign freely from the Party seemed partly to be the aftermath of the Party's history as a self-assigned vanguard of a new order that was besieged from without, in the form of antagonism from the West, and from within, in the form of reluctant citizens who would dismantle the Party before they had been successfully reeducated. For some members, especially the opportunists, there appeared from my observations to be a common bond that served as one of those irresistible lures in human nature: the lure of the Mission.

Since its inception the Party had been locked in a struggle with adversaries. Its view of itself as a revolutionary movement was made manifest in its rhetoric by such terms as "struggle" (*Kampf*) and by the large monuments it had erected throughout the country. A monument in Rostock on the Baltic Sea to "revolutionary sailors" stood thirty feet tall, bronze sailors with fists held high and striding confidently forward to socialist victory. The unspoken bond of the revolutionary fighter is one of the most intense bonds between humans, and to break this bond is to destroy the web of intense struggle for which sacrifice is made.

My conversations suggested that the siege mentality characterizing much Party action was well expressed in the conduct of Party meetings. Members never discussed anything of what transpired in their sessions, but nonmembers who for one reason or another had brief access to meetings suggested to me that they were conducted with an air of great seriousness. Since the Party was intendedly composed of enlightened members of the working class, and since cultural appreciation formed an important part of socialist enlightenment, a brief music concert preceded many regular meetings. The sudden appearance of a nonmember, who may have entered to bring a requested document, for example, brought sudden, absolute silence to the room, lasting until the outsider had left. Even such mundane matters as taking roll were carried out with precision. Actually, taking roll was probably not a mundane matter, since presence at meetings was vital for maintaining a healthy record. Saying "Here" during roll call was perhaps the most significant action required of all members, for it was recorded in one's societal engagement file. One could certainly participate in the discussions at meetings, but saying "Here" was the only act guaranteed not to bring disadvantage when the decision came back down the line.

The siege mentality was suggested as well in one of the required courses for students in the architecture school at Weimar, called "Handling Confidential Information," wherein students learned appropriate management of state secrets. In East Germany much that one could speak about freely in the West was regarded as sensitive. One could not publish any map that showed contour lines of the land, since such maps had military usefulness, although everyone knew such maps could be purchased readily in bookstores in the West. One could not photograph industries, bridges, or railroad installations even though they had all certainly been photographed in detail via satellite. Even the diminutive steam locomotives of the country's narrow-gauge railroads declared as historic monuments and maintained as tourist attractions could not be photographed.

I visited the Einstein Tower in Potsdam, a 1920s solar observatory of world importance in architectural history, though in observatory history probably not significant at all. The old building could not possibly hold military secrets. Once one had made arrangements to be admitted to the grounds escorted by a member of the staff, one could photograph the exterior of the historic building as well as the exterior of the research grounds in general, where I am sure a spy could learn more than inside the tower. Please to put your cameras away before entering the tower, however. "We don't actually do anything secret here, but the institution has its rules." When I was there the whole internal apparatus was dismantled anyway for its biannual mirror regrinding necessitated by air pollution in Potsdam.

Once when I visited the architecture school at another East German university, I had to wait for my appointment because the professor was in a meeting with an army colonel. He later asked me, "How much say does the army have in city planning matters in the United States?" "Well," I murmured, "the Interstate highways were built with defense in mind. . . ." In East Germany the military had a say in the layout of cities and residential districts. The siege mentality had thus penetrated to levels of decision making that had little to do with siege but much to do with daily life.

To be sure, not all Party members were led by intrigue, but those who were were easily encountered. One day when traveling to Leipzig I met a faculty member and two doctoral students at the Weimar railroad station, waiting for the same train to Leipzig. Few people attained either status unless they were members of the Party, but one learned for sure and gleaned the nature of their travel only by exchanging pleasantries. "Hello. What's happening in Leipzig today?" I enquired. The answer could have been something vague as, "We are consulting with the city architect about a research project." But when the answer was "We'll see," followed by absolute, total silence, one knew the Party had called. We traveled together on the train, to their evident discomfort, and they quietly discussed among themselves a few points from that morning's *Neues Deutschland* regarding the student uprisings in China that had happened a few weeks previously. I gathered their meeting had something to do with expressing solidarity with the Chinese government movement against the counter-revolutionaries, a policy adopted as the Party line. At the Leipzig station, the first words to me after "We'll see" were "Well, here is where we must part company. Have a good day." They spotted their contact person waiting on the platform and rapidly distanced themselves from me.

Before one could resign from the Party, of course, one had to join. This action was also not entirely voluntary. The Party in fact propagated itself by selecting its prospective members. One could not merely join if one so desired; one had to be recruited. Thus it resembled a private club in a tradition not unknown to Americans, and the Old Boy network was thriving quite well. The Party's self-selection of new initiates, indeed, was the final knot that tied up the Poodle's Core of democratic centralism so tight that people in East Germany had been absolutely unable to unravel it until it succumbed to spontaneous mass protest. The knot looked like this: The Party recruited its members from the larger society, itself selecting who should be admitted. Given the country's political organization, established by the Party, based on Party control of decision making in the workplaces, the Party positioned key decision makers in every organization in the country. These Party representatives in the organizations were beholden to the Party for their livelihood, and any threat to the stability or dominance of the Party was a threat to that livelihood. It was important to silence those who held unpopular views, for those views could be threatening. Indeed, it was important to exclude those who could not be trusted (i.e., non-Party members) from any position where they could effectively utter an opposing point of view. The knot could be tied because the enforcement authorities such as the *Stasi,* the state security police, were organized in the same way, also by the Party. Every productive enterprise was protected by *Kampfgruppen,* or "struggle groups," the Party's nationally organized private militia. It was as though the National Guard in the United States were an arm of the Democratic party, its mission to protect the Democrats from any threat to their power. The whole Socialist Unity party organization in East Germany thus functioned as an autonomous unit of society, self-perpetuating, self-governing, self-enforcing, and controlling everything else. In the end it resembled a huge perpetual motion machine that had reached a state of equilibrium that defied any attempts by any person or group to alter its course or speed.

During my tenure I found that people with whom I talked understood this state of equilibrium well, and for them it meant that there was no orderly way out of the East German dilemma. People said to me over and over, in fact, that new directions would have to come from above, not below, in order to change the country without destroying it, but that the higher echelons of the Party were as locked into an unchangeable system as much as anybody else. In the end, however, new directions came from below.

Not all Party members were indeed silent while I was there. Those of the idealist persuasion tended to be highly critical and discouraged, though the extent to which they expressed this to me varied with their positions, their personalities, and how well we had come to know each other. At one point a Party member friend said to me, "It's hard to have a real discussion with people about issues. A lot of people truly and deeply believe every opinion set forth in this morning's *Neues Deutschland*. If today the Party changes its mind and publishes an opposite opinion in tomorrow's paper, then these same people by nine o'clock tomorrow morning will always have truly and deeply believed the new Party opinion."

I became acquainted with a number of idealists who wished no longer to be in the Party because it hampered them in the realization of their own lives and they felt their voices were not being heard. However, once a member, one had been privy to the Party's workings but could not divulge them for fear of severe disadvantage. By leaving the Party one would have more freedom to criticize, as well as more knowledge to use as the basis for criticism. Thus one could only leave in disgrace, with a dishonorable discharge.

Some Party members had thus remained but were disgruntled and felt disenfranchised, since the Party appeared to allow almost nobody any real influence on decisions until one reached the top levels, by which time one was beholden to a network of people above and below who had elevated him or her to the position. One of my Party-member acquaintances, quite idealistic, believed in true democracy, in free speech, and in the humanist goals of socialism in providing an unstressful, rewarding life. I posed him the question that, given a fair number of like-minded Party members, could not one begin to achieve the goals of democracy and free speech in those Party functions over which one had control? Unfortunately the rigidity and hierarchy of the Party precluded even that, he responded. An aspect of democratic centralism that suppressed free speech was the multitiered organization of the Party, through which recommendations flowed upward only one level at a time. Rank and file Party members were several layers removed from the decision-making levels of the Party. Party members at lower levels, for example, recommended delegates to Party congresses but never actually knew which names were finally selected as delegates since the final decision was made in secret at higher levels. Given such anonymity, even a reform-minded person at the next higher level of the Party could not promise his subordinates protection from disadvantage if they expressed unpopular opinions. Disadvantage could be meted out from all levels above. Thus there was no way, it seemed, to adjust the system, and there was great frustration even within the Party. Another Party member, a high-ranking university professor, said a couple of times to me, "The Party cannot keep on going like this because if they do they're going to ruin the whole country."

During my tenure I also held several conversations with people who had not joined the Party and who had resisted efforts by the Party to recruit them. My conversants cited the incident of the student who wished to resign, as well as similar stories. They expressed concern about the Party's gaining total control over their lives, and asserted that in the long run joining would stifle whatever freedom of action they had as individuals, even though they knew that as long as the Party remained in power they would be hindered in professional advancement and excluded from any dealings with sensitive information. A few persons expressed hesitation about joining because its demands of absolute obedience resembled a similar requirement by the Nazi party, a memory that still lurked close to the surface.

Not only could Party members not question Party decisions, most had to pledge to renounce Western contacts until such time as one moved into one's own power position and had some leeway. So for young comrades, much of the opportunity to investigate knowledge was replaced by inculcation of Marxist and Party values, some of which were represented by clichés (*Phrasen* was the East German term) that were not to be probed. Despite the exhaustive discussions that took place, hardly any had real content, at least in public. Thus it was that one third-year architecture student, Party member, neighbor, and member of group 3B, approached me one day rather intensely and asked if I could please come over for tea that evening since she wanted to talk. I went, we drank, chatted, and then she leaned toward me and said, "Paul, please tell me the truth. Tell me what the West is really like."

As I contemplated the nature of the Party, its demands for obedience, its punishment of those who diverged from accepted speech and behavior, I thought of American institutions, public and private. I thought of what often happens to whistle blowers, of privileged information and the attempts to avoid public scrutiny, of bureaucratic power plays. In the end, I thought, despite the clashing ideologies between the two systems there were common strains of human nature in the function of both.

Here is a children's song from the Thälmann Pioneer songbook *Be Ready! (Seid Bereit!)*, called "Good Is the Party," learned by children ten years old. It rhymes nicely in German but not in my English translation:

> Good is the Party.
> For us it provides
> For today's play
> And tomorrow's deeds.
> As a friend it shows us
> Many enticingly beautiful goals.
>
> Smart is the Party.
> It must consider very many things,
> And many help it
> To plan and rule.
> Thus do colorful beets grow,
> And big new cities.
>
> Strong is the Party.
> It can achieve so much.
> And, for our protection,
> It also has strong weapons.
> We hold in strong embrace
> The hands of the comrades.

A joke circulated about the SED, the German initials of the Socialist Unity party, (*Sozialistische Einheitspartei Deutschlands*). "SED" really stood for *So endet Deutschland*. "Thus ends Germany."

6

Why Rosa Luxemburg Was Wrong: Notions of Freedom under Communism

The Party says: "Everything you have is mine. Everything I have is none of your business."

MAY DAY was one of the two big holidays in East Germany. October seventh was actually the national holiday, celebrating the declaration of the German Democratic Republic on October 7, 1949, but socialism was still ideologically regarded as an internationalist movement where solidarity among working classes was stronger than national loyalty. Hence the first of May remained a big day of parades, speeches, and street festivals marking another year of development toward advanced socialist society. East Germans proudly pointed out to me that May Day, the day of working-class celebration, was an American invention.

Indeed, May Day was an American invention, its roots set in the fight for an eight-hour day. The short-lived Federation of Organized Trades and Labor Unions resolved at its 1884 convention in Chicago that as of May 1, 1886, eight hours would constitute a legal day's labor. On that first May Day, workers in many American cities engaged in a one-day strike. By 1889 the call for an eight-hour day had reached international attention, and the founding congress of the Second International in Paris in 1889 called for May first to be celebrated as an "international labor day." With the demise of radical labor movements in the United States, May Day activities eventually withered there, but May first remained the observed "labor day" throughout capitalist as well as socialist Europe.

The same 1884 convention in Chicago had also proclaimed, along with the May Day protest action, that the labor movement should declare a celebration day each year, selecting the first Monday in September. Ten years later the United States Congress adopted this date as the annual Labor Day holiday, which has continued to be observed.

From outward appearances all of East Germany expressed a spontaneous enthusiasm about the first workers' and farmers' state on German soil when they celebrated May Day. Flags hung everywhere. Even the smallest village was festooned with bright, new DDR flags and the red flags of the international workers' movement. Not only flags and bunting draped the country for May Day, walls and fences were covered with banners bearing inspiring slogans. "Solidarity with the people of Nicaragua!" "Forever allied with the Soviet Union!" "A stronger socialism means a more secure peace!" In some instances slogans were apparently solicited from workers in a People's Own Enterprise and the best were selected by the Party secretary to be displayed. Not all were approved; one person wanted to make a poster saying "A clean environment—everybody's business!" He was denied.

Then there were the parades, the mass demonstrations of thousands of East Germans marching with flags down the main thoroughfares of cities. In 1989 *Neues Deutschland* proclaimed that seven hundred thousand Berliners had marched in that city's four-and-one-half-hour May Day parade, always the country's largest. That figure, if it was true, represented over half the entire population of the city.

In Weimar the 1989 May Day demonstration was held under the slogan, "High achievement for the well-being of the people and for peace—Everything for the implementation of the decisions of the eleventh Party Congress of the SED—Forward to the fortieth birthday of the DDR!" According to the neatly printed program, nine marching groups would present themselves to the local Party functionaries on the reviewing stand, beginning with students and sport groups from the architecture school, through representatives of the Heavy Equipment Production Conglomerate "Progress," then agricultural cooperatives, various people's own enterprises, and governmental agencies. On that day, thousands of flags were carried past the reviewing stand set up on Goethe Platz across from the main post office. Scaffolding on its facade, built to shelter postal patrons from falling debris, was neatly hidden behind red bunting.

Though photographs of these demonstrations in the Western press conjured up visions of millions of people happily spending their holiday cheering the system, I found the reality, as were most realities in East Germany, to result neither from powerful, uncontrollable forces over the human mind nor from a latent euphoria about communism. Some insight into May Day came when I overheard a group of students talking before one of my classes. Their problem was that every class year at the architecture school had to be represented in the parade by a group of students carrying flags and banners, and other organizations such as the university athletic club also had to have representatives, some of whom were also part of the other group and had to choose between them. Snatches of the conversation went something like this:

"Who's going to carry the flag this year? I don't want to do it."

"So many people are out of town working on their class projects. There are only a few of us left, so we all have to be there."

"And what if nobody shows up?"

"Come on, Professor Holz told us he is trying to work out some exchange programs with West German universities, but the Party is uneasy about it. If we don't make a good showing in front of that reviewing stand, our chances are nil."

"Our chances are nil anyway, so what are you excited about?"

"If we're not there it will bring us nothing but trouble."

"Carrying flags is outmoded. People did that in the fifties. It's just going through the motions now."

"Maybe, but if you don't participate it makes it tough for the rest of us, so be there, will you?"

"Well, I'll go but won't carry anything. I can't carry one of those stupid slogans."

In the end nearly all of them went, and nearly all carried something. Yet participating did not appear to be all that bad, after all. There was not much to do on a holiday in East Germany anyway, and everybody else was at the demonstration. One could meet friends, stroll around in what one hoped would be pleasant spring weather. There was a good feeling about doing something together with others even if one would not do so alone, and besides, everyone who participated received ten marks. That paid for a good meal. If one failed to show up, the boss would know about it on May second and one would have to explain being absent.

Participation was strongly encouraged partly because retribution for a system malfunction at a low level such as this could reach high levels. Every supervisor was responsible for assuring the participation of subordinates. If a worker decided not to participate, he or she could be reprimanded by the supervisor (and, therefore, if reproaches were serious or frequent enough, could be denied promotion, bumped from a housing waiting list, refused a desired vacation trip to a Black Sea resort, and so forth). If subordinates balked, the supervisor would be reprimanded, and so it would go up the system. Therefore an individual risked much by nonparticipation. It was better to spend a couple of hours being counted than to lose one's place in line for the fruits of the revolution.

Under massive protest this system would quickly collapse. My students understood this well, but in early 1989 protest was still largely untested. The students also believed that the first who tried would have to bear the brunt of disciplinary measures and, up to that point, few had been willing to be the first. Those who had been willing to stand up in opposition were imprisoned, and the worst were expelled to the West. By escorting dissenters from the country, in fact, the Party had been successful in getting rid of the leaders without whom opposition could not become well organized. When spontaneous demonstrations erupted in late 1989, in fact, it became clear that the hundreds of thousands then willing to take the first step had few charismatic leaders to follow.

May Day may have been the most exuberant celebration, but certainly not the only one. On International Women's Day in the spring of 1989, Theater Place in Weimar was full of people viewing the afternoon celebration. Hundreds of women and a fair number of men milled around the square, not paying particular attention to the festivities on the steps of the National Theater that served as a stage. As it turned out nearly all were given time off to attend and their presence noted by representatives of their workplaces. So people tended to stand around and chat with friends until they felt they could sneak away. The speeches from the theater's front steps addressed the woman's workplace as her place of struggle for peace and socialism, and lauded the fulfillment of production quotas at a baby carriage factory. Children of the Young Pioneers lined the steps, lending color with their white shirts and red bandanas, though their presence appeared to provide additional bulk to the quantity of participating people rather than contribute to the content. After the speeches, the crowds were sent home to the strains of military marches played by the local Soviet Army band.

I contemplated why a celebration such as International Women's Day would be so energetically observed in East Germany while largely forgotten in the United States. One functionary told me that it was a sign that the United States oppressed women, while East Germany had proclaimed them vital participants in building the socialist state. Yet I noted an East German form of sexual politics in that the event was planned by the Party, largely by men, and seemed to celebrate the traditionally subordinate role of women rather than their equality or capacity for leadership.

Though many apparently attended these events to be counted and spend an afternoon away from the workplace, and though others were there certainly because they believed in the Party, still others had their own reasons for attending. I spoke to a few acquaintances who went to see if any glimmer of change could be discerned in the speeches. There was none. It must also not be forgotten that, given the paucity of interesting things to do, the Soviet Army band playing on the steps of the National Theater was an event relatively worth attending.

Anniversaries were also very important days in East Germany, tracked carefully and used to advantage in taking another step toward advanced socialist society. An important day might be a milestone anniversary of a city's founding, say 750 years, or the anniversary of an event in history deemed important for socialist history, as the 450th anniversary of the German Peasant War when farmers rose up against feudal landlords, or the anniversary of a significant event in German cultural history such as the 300th anniversary of Johann Sebastian Bach's birth in Eisenach.

Berlin's big birthday celebration a few years ago demonstrates how the anniversary system was incorporated into state planning goals. Berlin had been founded in the year 1237, and the city's 750th anniversary was coming up in 1987. It was important to make the city look good for the occasion, especially since West Berlin, being also Berlin, was celebrating the same birthday. The competition was on to see who had the best Berlin: the one on the east side of the Wall or the one on the west. The eastern one, by the way, was always "Berlin, Capital of the DDR." Just as you do not call it Frisco, you never called it "East Berlin." The other one, the one shown as a blank on East German maps of Berlin, was known as "Westberlin," usually written as one word.

Each of the fifteen administrative regions in East Germany had its own WBK. The WBK was an industrialized housing construction conglomerate, or *Wohnungsbaukombinat*, charged with building new multifamily housing in its region. For several years in preparation for Berlin's 750th, the WBKs in each of the outlying fourteen regions (Berlin was its own region) were given a construction quota in East Berlin. Each was required to divert a certain percentage of its output to Berlin—ship the materials and provide the workers to construct housing in the capital city. East Berlin was to become a showplace for socialist housing. This and other diversions of productive capacity, which had in fact continued even after the 1987 birthday, managed to worsen conditions in the rest of the country, as needed housing was not provided and needed goods were not available. The government published a handsomely illustrated booklet, "The Regions Build in Berlin," to show off their work, but many people expressed bitterness about the policy—even East Berliners, for some of whom the city seemed to be growing out of control.

Among the primary beneficiaries of the policy apparently were construction workers themselves who came from the outlying districts to build in Berlin. Since there was a housing shortage in the capital, the first dwellings they built in Berlin tended to be their own. They would live in these dwellings while building others, intending eventually to return home and free the dwellings for Berliners. In reality many remained permanently, since economic opportunities there were better than in the provinces. Under socialism one did not evict tenants from dwellings, and since availability of a dwelling was the chief practical determinant of where one could work, to have a dwelling in Berlin opened up many possibilities.

Living in East Berlin had an additional advantage. The city was flooded from across the Wall by the programs of Radio Free Berlin, rather Radio Free Westberlin (*Sender Freies Berlin*), and of RIAS (Radio in the American Sector)—despite its name a fully German station—so that one was better informed. These two influential West Berlin radio stations not only provided East Berliners with news about the world outside the Zone, they also broadcast more meaningful news about developments inside East Germany itself than did the Party-controlled DDR stations.

In further preparation for the 750th birthday of the capital city, East Germans were asked to place "Berlin 750 Years" stickers on their cars. Some people, displeased at the decree that the country should show solidarity for building up its capital at the expense of other regions where housing needs were often greater, placed their own stickers on their cars. These said things like "Dresden 780 Years," or "Leipzig 970 Years." Such behavior was not deemed sufficiently societally committed, however, and police proceeded to remove the non-Berlin bumper stickers.

Such displays on one's automobile were often a popular instrument of subtle protest. In rear windows one frequently saw stuffed ALF dolls (the beloved critter from the American television show), or the banners of West German soccer teams. A favorite sticker on the back of the diminutive Trabant automobile was the international black and yellow "long vehicle" sign. Many people who had requested permission to emigrate to West Germany tied white streamers on their car antennas as their own expression of solidarity. Those whose applications had been denied often displayed black streamers. A friend deadpanned that people who had requested emigration to the Soviet Union would display red streamers. In October of 1988, however, the People's Assembly passed a new law that prohibited attaching anything to the antenna of a car.

The notion of "solidarity," ingrained in Marxist thought, by which one was expected to participate in the building of socialist society and not act against the interests of the working class as represented by its vanguard Party, led to a quality the East Germans called "apparent participation" (*Scheinbeteiligung*). Sometimes a person was represented as showing solidarity with building the socialist state, irrespective of what one had actually done. The local Weimar paper interviewed a student about anticipated changes in the architecture school's academic program. When he read the published article, the student noted several quotations attributed to him that he had not uttered and that portrayed him as an enthusiastic supporter of the changes, which he was not. Concerned that his friends would wonder about his true beliefs, he decided to write a letter of complaint to the newspaper. Because the letter referred to a school issue, he had to submit it to the school administration for review and approval before sending it. The administrators did not deem such a letter appropriate, but they did approve a mild statement expressing concern over "an extension of my remarks beyond the actual words spoken." The letter was finally forwarded to the newspaper, but the student received no reply or acknowledgment, and it was not published.

An attribute of life in East Germany that resulted in a high degree of frustration was the expected "apparent participation" in discussions relating to issues facing the country, when the limits of such participation were confined to expressing support for the Party. The feeling that one had continually to attend meetings and say something without really helping to find the best solution, since decisions would be made secretly by higher Party levels according to their own agenda, led to a large population that seemed not to have learned to engage in public discussions, as I noted in chapter 4, and also not to have learned to listen. People did not listen because they believed there was nothing interesting to hear. Students in my classes would read newspapers, for example, and when I asked them if what I was talking about was really so boring that the newspaper was more interesting, what they said was that I was indeed not boring but that it had not occurred to them to listen to me.

Students were expected to attend class at East German universities, but attendance was actually mandatory in only two courses. The first was athletics, and the second was M-L. All students had to take a series of courses on Marxism-Leninism. These courses were in fact notorious among the students as an opportunity to do everything but listen. If one really listened to the lectures in these courses, one was suspected of being a Party sycophant, a Ministry for State Security informer, or at best a goody-goody not to be trusted. Students would knit, write letters, clean their pens, pass notes, catch up on the gossip. They did pay attention when roll was taken, since it was quite important to answer "Present" when their names were called.

The notion of apparent participation was also evident in the relationship of parents to the elementary and high schools. In the United States, of course, elected school boards are often caught up in parent-generated controversies about educational content, ranging from the recurring debate over creationism vs. evolution to issues of sex education and library censorship. The situation in East Germany was different. Parents did not have the right to know, and thus could not ask, what their children were being taught in school. That was a matter for the Party to determine, in its role as vanguard of the working class. There were parent-teacher meetings, to be sure, where the teachers would explain to the parents some aspects of the program. The parents would hear what was said and perhaps ask polite questions. Teachers were invariably Party members, and Party-member parents had the opportunity to meet with teachers privately before the official evening sessions with other parents.

Children were to be taught correct socialist values in school and in their youth groups, the Pioneers. Thus, for example, despite the serious air-quality problems caused by coal smoke emitted from the country's few million polluting chimneys, children would learn songs like this one, also from the Thälmann Pioneer songbook, entitled "No Smokestack Could Smoke." It rhymes nicely in German.

No, oh no, no smokestack could smoke
Without using coal.

Without coal one cannot
Heat an oven, burn a light.

Refrain: Everywhere, in every case,
    We need black coal.

Our huge factories and machines
Must use black coal.
Only with coal is it possible
To run our fast trains.

From black coal is born
The fuel for our motors.
Only with coal, you should know,
We make electricity and we make gas.

So many important and good things
One can make with coal!
Colorful paints and pharmaceuticals
Oil and tar and so much more.

One acquaintance reported to me the first lesson in socialist civics that his first-grader came home with: the National People's Army is good because it protects our republic, with the help of the Soviet armed forces. The West German army is bad because it is a pawn of American capitalists who want to invade the DDR and exploit the people for private profit. I noticed most of these types of comments from children tended to drift through home conversations without much notice by parents who obviously thought otherwise. I asked one friend if this inculcation of values in his child bothered him, and I appreciated the astuteness of his response. He told me that it was very complex. If he convinced his child that what was being taught in school was wrong, it would set up a kind of schizophrenia that the youngster was too immature to handle. If he did not convince his child, he would have driven an emotional wedge between himself and the youth. So he said little and waited for the inevitable questions, which he attempted to answer as forthrightly as possible. "After all," he said, "everybody else has figured things out, so my kid will too."

Then there was the time a child came home and reported to her parents what she had learned in school that day: the Russians had given the Germans their culture. Her mother told me she had to sit the child down and tell her a bit about how the world really works. Just don't say it in school.

Given the different value systems by which people had to live simultaneously, a form of value plurality seemed to be mastered quite early by children. One said certain things in school and in the Pioneer meetings, one said a different set of things at home, and for those involved in the Church there was to some extent a third set of values imposed. At home, some children would watch West German television and converse freely about such things as the latest daring escape over the Wall. None of this would be part of their schoolday conversation, at least in public.

A minister was discussing this problem with me one day, and he told me a story about a recent Sunday school class. He was giving a lesson about Moses to a group of third graders, when one of the students spoke up. "Didn't Karl Marx say something similar about. . . ." The child's neighbor elbowed him in the ribs. "Aw, c'mon, man, this is Church school."

Strongly encouraged "apparent participation" and restricted opposition had a long history in communist thought and were principal contributions of Lenin to the theoretical basis of Marxism. They constituted much of the difference between Marxism and Marxism-Leninism, the latter term used almost exclusively in East German writings. From the communist perspective, enforced positive participation was still viewed as an important protection against oppression of the working class. The attitude toward Rosa Luxemburg is a case in point. In January 1989 the Party organized its annual official demonstration in East Berlin to commemorate the anniversary of the deaths of the socialist activists Rosa Luxemburg and Karl Liebknecht at the hands of rightist German troops in 1919. Though the two were revered in East Germany as martyrs, they said some things that did not find particular favor with the Party. In "The Problem of Dictatorship," a 1917 essay on the Russian Revolution and Leninism, and directed specifically to the evils she had already observed in the workings of democratic centralism, Rosa Luxemburg wrote a passage that had come to be of particular interest for East Germans:

> Freedom only for the supporters of the government, only for members of one party—however numerous they may be—is no freedom at all. Freedom is always and exclusively freedom for the one who thinks differently. Not because of any fanatical concept of "justice" but because all that is instructive, wholesome and purifying in political freedom depends on this essential characteristic, and its effectiveness vanishes when "freedom" becomes a special privilege.

The official demonstration in 1989 bore special importance, given the stress on round-numbered anniversaries, since it marked the seventieth anniversary of the martyrs' deaths. On that day, concurrent with the official Berlin demonstration, an unofficial celebration in Leipzig honoring Luxemburg and Liebknecht prominently featured banners bearing the slogan "Freedom is freedom for the one who thinks differently." Leipzig was already becoming known as the country's center of opposition, and the demonstrators, about eighty I was told, were arrested. By October of 1989 there would be a thousand times as many demonstrators every Monday night on the streets of Leipzig, but at that time eighty demonstrators was quite something. The event and its consequences were fervently discussed by students at the architecture school. I entered into it one night with a group of Ph.D. students, all Party members.

"Why do these words cause such controversy?" I asked. "They were said by one of your heroes, and it seems obvious from the attitudes of so many people in your country who are unhappy that one should heed them."

They responded with the Party line (East Germans also used the term "Party line"), which was rather crafty: The very people who "thought differently" and whose rights Luxemburg so fervently defended were the ones who killed her. Therefore she was wrong, and antisocialist minds that "think differently" about societal issues should not be allowed such freedom ever again. My argument about revering that statement as a guide to make sure such injustice did not recur failed to penetrate their logic. At least they did not admit such. Non-Party members saw the logic quite clearly.

> The child had learned a song in school and began to sing it in the back seat of the car.
> "I carry the red flag. It is the workers' flag. . . ."
> "Hans!" admonished the father.
> "The flag has never fallen, though many bearers have given their lives. . . ."
> The father grabbed a cassette and slammed it into the stereo.
> "WE GET HIGH ON THE SUNSHINE. . . ." It was the rock group WAR, approaching the threshold of pain.
> He leaned over and yelled in my ear, "You gotta meet power with power!"

7

Going Folding:
The Last Communist Election

I VOTED IN East Germany. It was the last election before the communist government's demise, an election the East Germans would not forget. "The Citizens of the German Democratic Republic exercise their political power through democratically elected Peoples' Representative Bodies," stated Article V of the East German constitution. This charge was taken seriously, and elections were held every few years for members of the national and local legislative bodies. Officially, elections in East Germany proceeded much like elections in the United States. A registered voter would go to the polling place, have his or her name checked off, receive a ballot, could if desired retire to the voting booth to mark the ballot, and then fold it and place it in the ballot box. Within this framework, however, some adjustments were made that differentiated East German socialist democracy from the pluralist democracies of the West.

Given the air of tension building in the country in May of 1989 over *Sputnik* and other frustrations, these elections were greeted with an unprecedented intensity and were preceded by several months of speculation, even though the National Front composed of the Party, the other four nominal parties, and the important societal organizations as usual offered only one candidate for each position. Though one did not choose among candidates, the election served to affirm support for the National Front, which was really the Party in various disguises since the Party had placed its members in strategic positions in all the constituent organizations.

When the election approached I decided to discover what I could about how East German elections really worked and what their significance was, so I decided to register and vote.

"Foreign residents have equal rights in the DDR," exclaimed Egon Krenz, then chairman of the state election commission as well as head of the state security agency. The Party's Central Committee had decreed in March 1989 that foreign citizens aged eighteen years and older, having lived in the DDR for over six months, were granted the right to vote for candidates to the *Volksvertretung,* which I shall refer to here as the "city elective body" since the term "city council" suggests a degree of authority this organ did not possess. It was not a matter of voting for national candidates who would guide the country, but merely for local candidates who would deal with questions relating to what might be termed livability issues in their towns and districts.

Prior to the election, the candidates selected by the National Front held public meetings in their districts to hear the opinions and problems of the population. One did not expect heated discussions at these meetings given the presence of democratic centralism, but people looked at least for innovative approaches within the prescribed framework and possibly for indications that higher authority had made some policy shift that would be of interest. Thus despite the near certainty that the candidates would be elected, the meetings were popular for people seeking hints of new directions. For that matter, I presume they were also popular for those who feared the same new directions.

Candidates were widely publicized through two printed media. Store windows were emblazoned with photographs of the local candidates under the slogan "We are voting for the candidates of the National Front!" In addition, for several weeks before the election, *Neues Deutschland* carried lead articles with enthusiastic exhortations about the candidates, the issues, and the stand of the Party on policy matters. A front-page photograph of Harald Mensch, chairman of the agricultural cooperative "Joyful Future" (*Frohe Zukunft*) in Berlin, showed him poring over ledgers. "We have accomplished much," he stated. "The annual milk yield per cow has risen in the past four years from 5,010 to 5,822 kilograms. . . . All those are things I can report as representative and candidate for reelection to the Pankow District Elective Body, and which give me the certainty that we can shape an even more beautiful future through our daily accomplishments."

Neues Deutschland also carried photographs and testimonials of non-proletarian role models. Petra Zieger was a DDR rock star: "It is important for us that our music contributes to our independent national culture. National Front candidates will commit themselves to this end." Or Gloria Siebert, track star and medal winner at the Seoul Olympics: "I am happy to live, work, train, and study in this land. Unlike in the capitalist world it gives me athletic and professional support, but above all human and social security. It is the socialist way that the producing classes have the say."

Given the political organization of socialist society around the workplace, voters were registered where they worked rather than where they lived, though voting precincts were arranged by dwelling district. A Party-appointed election official in each enterprise was responsible for registering voters, and before the election each registered voter received a red card with his or her name and precinct. One could choose to vote on election day or during specified hours during the previous two weeks, when polling places were also open. Since there was no absentee balloting, the multiple-day opening of the polls assured that all would have the opportunity to vote.

The polling place where I voted, a student club in Weimar, looked similar to one in the United States. Crossed flags—the black-red-gold DDR flag with the central garland of wheat, and the red flag of international communism—graced the entrance. Inside, three election monitors sat at a table. The first took the red card, the second checked my identification, and the third handed out the ballot. As a foreigner I was allowed to vote only for candidates to the city elected body, so I received one pink slip with the voting precinct printed at the top, followed by a list of about twenty names. Nothing else, just the names, without affiliation or position. One could, and citizens supportive of the National Front were expected to, merely fold the ballot in half and place it in the ballot box without marking on it, thereby casting a vote for all the candidates. One could, however, retire to the voting booth to cross out the names of any candidates one chose not to support. If one wished to strike out any candidate, one had to follow an exact procedure. A single "X" through the entire ballot did not indicate disapproval of all candidates; it merely rendered the ballot invalid. One had to strike through each individual name.

By the time of the election I had lived in East Germany for eight months and had already experienced much of what I report in this volume. I had come to sense the idealism with which the state had been formed, I had come to appreciate the orderly life one could lead in the DDR, and I came to understand the desire to maintain a society without the unfortunate extremes that plagued Western countries. Yet I also wondered about the price one had to pay for this life, and I contemplated how I should vote. I did not want to present a simplistic anticommunist reaction, the caricature of an American; and as a guest in the country I considered the polite response of folding and leaving. But in the end I considered how I would have voted in this situation in my own country, and I exercised my democratic right by dutifully entering the booth and striking through every name on the ballot. Then I folded it and dropped it in the box.

The procedure was handled with the same quiet efficiency that characterizes American polling places, with one exception. The heads of the poll officials perked up as I entered, and one of them said, "Oh, here is our American." They watched me enter the booth, and I have no doubt they knew exactly what I was doing. I thought it would probably be the last time the East Germans would ever allow an American to vote in their local elections.

So far the election process would not appear remarkable. There is, however, more to the story. It is true that candidates held meetings before the elections, but it appeared that neither the candidates nor the electorate were sure what their authority was. A difference between East German elected officials and American city council members became quickly evident. After the candidates were affirmed by the East German voters, the local elected bodies would meet about twice a month to discuss various issues, but their meetings were not public and records of their deliberations were generally not publicly available. I spoke with one young, newly elected representative who told me that prior to his selection as a candidate he had in fact never had contact with a local representative and was unsure what he was supposed to do. These bodies were not a "city council" because decisions on policy, budget, and program priorities for a city were not made by them but by the department heads of city agencies who were Party members appointed by the Party. These decisions were made in secret session, not open to public comment, with entire deliberations announced only after a decision resulting from them had been made.

In reality the local elected body was apparently so unimportant that the ballot one received might not list the candidates who represented one's own district. I voted prior to the official election day, and the candidates on my list were from another part of the city. I discovered later that *all* voters submitting ballots at my polling place before the final election day were presented with the same list, irrespective of where they lived.

Pity the poor representative democracy. It is doomed to a contentious and ineffective existence no matter how it is formulated. If a few delegates represent the interests of the many, each delegate has considerable power but it is wielded far beyond the control of individual members of the electorate. If many delegates each represent the interests of relatively few voters, the people can exert more direct influence over their representatives, but each representative has little power to influence the system. The Party apparently understood this paradox and had invested heavily in the latter form. There was, in fact, so much democracy, at least apparent democracy, in East Germany that it could not possibly have influenced the system. In the May 1989 local elections, a total of 273,444 candidates ran for 273,444 offices. One candidate per office was standard, of course. The candidates were selected by the Party from among its own trusted people and ran without opposition. This "socialist democracy," as it was called, was obviously a manipulation that assisted the Party in cinching its knot of control ever tighter. East Germans were aware of the deception, and for this reason focused their expressions of dissent on striking candidates' names. Yet regardless of the actual degree of true democracy in this election, this number of candidates in a country of sixteen million people amounted to one local "elected" representative for every sixty residents nationwide. In the United States, by comparison, it is almost impossible to find an elected body whose members represent only sixty people each; that would be the case only where a town of three hundred people elected a five-person city council.

It is further instructive to note the age distribution of the candidates. Of these 273,444 candidates, about 46,000, or 17 percent, were under twenty-five years old. The Party suggested that the youthfulness of many elected representatives demonstrated the commitment of young people to socialist ideals. Another interpretation of course would be that the youthfulness of representatives suggested the relative powerlessness of the office.

As the May 1989 local elections approached, many East Germans believed that if people voted as they actually felt, the Party would suffer a resounding defeat. It was not expected, however, that this sentiment would be reflected accurately in the voting results, for three reasons. First, the history of voting intimidation in East Germany meant that many would still not dare enter the voting booth to cross out names for fear of receiving disadvantage. Second, the exacting requirements to register a negative vote made it difficult to do, and later discussions revealed that many people had actually cast positive votes while believing they were casting negative votes. Third, many thought the Party would falsify any results that made it look bad. The vote counters would count all votes as positive, irrespective of what the ballot said, until the desired 95-plus percent support level was reached, and only afterward would negative ballots be counted as negative. Election monitors were Party members, monitoring the election that would show support for their own party to which they were beholden for their professional positions.

The voting booth at my polling place was actually a regular table, on top of which was placed a three-sided screen two feet high, open only at the back where the voter stood. Officials could tell exactly who went into the booth, and it would not be hard to figure out what one was doing therein. Further, the table was laid out nicely with a clean white tablecloth and provided with two razor-sharp hard-leaded pencils for the voters who wished to enter the booth. Of course attempting to strike through names on the flimsy paper ballot with these pencils on top of a soft tablecloth without ripping the ballot, which would render it invalid, was quite a feat.

Some people believed that the only sure way to register a protest was not to vote at all. One acquaintance, a nurse, had decided she would not vote in the 1989 election and had prepared a list of grievances to justify her decision if called upon to do so. Her list cited the limited supply of surgical materials at the hospital: one set of tweezers for an entire station, splints sufficient for only one broken leg at a time. Materials were at hand to do almost anything, but only once. If an emergency arose most patients would be out of luck. The Party, she said, cared only about the statistic showing everything was available, not the one showing how much, where the quality of the country's medical services would actually be tested.

The afternoon of election day, a Sunday, I was visiting friends who had decided to refrain from voting. A knock came at the door. Good afternoon, we are local election officials who have noticed that a few people in the precinct have not yet voted, and as a service we are going door to door to help people vote. The officials, wearing their Party lapel pins, happened to have some ballots and a ballot box with them. My friends, not able to state directly that they chose not to vote for fear of receiving disadvantage, had to vote. The officials handed them the ballots and proffered the ballot box for deposit. The two voters, however, having been through this before, took the ballots into the living room, brought them back folded and pushed them into the ballot box slot. Since we had been discussing the issue of voting versus nonvoting when the officials knocked on the door, I asked them how they voted. "We crossed out every name."

After the election there was much discussion about this matter of crossing out names to express disapproval of candidates. Since one was expected to approve, the procedures for disapproving had never been made public. Indeed, it was the first election in which it was general public knowledge that one had to cross out each individual name rather than draw a big "X" through the ballot. A ballot crossed out with an "X," and therefore invalid, would not be registered as voting against the National Front and would not affect the outcome. In fact, 1989 was the first year that many people knew that if one crossed out all the names but one, the ballot would still be counted as voting for the National Front, only that certain candidates would be recorded as having received more votes than others. It was also the first election that saw a substantial number of people entering the voting booth at all. People told me that as late as the early 1980s, those who even went to the voting booth, irrespective of how they voted, could expect disadvantage later.

In many places in East Germany, citizens concerned over possible falsification of the vote tally showed up at polling places at their close to observe the vote count. I cannot say in general how this vote count proceeded, I can only relate the events at a few polling places where people with whom I spoke were involved. As the polls closed in the evening, agents of the Ministry for State Security cordonned off one polling place in Weimar, barring the group of intended observers from entering the building, saying the room was already full. "But I can see in the window that the room is empty," said one of the group. These people did not gain access. Another acquaintance determined to enter his polling place to vote five minutes before it closed, then remain there when it closed to exercise his citizen's right to observe the count. He said he had done so the last time and was allowed to remain but not allowed to speak. When he had questioned the decision about one of the ballots, an official had cut him off with, "Counting the ballots is our job, not yours." This time he was determined to speak up if he saw irregularities, but this time when the polls closed he was ushered out and not admitted to the count at all.

On the other hand, I spoke to a faculty member of the architecture school who held idealistic goals for socialism and fundamentally believed in the system, though frustrated with its current state. He had been charged with counting ballots at a polling place in Weimar where many students voted, and he assured me that the ballots were correctly counted before an audience of citizens. He held each ballot up for inspection and placed it into one of four piles: for all candidates, against some candidates, against all candidates, and invalid. The students, however, told me that of course the students' polling places would be handled carefully, since the Party was afraid of student unrest.

One may wonder why East Germany took what would seem to be a risky step of allowing foreigners to vote in local elections. It is almost unprecedented for a country to grant noncitizens the franchise. This decision can perhaps be understood in the context of East Germany's unique relation to West Germany, where the political issue of foreign "guest workers" was warming up in early 1989. At issue in West Germany was whether the guest workers and their descendants, some of whom had lived there for three generations but were excluded from citizenship and therefore had never gained voting rights, should have a say in local elections. The West German Greens and other progressive factions supported giving guest workers the right to vote, while conservatives, often accused by East Germans of being latent Neo-Nazis, were deeply opposed. Here was an opportunity for East Germany to demonstrate how warmly it welcomed its foreign factory apprentices and the handful of others such as myself.

A second reason for the East German voting policy was also discerned by some. The Party was so skittish about possible dissent in the election that it may have taken steps to assure a higher percentage of positive votes. As a foreign academic I was certainly an exception in East Germany. Nearly all other foreigners were from Mozambique, Cuba, and Viet Nam, "apprentices" for up to ten years in East German factories, who certainly found conditions of life in East Germany much better than in their homelands and could be expected to support the government that granted their stay in the country. If the East German government felt challenged, it might send them home.

The day after the election, *Neues Deutschland* carried the banner headlines, "98.85 Percent Vote for the Candidates of the National Front! Impressive avowal to our politics of peace and socialism! 12,182,050 citizens presented their trust in their elected representatives! High election participation: 98.77 percent of voters exercised their voting rights! Workers' collectives came with fulfilled and surpassed plans! New initiatives toward the 40th birthday of the German Democratic Republic!"

Upon reading these results, many East Germans were angry for days, weeks, months, and the anger became more intense as time went on.

Nearly everyone, it seemed, was convinced that the Party had falsified the results; there was no way that almost 99 percent of the people had actually supported the government. When I left East Germany two months later, people were still saying to me, "Man, that was some election, *wah?*" Restaurants and private homes were full of outrage about how impossible such a result was, yet what do you expect, people said. Two leaders of a Christian organization in East Berlin officially challenged the results and were immediately expelled to the West.

During my ten months in the country, the Party seemed to make two hated, unpardonable mistakes in the eyes of many people. These mistakes may have been more effective than any other recent actions in drawing hundreds of thousands of people into the streets in the fall of 1989 when the refugee trains rolling from Prague into West Germany finally provided the spark. The first was the banning of *Sputnik,* and the second was the extremely blatant falsification of this election.

Soon came the jokes, such as the one extolling the "Seven Wonders of the World of the DDR":

1. Although there is unemployment in the world, all East Germans have work.
2. Although all East Germans have work, not everyone works.
3. Although not everyone works, they continually overfulfill their economic plans.
4. Although they continually overfulfill their economic plans, there are many shortages.
5. Although there are many shortages, the people have everything.
6. Although the people have everything, everybody complains.
7. Although everybody complains, they continually elect the government slate by a 99 percent margin.

People called the election *falten gehen,* "to go folding," a play on the expression *flöten gehen,* literally "to go play a flute," but actually an idiomatic expression corresponding to the English "to go to the dogs."

8

Pre-Chewing:
The Manipulation of Knowledge

PUBLIC ART was everywhere in East Germany. Statues stood on market squares, in the grassy areas between the new industrialized highrise dwellings, in building courtyards. New building facades were covered with mosaics, bas-reliefs, and decorative metalwork. Some of this art was abstract, but much portrayed the likenesses of people. The revolutionary heroes of East Germany stood tall in city after city. In Merseburg a monumental sculpture portrayed Lenin, his arm raised, striding forward to lead the revolutionary workers to triumph. In Rostock's *Monument to the Revolutionary Sailors,* the men on their pedestal raged at the city, fists in the air, bronze jaws clenched and faces stern, defiantly taking power. The huge bronze bust and fist of Ernst Thälmann rose out of a bronze unfurling flag of East Germany in front of the gigantic new dwelling complex in East Berlin named after the communist martyr killed by the Nazis at Buchenwald. Sinewy, naked bronze families stood before the entrances to housing blocks throughout the country. Other pieces portrayed another type of hero, the revolutionary worker. Shovel-bearing laborers marched with the same stern face of Lenin toward some unseen goal.

Statues of revolutionary heroes and other public artworks were approved and placed by an Office of Architecture-Related Art in each administrative region, assuring that art in service to the socialist state would form a ubiquitous part of the architectural environment. This art could work a powerful influence on the viewer, but it also brought a question: where, actually, was Lenin headed? The workers, mothers, and children cast in bronze and carved in stone, what was their message to the people about life in advanced socialist society? In socialist art, the worker in whose name the state was created, was often portrayed in one of two ways, either as part of a faceless multitude or as a superdominant operative—a hand commanding the power of a huge machine. In both cases the appropriate attitude of the workers was set, literally, in bronze or stone.

East Germans spoke often of things that were "*vorgekaut*," prechewed. The message of this art was pre-chewed, information was prechewed, interpretations of Marxism-Leninism were pre-chewed, correct socialist policy was pre-chewed, acceptable lifestyles were pre-chewed. The Party often presented concepts as clichés without the need for contemplation or effort at understanding, rendering the listener in fact passive rather than actually engaged in the society.

I understood this feeling more completely after having read a November 1988 speech in *Neues Deutschland* commemorating the seventy-first anniversary of the Russian Revolution, given by Werner Eberlein, member of the East German politburo and the Party's central committee. He noted that the workers' and farmers' state was "a thousand times more democratic than any bourgeois democracy and, in contrast to bourgeois democracy and for the first time in history, offered real democracy for the people. Nowhere are more rights and freedoms granted to the citizens than under socialism. Naturally, our Party and our democracy understands 'democracy' not as a carte blanche for antisocialist machinations. Of course the opponents of socialism would like that, but we will not do them such a favor. We shall never leave them with any uncertainty that our power lies firmly in the hands of the workers. We consider that as our duty toward the heroes of the October Revolution. . . ."

I discussed the speech with an associate, who said, "Of course that's true. You have freedom, we have freedom. You have democracy, we have democracy. Except that you determine what yours is, and the Party determines what ours is."

This pre-chewing was evident in the *Mein Kampf* affair. For years East German television featured a weekly program called "The Black Channel." Its moderator, Karl Eduard von Schnitzler, would weave together excerpts of news and documentary programs from the two national West German television networks to show, supposedly from the horse's mouth, that West Germany was Neo-Nazi, oppressive of its underclass, revanchist about World War II, and generally morally corrupt. "The Black Channel" was not a particular favorite among East German television viewers. Von Schnitzler's nickname was "von Schni," since that was all one heard of his name before switching channels. At any rate, one week his program centered around the theme that the American army in West Germany was a hotbed of Nazism, showing excerpts from West German television reports of a slightly embarrassing incident in order to prove his point. The report had to do with copies of Hitler's book *Mein Kampf* being discovered for sale in the book departments of United States Army post exchanges in West Germany. True, the book had a lengthy introduction that placed *Mein Kampf* in historical perspective, but when certain West Germans discovered its presence they protested, and the book was removed from sale. The event made the West German evening news, and von Schnitzler reported it to the East Germans as proof that the American military was attempting to incite Neo-Nazi feelings among its troops. *Mein Kampf,* of course, was strictly banned in East Germany, as were all documents of the Nazis or of the period in which they ruled.

As I watched von Schnitzler's program, I realized that the Americans had indeed made a mistake in the *Mein Kampf* affair. The mistake, however, was not to place the book on sale in post exchange bookstores; the mistake was to remove it. *Mein Kampf* was a period piece in its ridiculous claims and rambling prose. It is hard to believe that anyone could have read that book in 1989 and be converted to fascism. On the other hand, if one wished to understand the incredible brutality of the Second World War, the book, with its clarifying introduction, could be an important piece of the puzzle.

The Party's need for pre-chewing, I thought, arose from a false assumption. One assumed that to read something was to believe it. In the West one hoped to operate on a different assumption, that to read something was to understand it, not necessarily to believe it. On the other hand, perhaps the Party's assumption was correct. One might have read some things from the West—newspapers, for example—and might have a tendency to believe what was said therein.

Pre-chewed notions of the state of affairs in East Germany did not only flow downward to the people, they also flowed upward to the higher levels of the Party. One day the mayor of the district capital city of Erfurt visited the architecture school in Weimar. The police were out patrolling the streets for some time before his arrival, and people around school generally appeared quite anxious that the visit should proceed without mishap. He finally arrived with his bodyguards, was ushered through the building apparently noting the fine displayed work of the students and the pride with which the school maintained the historic structure, held his meeting, and left. All were pleased that the visit had been satisfactory.

Of course, the day before his arrival the building had not been quite so well maintained. Mildew was creeping up the walls, and cracks had been working their way up through the plaster. The week after he left the mildew and cracks were indeed still creeping up the walls, though while he was there they were not to be seen. Part of the nervous preparations had been to slather the corridors between the building entrance and the director's office with paint, temporarily covering everything up that the mayor may not have been so pleased to see.

In another instance the architecture students were given an assignment to beautify the facades of a certain street in East Berlin. They were instructed to prepare their facade plan only from the ground to a height of three meters, wherever that happened to be on the building. Three meters was slightly higher than one could see from the back seat of a car driving along the particular street, one of those called a "government protocol street" (*Regierungsprotokollstraße*). Every major city had such a street, though officially never named as such. It was the street Party officials were driven down on their way to a big meeting. When Party officials passed along the protocol street they would view neatly manicured facades, the red and white pedestrian barriers freshly painted, and store windows full of consumer goods. They would not see lines waiting at the doors. One observed, of course, that immediately before their arrival the shops were closed and the windows stuffed with goods, to be removed immediately after the motorcade passed.

The students' assignment was not, by the way, merely an exercise to help expand their creativity or learn the technical aspects of architecture. Given the shortage of labor, including that of architects, students and faculty had little time to play with ideas or explore new architectural visions. Student exercises were, in a sense, solid training for the rigors of professional life. They were intended to be implemented.

One student wanted to design a new television tower for Dresden. The city already had such a tower, but it was set high on a hill away from the city, and the student wanted to explore ways of integrating such a structure into the city center. He presented his idea to a faculty member, who looked at the student with a kind of resigned indignation. "Dresden," he said in no uncertain terms, "does not need a TV tower."

Sometimes, it appeared, the upper echelons of the Party even pre-chewed what the middle echelons would experience, such as their degree of contact with opposition groups. By early 1989 Leipzig had become the center of opposition in East Germany, at least of the publicly demon-strated sort, and several minor skirmishes had taken place there during 1988 and early 1989. Before the May 1989 communal elections, a group of about a hundred persons in Leipzig arranged a meeting with their local representatives from the "city elective body." Word apparently ascended to the Party central committee that some of its local officials had agreed to meet with nonsupportive citizens, and the central committee deter-mined that such a meeting should not take place. The state security forces were instructed to arrest the perpetrators of the meeting. Word leaked out to the group of one hundred, however, the members of which hid them-selves (one behind closed curtains in an acquaintance's apartment) and avoided arrest. The meeting actually took place, but without the people who had called it. The elected officials met with a hastily gathered assem-blage of "normal" citizens and apparently had a fruitful discussion.

The orchestrated simplification of issues without the opportunity for open public discussion caused what appeared to me to be the same prob-lem that would be caused anywhere by such situations, namely an arro-gance by decision-makers. The city traffic engineer and city architect of a medium-sized city in East Germany, both employees of the city govern-ment, were discussing the need to demolish a historic building to make way for a new highway.

"We can't just apply for a demolition application," said one, "because the building is a landmark and it won't be approved. We should apply to dismantle the building, move it back thirty feet, and reassemble it."

"That's impossible to do," said the other, "even if it were physically feasible, it would be economically prohibitive to dismantle that building."

"It doesn't matter. We must only contend in the application that we are going to dismantle and reassemble it. If we never get around to reas-sembling it, who cares?"

The exchange is notable only because it was held in the presence of the regional historic preservation director in charge of protecting the historic building. Though officially he had the power to assure that the interests relating to the historic monument would be protected, in reality he was powerless because the actual decisions were made within the Party at higher levels, based on what the Party saw as a straightforward, uncompli-cated agenda to build a highway. The officials knew this and could disdainfully exclaim their intent before their adversary, knowing he was powerless to act.

A relatively small group of ethnic Slavs called Sorbs, who had populated the region around the town of Bautzen, lived quite integrated within German language and culture until after World War II, though they had been persecuted by the Nazis. After the war, the East German government, in an effort to manipulate history, apparently sought to establish the Sorbs as the country's official ethnic minority group. There may have been sincere humanitarian goals behind this decision, but the motive commonly attributed by jaded East Germans in 1989 was that accommodating the Sorbs could serve as a statement of socialist brotherhood with the Soviet Union, where minority groups formed major populations within the country. The way my acquaintances told it, after the war a Sorbic written grammar was first codified, the language officially adopted as an equal official language with German in that region, and the Sorbs officially declared a minority group that would retain its culture but be fully integrated into socialist society. Not only did East Germany thus share the burden of having to deal with a minority group with the mentor-state Soviet Union, it could also proudly proclaim that this small and peaceful group lived harmoniously, with full rights of citizenship, within the new socialist state.

At the same time, one would search in vain for Gypsies in East Germany. Traditionally the Gypsies had roamed through the region as through other German territories, thereby forming another important minority group. Some of my acquaintances remembered them riding their wagons through East German towns in the 1950s. However, the Gypsies were problematic. They did not speak much German and were assertively adverse to political or cultural assimilation. Therefore in the 1950s East Germany systematically expelled the Gypsies who remained after the Nazi persecutions, neatly removing that thorny minority issue.

Though the Sorbs were seemingly effortlessly integrated, there was of course trouble on the street. Few Germans understood the Sorbic language, which sounds somewhat similar to Polish. Given the reemerging tensions between East Germans and Poles, one would hear comments about "Damn Polacks" referring to the Sorbs. A Sorbic friend who was bilingual in German and Sorbic and an elected official of one of the cities in the southeastern DDR that was officially bilingual and bicultural both spoke of the disdain heard from German youths and the working class— the same source of racial tension in most countries.

The East Germans were so intent on making a display of accommodating the Sorbs, that the forced intensity grated a bit even on some Sorbs themselves. The annual Sorbic Festival in Bautzen was a celebration of Sorbic food, dance, music, crafts, and other traditions. But the street festival was so intensely arranged for national East German television coverage that, for example, two bands were playing on two stages so close to one another that the television cameras could cover both easily, but the music of neither could be heard over the other on the street. As usual, participation was logged as part of one's societal engagement.

East Germany had undertaken a monumental housing program that, whatever its shortcomings in style, comfort, and quality, represented a major commitment on the part of the government since 1945. Groups of six- to twelve-story apartment blocks ringed nearly every city, the dwelling complexes provisioned with grocery stores, restaurants, and often sports facilities for the maintenance and nurturing of the socialist family. Yet as I ventured into the new housing districts and walked through the neatly planted district centers past the sculptures of mothers and children, I was struck by a certain empty feeling. During business hours one could buy bread and red cabbage at the *Kaufhalle* grocery store, or perhaps find a place in a restaurant for a beer. Other than that, and for all my enthusiasm for even the most mundane urban places, I often encountered a resounding silence, the silence a traveling salesman would find in the center of a small American town on Thanksgiving morning. I found that in so many of these showplaces of socialist life I had the feeling of absolutely nothing going on. There may have been a few people shuffling around, talking quietly, perhaps someone sitting on a bench, a mother watching her child play in the sand. Yet there was no bustle, little noise, no joy to be seen. Thousands of identical dwelling units in highrise blocks were lined up like dominoes, separated by wide, empty, somewhat neglected dirt and grass, sometimes enlivened by remnants of building materials that had lain for years uncleared. Indeed nearly everywhere one needed to walk only one block away from a well-maintained important street or square to find a neglected district. Often the signs of humanity seemed to be found only in the decorated balconies of apartment blocks, which some people had turned into a kind of private fantasy world. Here a balcony was painted like a medieval half-timbered farmhouse, there a balcony was painted shocking pink, and elsewhere someone proudly displayed a collection of garden dwarfs, those kitschy plaster figures similar to Snow White's friends. (The word *Kitsch* is one of the German language's lasting contributions to the world's vocabulary.) East Germany supplied much of the world's garden-dwarf quota, but nearly all were shipped to the West for hard currency and were hardly to be found in East Germany itself, unless one had connections.

I contemplated that certain things make life wonderful, and these things are not dwellings and potatoes, necessary though they are. Life is made exhilarating by raising prize collies, playing the harpsichord, restoring a Model T, collecting world's fair memorabilia, hang gliding, visiting a new land. Much of life's excitement is found in observing the creativity of others—finding an unusual restaurant, exploring a new part of town, listening to a new rock band, cruising the art galleries. In the West, one of the primary characteristics of most successful tourist towns is that human creativity is in full display, whether to be bought or merely experienced. It is these things that were expunged from East German life, partly because some were not allowed, moreso because the wherewithal to do them did not exist, and most of all because nearly everything, everywhere, was the same.

Nearly every city had constructed a pedestrian zone at its center, but most had the identical globe-shaped street lights, the same shops operated by the national retail enterprises, all carrying the same limited assortment of goods. Nearly every restaurant had the same few items on its menu: sauerbraten, roast pork, beef, and the vegetable was nearly always cabbage, white or red, raw or cooked. A chain of chicken restaurants offered a reprieve, offering a choice of a quarter or half a chicken smothered with one of three or four sauces, with cabbage. Only the largest cities had exotic restaurants. There was an excellent Cuban restaurant in Leipzig, with long lines waiting to be seated. Food booths could be found in the centers of many cities, or in railroad stations, but the fare was nearly always one thing: bratwurst on a roll with mustard. Occasionally one found at the kiosks not bratwurst but bockwurst on a roll with mustard. It is not that any of these things were bad, but after a while they were merely boring. Fast-food chains and shopping malls in the United States may be equally boring, but at least one can find an alternative if one looks hard enough. The primary descriptor of so much of what I saw in East Germany that its founders had so proudly created was a ubiquitously pre-chewed, monotonous, passive, boring environment. A few towns like Quedlinburg were tourist attractions, but the attraction was the remnant of Old Germany. Few people seemed inclined to visit other towns on a Saturday outing, because whatever was created by the socialist state was identical to what one saw in one's own town.

Dresden had a transportation museum full of historic locomotives, automobiles, and boats. It also had a small gift shop. In the West, such a gift shop would be full of gadgets that enhance one's knowledge, satisfy one's curiosity, and challenge one's creativity: books on how a steam locomotive functions, ant farms, physics games that teach the principles of motion. In the Dresden museum gift shop there were pictures. Pictures of old motorcycles, picture books of locomotives, postcards of historic vehicles. There was also a plastic model streetcar kit. Not one of the items would help one learn how something works—only passive pictures and a streetcar kit.

Thinking about how one would pursue some interest in the face of such monotony, I decided to set off on a quest for practical knowledge to see where it would lead me. In the Dresden museum's maritime section I remembered having seen an exhibit of sailor's knots. The knots were all there, glued on a board like a Boy Scout would present for a merit badge, but they were tied so tightly one could never figure out from the exhibit how they were tied. So I decided to find a book on knot tying, which beyond the thrill of the hunt would teach me the names of knots in German. I visited several bookstores with no luck, but eventually a salesperson told me that the DDR's Sport Publishers had published a book entitled *Knot Tying and Splicing.* I went to bookstores that handled this publisher's works, to be told that yes, the book had been published, but it was currently out of print and no reprint date had been set. As an alternative I was shown a volume in a series on seamanship which contained pictures of various knots in those blown-up versions with arrows that supposedly show how the knot is tied. However, to tie a bowline from looking at a finished knot is next to impossible. Two public libraries also did not have the desired book, though I presume further sleuthing may have turned up a copy somewhere in a library. I concluded that such practical knowledge as learning to tie knots was not readily available. Without doubt if one were officially engaged in a seamanship program of the Society for Sport and Technics (membership denied to persons suspect of being antisocialist), could learn knot tying, but if one merely wanted to learn, the path was frustrating.

I even came to believe that curiosity itself was regarded as a suspicious activity in East Germany, it being thought that one was intending to gather knowledge for use toward someone's disadvantage. I encountered suspicion when asking questions about how things worked, why things happened—questions that seemed to me to be well within the threshold of an inquiring mind. "Why exactly would you like to know that information, Professor Gleye?" was a response I sometimes received, often accompanied by an askance look.

The one place I did observe creative thinking, even enthusiasm, was in discussions relating to dissent: what was wrong with actually existing socialism, what was really happening in the corridors of East Berlin, how to interpret some article in that morning's *Neues Deutschland*. I had left East Germany by the time the big demonstrations started in late 1989, but the previous spring people everywhere, young and old, workers and professionals, Party members and not, were letting loose with vilification about the "shit-state" (*Scheißstaat*) and "shit-communism" (*Scheißkommunismus*) that came to dominate nearly every conversation.

Some people seemed to harbor a special resentment for a monument overlooking Ernst Thälmann Platz in Halle, a huge traffic circle with a soaring overhead highway under which a streetcar stop was sheltered by concrete mushroom pods, under which in turn a subterranean pedestrian passage linked the main railroad station to the main shopping street. Together it formed a fantastic Flash Gordon Modernist environment. "The Fist," as the monument was called, was a stalk of huge stone fists rising forty feet from the pavement, officially called the "Monument to the Revolutionary Workers' Movement." One could not miss it, this blunt firework of fists in stone, covered with dates significant to the history of the socialist movement. I asked a few people what the dates stood for, and people did not know, though I must admit that many Americans probably do not know the significance of many dates in their own country's history either.

This "Fist" was mentioned to me by somebody every time I said I was going to Halle. Many other monuments to the history of socialism stood in East German cities, but this one seemed to stick in the craw of many people. Almost as prominent in Halle was the thirty-foot-high concrete unfurling red flag monument to international communism, surrounded by flowers and fountains, but nothing seemed to compare with "The Fist." Though nobody could express why, I concluded that it conveyed a dual message. The clenched stone fists were supposedly raised against the capitalist oppressor but could be seen as the Party's hammers waiting for some unlucky East German to walk by. Its brutalist massiveness suggested not the power of the workers' movement but the power of the state. Most powerfully perhaps, it may have represented the coopted "struggle" for peace and socialism that continued to dominate public pronounce-

ments by the Party. Though the struggle to overcome capitalist exploitation remained a central program of the Party, this struggle had long been
institutionalized. It was mentioned in the East German constitution as a
basic duty of every citizen. "Struggle groups," the Party's own militia
based on workplaces, had erected the "antifascist protection wall" in Berlin in 1961, for example. Posters and billboards emblazoning public
squares on holidays exhorted the people to struggle toward advanced socialist society, much like American billboards exhort people to buy something.

In fact this social struggle is important. Not necessarily the struggle
for socialism, but a struggle to succeed in one's quest for a satisfying life
by overcoming difficulties placed in the way by adversaries, causes the
adrenalin to flow. Yet in the end this struggle must be a personal one, I
think, whereby one finds one's own success, one's own sense of fulfillment. The pre-chewed duty to struggle handed down by a central authority
destroys the very impetus that makes it work. Once "struggle" is reduced
to sloganeering and advertisements on bus benches, it has lost its power.
Indeed it quickly becomes oppressive.

In Rostock somebody said to me, "Look at that building with the plaster coming off the facade and the hole in the roof. When it's windy you
can't park in front because something might fall on your car. But," he
pointed to the newly painted sign hanging on the front bearing a slogan
about struggling for socialism, "what's most important is that they display
their slogan."

I could not help but think how pre-chewing unfortunately sheltered
people from the realities of the world, both good and bad. It sheltered them
from dissatisfied minority groups, nationalist sentiment, even from the
dropouts who exist in every society. There may have been plenty of dropouts in East Germany, the *Aussteiger,* but even they received ten marks
per day, on which one could manage to live. Since alcohol was the only
available means of substance abuse, the drug problem did not need to be
faced. So many of the social challenges confronting and, one might even
say, in the long run strengthening Western society were outside the consciousness of East Germans, because they could not probe the policy regarding minority groups, could not read *Mein Kampf,* could not question
the socialist system, could not. . . . I kept thinking of John F. Kennedy's
response nearly thirty years ago to charges that the Voice of America was
broadcasting critical news about the United States, that a nation afraid of
the truth is a nation afraid of its people.

Despite the sanitization, at least some of the nagging social problems found in the West were inchoate in East Germany. A sociologist circulated a *samizdat,* a mimeographed underground document, documenting Neo-Nazi activities in the country, and skinheads were known to beat up people. At the same time, perhaps being the greater tragedy, pre-chewing precluded the creative streak in human nature from finding expression, thus denying so many of the wonders of life, as well as its responsibilities. Life in East Germany, in the end, was like living on a diet of brown rice.

The very nature of pre-chewing also made it difficult for anyone even to begin formulating arguments against the system the Party had established, let alone take action. The Party would return with threats of unemployment, homelessness, and starvation, with examples from the United States. The socialist person was provided for; there was cheap housing, food, and public transportation. It was hard to argue that, "I want to discover the world," because the response would be "Why? Our world is better." As I contemplated the demonstrations in the fall of 1989 I noticed that many of the banners carried in the streets proclaimed the desire for "freedom." I also wondered how many people really understood the responsibility that went with that freedom, a responsibility most East Germans had not had to face in all its complex subtleties, where rights, privileges, opportunities, and protections had to be balanced for all members of the society without their determination by a central authority operating under a single truth.

When people would confront me with an accusation about the United States as a society that looked with disdain upon its members least able to cope—the homeless, for example—I found myself saying that it might unfortunately be true, but at least where the problem was openly discussed there was hope for an enlightened people to address it. Yes, people sometimes said, perhaps. I may have added another bit of confusion about a world that for them was already confused.

9

Large Animal Units:
East Germany's Quest for Legitimacy

SINCE ITS founding in 1949, the German Democratic Republic had engaged in a continuing quest for recognition as a legitimate member of the international community, a quest driven partly by the West's general nonrecognition of the East German "Soviet satellite," and partly by West Germany's increasing stature in world affairs. To this end East Germany took steps to differentiate itself from West Germany as a separate but very equal state, claiming itself to be "the first workers' and farmers' state on German territory." Forging a differentiated German language was one manifestation of this quest for recognition. In popular speech this attempt had hardly borne fruit by 1989, given the Western orientation of many citizens and given the access to West German radio and television in most of the country. In official speech, however, one could note a couple of East German reformulations of the German language.

First, the nationally centralized planning of the country, combined with a need to address Marxist-Leninist principles, led to the development of certain complex verbal concepts. Much East German technical language revolved around terms such as the "societal-spatial urban structure" (*gesellschaftlich-räumliche städtebauliche Struktur*) or "intellectual-cultural life" (*geistig-kulturelles Leben*). A state agency exercised its "scientific-organizational function" (*wissenschaftlich-organisatorische Funktion*) to help realize the "scientific-technical revolution" (*wissenschaftlich-technische Revolution*). Such terms might be seen as the East

German equivalent of the American "and/or" which allows an expression to rope in all possible permutations of a vaguely understood concept so that one appears to be in masterful control of some impossible situation. The American "and/or" leads to expressions like "Care for each dead and/or injured victim," and the East German "cultural-artistic activity" (*kulturell-künstlerische Betätigung*) led to some pretty blank stares when I asked what that actually meant.

Second, since the productive processes had been constituted to perform at a large scale as a statement of socialist power, and this large scale indeed revered, the processes were accompanied by a pretentious vocabulary, especially when the concepts in ordinary language were rather mundane. Of course, pretentious terminology is nothing new to Americans either. A bus driver is a "coach operator," and a "stationary engineer" runs the furnace. Names become so long they must be referred to by their acronym: American architects dread E&O and planners discuss AIRFA as if everyone knew what they meant (for the uninitiated: errors and omissions insurance, and the American Indian Religious Freedom Act). The East Germans were particularly creative in this regard. A cooperative farm LPG was a *landwirtschaftliche Produktionsgenossenschaft,* or "agricultural production cooperative." And on this farm he had an RGV: a *rauhfutterverzehrende Großvieheinheit,* or a "silage-consuming large animal unit." A cow.

A few acronyms had made their way into everyday language, and during the "discussion" session after one of my lectures in the city of Suhl I played with two of them. The official German term for automobile is *Privatkraftwagen* ("private motor car"), often referred to as a PKW. The East German identity card number was a *Personenkennzahl,* known as a PKZ. A member of the audience stood up and asked, in a quite formal manner, what I believed to be the essential difference between American society and East German society. Such questions were difficult to deal with anyway, and this audience seemed particularly reserved, given the certain presence of *Stasi* informers.

"Well," I pondered and responded with a big grin, "I think the difference is that we all have PKWs and you all have PKZs." Everyone in the audience started grinning too.

Beyond acronyms, the attempt to express mundane functions as efficient, large-scale processes could extend sometimes to the attitudes toward workers. Americans refer to an employee's "performance" in an attempt to be coldly impersonal. Dr. Fritz Müller, party secretary in the

Fruit, Vegetables, and Eating Potatoes Conglomerate in the Erfurt district, referred to his employees' performance as if the vegetables were the audience, in a November 1988 *Neues Deutschland* newspaper interview.

> INTERVIEWER: Congratulations on your reelection as party secretary. What have the comrades set as their next goals?
> MÜLLER: We want to do everything in our power to improve the fruit and vegetable provision in our district. That is the A to Z of our daily work, and we discussed it at the election meeting. So that all comrades and colleagues take on the appropriate point of view toward the vegetables, we emphasize consultations in the workplace and quick response when hindrances appear. . . .

Listening to East German administrators discuss "professional-methodical support for the artistic output of the people" (*fachlich-methodische Unterstützung des künstlerischen Volksschaffens*) was like listening to the Coneheads on "Saturday Night Live," except that it was not supposed to be funny.

East Germany had often been viewed by many in the West as a militaristic state, and from outward appearances one would quickly decide this was true. Since one hallmark of a "legitimate state" appears to be a large army, East Germany often displayed goose-stepping soldiers and massive shows of military might, as during its holiday parades in Berlin. Soldiers, even off duty, were always in uniform, and army vehicles were common sights in towns around the country. The militaristic view was enhanced when one visited a kindergarten classroom and saw toy tanks and armored personnel carriers with which the children played. Toy stores sold a series of miniature military vehicles such as the "MAB tactical rocket carrier," a realistic scale model of a tracked rocket launcher offered as a "patriotic toy" for children ten years and older, though most children actually stopped playing with such toys by the time they reached ten years of age. It reminded me of the PG–13 movie that nobody over thirteen wants to see. Coloring books were sold in which children were asked to color soldiers and military equipment and send their finished work to a soldier.

Children also learned to sing the praises of the East German army. Here is another song from the Thälmann Pioneer songbook *Be Ready!*, entitled "Soldiers March By."

> Soldiers march by.
> In exact marching step.

We Pioneers know them
And gladly march alongside.

Good friends, good friends,
Good friends in the People's Army,
Protect our homeland
On land, in the air, and on the sea.

Soldiers march by,
The entire company.
And when we are all grown up
We want to be soldiers too.

In addition, basic military training was part of every male East German youth's upbringing. For two weeks in summer, ninth-grade boys were sent to a military camp where they learned the rudiments of military life—how to march, how to salute an officer, how to handle weapons. All was accomplished with some air of resistance-movement secrecy: "cadets" took turns standing guard at the camp gate, always in pairs as was the East German tradition. I gained access to a camp during a drill session purely by chance and by remaining silent, since an American intruder would certainly not have been welcomed. An architect showing me around town had designed one of the buildings at the camp and wanted me to see it. He announced himself at the gate as bringing a guest, and we entered with a wave of the hand from the employed gate watchman; the two ninth-grade cadet guards were busy pounding each other in the universal behavior pattern of fourteen-year-olds.

I had heard of these paramilitary training camps and had regarded them as an evil influence on human nature, inculcating militaristic thinking that would somehow create less humane adults. But I so thought only until I saw them in action—the boys being playfully sloppy in their marching, giggling behind the instructor's back, sticking each other in the ribs. I came to doubt that such training had any adverse effect on the young people. It takes a whole national mood to militarize a mind, and this mood was strikingly absent in East Germany. The military was held in such disrepute among nearly everyone with whom I associated that people who made any voluntary commitment beyond the two-year term of conscription were generally disparaged. It was not a matter of pride to serve in the "National People's Army."

While the ninth-grade boys were learning how to handle a rifle, by the way, ninth-grade girls spent their two weeks learning first aid.

As I watched the boys in their training, it occurred to me that such forced rituals were perhaps less successful in socializing youth than in allowing the Party to deceive itself that its children were accepting its values. This pseudo-military training was another ritual of the "apparent participation" I noted in chapter 6. It certainly did not deceive the inhabitants; if any people were deceived by this action, it would be the country's leaders who were so out of touch with citizens' attitudes.

The ninth-grade training exercise reminded me of the feeling I had when witnessing debates in the United States over whether schoolchildren should be required to recite the Pledge of Allegiance, another form of forced participation that does not reveal or affect the true beliefs of those who recite it. East German schoolchildren also began their day with a form of pledge of allegiance ritual. The teacher would not enter the classroom and say "Good morning, children." Rather, the first words uttered by the teacher each day were *Seid bereit!* ("Be ready!"), the slogan of the Pioneers, the state-organized counterpart to the boy and girl scouts. The children responded with the required, "I am ready!" Adolescent boys, of course, all knew that the real command was *"Seid bereit! Beine breit!"* ("Be ready! Spread your legs!") and it offered an endless source of snickering when their female classmates affirmed their readiness. Later, however, when East German society began to unravel, I noted that when the final reckoning came, the children were indeed not ready in the way their Party had trained them to be but in fact generally held fast to a set of attitudes quite different from those they expressed deferentially in such rote exercises.

Children active in the Pioneers were organized into pseudo-military groups, and part of the terminology by which they carried out their activities had military origins. Children under ten years of age would join the "Young Pioneers" and at ten were advanced to membership in the "Thälmann Pioneers," a group named, as was much in East Germany, after the German Communist party leader killed by the Nazis at Buchenwald. Admittance was gained by passing such tests as learning the oath, which a nine-year-old girl was busy memorizing one day when I visited her family. She wrote it down for me:

> We Thälmann Pioneers . . .
>> Love our socialist fatherland, the DDR;
>> Love and obey our parents;
>> Love and protect peace and hate warmongers;

> Are friends of the Soviet Union and all socialist brother peoples,
>   and maintain friendship with all children of the world;
> Shall familiarize ourselves with technology, explore the laws of
>   nature, and get to know the treasures of our culture.

"Who are the warmongers?" asked her mother.

"The bad capitalists."

"In school you learn that Americans are bad capitalists. But you played with Paul in the park the other day. Do you think he is bad?"

The child pondered for a moment, looked at me, and looked down at her oath in silence. The concept was beyond her understanding as was, I presume, much of the oath.

Apparently the Pioneers were originally organized as a quasi-military youth group, where children were expected to defend the new order against what was sincerely believed to be a direct military threat from the NATO allies. This attitude had since abated, but vestiges remained in such terms as "Pioneer maneuver," which was actually a group learning activity such as judo classes or lessons about the Soviet Union. Participation in such maneuvers was competitive, with certain criteria employed to select children who would participate. The criteria had to do with their public attitude toward socialist society.

Part of the impetus to develop a DDR national recognition certainly stemmed from the postwar efforts to forge a new order of Marxist socialism on German soil. Stories of activities, later regretted by many, carried out by zealous communists in the 1940s and 1950s were frequently told. In the early years after the war, Christianity was seen as an evil by the Marxists—with some justification, given the Church's general silence during the Hitler period—with the result that children were forbidden to enter religious edifices. The penalty was disadvantage for the parents. Not only was religion the target but history as well. The statue of King Johann in front of the Semper Opera House in Dresden was, early in the postwar years, intended to be replaced by a huge statue of a farm tractor. A medieval castle in a small village near Weimar survived World War II intact because it had been used as a retreat for Nazi officers during the war and was bypassed by the Allies during the invasion. Because it had been associated with the Nazis, the postwar communists let the entire castle fall into ruin and apparently helped it along in order to eradicate relics of the old order. The mayor of the village asked me to find some American foundation that would fund the restoration work, but unfortunately I had no good suggestions.

Postwar attempts to disregard the fruits of previous, deemed evil cultures and to build a new order that would supersede the past led to a general neglect for years not only of historic monuments later seen as important but also of the entire prewar building stock. Specific monuments believed connected to the roots of socialism were preserved, as were some representing Germanic achievements. Places associated with Johann Sebastian Bach, for example, were maintained. Yet the emphasis since the early 1960s on industrialized, prefabricated housing had meant that the prewar building stock had been left largely unmaintained since 1945, and large central-city areas were in an advanced stage of deterioration by 1989. Historic preservation specialists believed that approximately one-third of the country's historic housing stock had been lost to deterioration between 1975 and 1989, as thirty years of deferred maintenance, to use the American term, had allowed water to seep into walls and fungi to destroy half-timber framing. By 1989, older buildings throughout the country were deteriorating beyond repair at such a rapid rate that the situation was seen as a catastrophe. And not only were prewar buildings crumbling faster than they could be maintained but many newer ones were as well. During the 1970s, East Germany covered many buildings with a new latex paint. Unfortunately, in ten years' time much of this paint was peeling off, taking with it the outer layer of stucco. East Germans had composed a bit of doggerel to describe the fate of their cities: *"Ruinen schaffen ohne Waffen"*—"Create ruins without weapons."

Much housing was provided in former single-family dwellings divided into apartments, and many remained in private ownership. The state did not nationalize most housing but engaged in a war of attrition with the owners. State-determined low rent levels adopted to meet socialist goals, while successful in providing massive amounts of housing at very modest cost, did not allow owners of any rental housing to maintain the units, and many owners eventually turned their housing stocks over to local authorities who had insufficient funds, workers, and interest in maintaining them. Renters tended to feel little responsibility for buildings that were not theirs, with the result that well-maintained apartment units were ubiquitously found in dilapidated structures. The difference in condition between the public stairwells and the interiors of apartments was often striking. One person said to me, "The people can't say anything; the people can't do anything, so they tend to take on an 'It's not mine, what do I care' attitude."

Even given the widespread realization that building deterioration had reached unmanageable proportions by the late 1980s, there were neither the materials nor the craftspeople to deal adequately with the problem. During the 1970s most craftspeople such as carpenters, plumbers, and roofers were taken in by the industrialized housing enterprises and no new generation of apprentices was being trained to take their places.

Despite the poor condition of much housing, it had been officially declared by the Party that the dwelling problem in the DDR would be solved by the end of 1990. That is, there would no longer be a shortage of dwellings, bringing to fruition another policy intended to demonstrate the viability of the German Democratic Republic. It was not certain in 1989, however, how it would be determined that the housing problem had been solved, since it was clear that a solution was far from being at hand. Many people assumed that the government would merely proclaim the housing problem solved and declare that whatever the situation was in 1990 would be sufficient. The concern was heightened by the actual wording of the original decree, which did not specifically state that there would be plenty of housing in 1990, but that the matter of housing "would cease to exist as a social problem" by that year. My East German acquaintances were quite skeptical that the solution would be anywhere in sight, and thus they circulated a joke:

"In 1990 retired people will be allowed to cross the street against a red traffic signal."

"In 1991 they will be required to cross on red."

I think the notion of what constitutes "news" also has something to do with how a country views what is important in its society and how to present itself to the outside world. For a country in search of recognition, the news emanating from it must be a matter of some concern. In the Western press, sensationalist human tragedy often takes precedence, but the East German broadcast and print media reported little human tragedy. If Western news media tended to exploit *Schadenfreude*, the joy at others' misfortunes, East German news tended to play a more exhortative role. Though the media regularly reported on human misfortunes in the West, such as unemployment and gang violence, much domestic news concentrated on achievements in building socialist society.

Television news and the newspapers regularly featured prominent reports on plan fulfillment, and the television reports were usually accompanied by long interviews with workers in the factory or field who gave their views on how it was achieved. These interviews reminded me of questioning athletes after the big game ("Yeah, they were really tough, but we just got in there and fought, you know") where absolutely nothing useful is actually communicated. Since plan fulfillment was central to the socialist program, one could understand the priority. One could also understand that not only plan fulfillment was reported but also the announcements of plans to be fulfilled in the future as well. "In their program of socialist struggle, the comrades of the circular weaving department of the People's Own Enterprise Worsted Knitting Mills in Niederschmalkalden have committed themselves to produce fifty kilograms of yarn per day beyond the planned quota. This quantity will suffice to produce 150 more sweaters per day for the people and for export," reported *Neues Deutschland* in February 1989. In fact nothing had happened here, and there was no assurance that anything would happen, but it read as though the productive capacity of the country was increasing at a substantial rate.

The problem with reporting human tragedy in the socialist press may have had less to do with high standards of integrity than with the problem of legitimacy. Human tragedy was a condition of life socialism was supposed to eradicate. Most human tragedy, except for the regularly reported accidents on the autobahns which provided recurring reminders of the dangers of fast driving, brought embarrassment to the state. Thus when an airliner flown by the East German airline Interflug plowed off the end of the runway and exploded at East Berlin's Schönefeld Airport in June 1989, one witnessed not only a human tragedy but also an extremely embarrassing event for the Party, which intensely attempted to convey the impression that it had everything in the country under control. Television reporters were in the hospitals within about two hours of the crash, interviewing patients bandaged from head to toe and strapped up in slings. The patients had little more enlightening to say than the factory workers about plan fulfillment. Investigators with television cameras led viewers over the crash site as though each viewer were a decision maker on the investigative panel, to engage in scientific explanations in more detail than I ever wanted to know about how the probable cause of the crash was aileron failure. I did not perceive the report to be sensationalist, but one intended to prove that when tragedy did occur, the Party could handle it in stride.

Despite the coverage of the Interflug tragedy, however, the East German view of what constituted news, and in what detail it should be reported, perhaps lent merit to the socialist version of news that attempted to place more emphasis on less dramatic events having more importance for one's own life than do others' misfortunes. One assumes, of course, that the overfulfillment reports were correct, and many East Germans assumed they were not.

East Germany was known internationally for its classical musicians, which it had trained with great care in an effort to enhance the state's stature and legitimacy. A special performance music school was placed in a former palace in Weimar, where children with musical promise were boarded to be intensely developed as world-class musicians. Many parents were apparently eager for their children to be placed in such schools, for the rewards for success were great, including automobiles and fine apartments. At the same time, the quest for performance-achievers coupled with a limited supply of teachers and instruments rendered it out of the question for most young people to study a musical instrument purely out of interest. Beyond basic instruction, continuation was not possible unless the child showed promise and entered a state program.

Unless, of course, one was a budding rock musician. The East German rock music industry was thriving, its records were for sale in West German stores, and many lyrics had to do with protest. The degree of protest expressed in rock music was surprising until one learned the concept of "critical solidarity," whereby one said, "We support you, but in order to show this support we must criticize you." Whatever the logic of this thinking, in reality the protest lyrics about such things as wanting to travel or hating to stand in line seemed to serve as a kind of safety valve that channeled protest into harmless endeavors such as singing and listening to music, away from taking a stand in an arena where power was actually brokered. Given democratic centralism, critical solidarity would at any rate fall helplessly on deaf ears since it was outside the Party's decision-making framework, so it posed no real threat. Rock music was culturally regulated, however. Groups could not record in English, even though nearly every rock group in the world records in English. Traditional American jazz songs could be sung in English by East German artists, but their own music had to be in German.

Then there were the Puhdys. The POO-deez, venerable war-horses of the DDR rock scene. A musician acquaintance snorted when I told him I had bought a Puhdys album. "Oh, man, hardly anybody can stand to listen to them any more. Do you know who they are? Check out their picture on the album cover. All in their fifties still trying to look like they're twenty, wearing those leather pants." Originally in the 1950s the Puhdys were an outlaw band, but they survived and eventually became the establishment rock band showcased to the world—like the Beach Boys during the Reagan era. So went the popular belief, rather than realizing when it was time to quit, the Puhdys continued recording basically the same music for years. Their informal slogan was reported to me: "*Es gibt kein Ende. Wir rocken bis in die Rente.*" Translated it meant something like, "We're gonna rock until retirement."

10

Who's Minding the Store? Central Planning in Action

"What would happen if the Sahara Desert were to become Socialist?"

"Nothing for fifty years. Then there would be a shortage of sand."

A PRINCIPAL organizational maxim of Marxist-Leninist societies, including East Germany, held that the country's resources, both materials and labor, would be allocated at the national level by the governmental administration rather than by private interests. Central planning had been offered by socialist countries as a socially equitable alternative to market economies where resources naturally gravitated toward the rich. For example, central planning could determine that the most desirable locations in cities should be devoted to worker housing easily accessible by public transportation to shops, services, and places of work, and that the desirable dwellings could be assigned according to need rather than wealth. In theory, central planning meant that social goals could take precedence over private, profit-oriented goals to eliminate inequalities. In reality, central planning set off an incredibly complex decision-making process that caused deep frustrations in East Germany because it responded so slowly, if at all, to individual needs while it set up its own system of inequalities.

Though Western scholars have written much about the vagaries of socialist central planning, my observations result from being a consumer of its actions during a year in East Germany. Comparing my experiences in market economies such as the United States and in the planned economy of East Germany, I came to the conclusion that the two putatively contrasting systems shared a basic characteristic: both were driven by a form of anarchy.

Market economics accepts the anarchical form that a web of decisions based on individual self-interest will forge both the incentive to provide goods and services and some equilibrium of supply and demand to create a self-perpetuating system. At least so goes the theory. The planned economy, at least also in theory, replaces this anarchy with equitable policies formed by the Party as the vanguard of the working class. Yet in East Germany, the nearly unmanageable complexity of large-scale planning, coupled with the elimination of opposition through democratic centralism which would represent competing interests in the decision making process, led to some fairly serious dysfunctions. Among other things, it led to orders from above that could not possibly be fulfilled from below. Threatened with disadvantage, however, people at the lower levels who knew a centrally promulgated plan could not be fulfilled could not report this fact to their superiors. In fact, it appeared that *no* level in the hierarchy could report any unfavorable results whatever to their superiors, irrespective of the true situation, since persons at every level were subject to disadvantage from above. Only the persons at the very top were in a position to understand the entire complexity of the system and its true situation, but they apparently did not, for two reasons.

First, decisions emanating from the Party's central committee were invariably reported back to it as having been fully implemented, whatever may have truly happened. Second, all people in subordinate positions made sure that people above them did not see things they should not see, as with the mayor of Erfurt's visit to the architecture school. The highest leaders, known as the "upper 10,000" although there were substantially fewer than that, were thus shielded from knowledge of the society by all the subordinate layers below them. Indeed they were whisked daily by chauffeured limousine from their gated community in the forest north of Berlin, along broad streets through timed traffic signals—called the "green wave"—so they needed never stop, to their offices in the heart of Berlin, and whisked back through a green wave in the evening. When I was there many East Germans assumed that the leaders actually believed that everything was fine in the country since they were so isolated from its reality. No wonder then that the leaders' initial response to the street demonstrations in the fall of 1989 was to liken the demonstrators to rowdies and enemies of the socialist revolution.

Since the Mercedes was frowned on for ideological reasons, being West German, the upper 10,000 were whisked about in Volvo sedans. Their secluded residential community was actually called Wandlitz, but East Germans had a better name for it—Volvograd.

Anarchy came into play where two situations existed simultaneously. First, the complexity of the system often left a fair amount of free rein at each subordinate level of the hierarchy, so long as certain rigid boundaries were not passed. Second, each level of the system appeared primarily intent on protecting its own position, irrespective of overall goals, in order to avoid disadvantage. One may see how this worked by observing the *Deutsche Reichsbahn*. The East German railroads were plagued by broken rails, which created sudden disorder in the tightly scheduled railroad network. Broken rails generally resulted from two problems: poor-quality steel or poor roadbed preparation. The central planning system with its caveat continually to increase efficiency led to several contradictory forces working simultaneously. The railroad management itself placed high priority on constructing track sections that would last the longest without requiring replacement. The Party, however, whose decision makers did not necessarily understand the technology of railroading, desired that the development of advanced socialist society proceed as quickly as possible, meaning gleaming rails quickly laid. At the same time, the construction manager might be commended for saving gravel in laying new roadbed. Likewise, the steel producers would receive commendation for producing steel as inexpensively as possible.

The combined interests of these three parties resulted in track being laid with the greatest speed and least cost, which resulted in the defeat of the railroad management's goal of longevity of the installation.

A quality engineer with an overall view of the project could slow up the work and disrupt the independent priorities of the various functions, but anyone was placed in a difficult position when he or she delayed the work for whatever reason. Not only were the interests of the Party, the steel enterprise, and the construction manager thwarted by actually pursuing the policy of maximum life of railroad tracks, but so were the interests of the quality engineer, since disadvantage lurked for reporting problems.

The railroads' on-time performance had become so poor by 1987 that people were regularly taking one or two trains earlier than their scheduled train if they had a connection to make. Then the *Reichsbahn* extended all schedules in their annual timetable, so that the trains ran no faster but at least the timetables corresponded somewhat to their actual running times. Airlines in the United States have done the same thing to compensate for takeoff and landing delays caused by congestion. At any rate, the DDR Museum of Transport in Dresden had to remove a displayed railroad time-table from the late nineteenth century when people noticed that it took *less* time a hundred years ago than it did in the 1980s to travel between major cities within what became the DDR. Of course, this prompted a joke:

"Did you know that the DDR is becoming ever larger?"

"Larger?"

"Yes, it must be, since it takes ever longer to get from place to place."

Despite such blemishes on the record of socialist accomplishment, the socialist worker thrived on productivity, according to ideology, and the word "productivity," *Leistungsfähigkeit,* figured prominently in East German sloganeering. To be sure, the country's large-scale industrial conglomerates were organized to maximize productivity through vertical integration by taking control of decisions in all realms of their own production. Thus the country's productive power was always presented as awe-inspiring. Yet it appeared a puzzling contradiction that actual productivity at the level of the individual worker was fairly low, and even obvious, easily grasped opportunities to improve it seemed to be missed.

Observing the way bricks were delivered to a building site demonstrates the point. At the brickyard a typical load would be dumped, like a pile of rock, into the back of a dump truck, with considerable damage to the contents. The truck would be driven to the building site and the load dumped on the street next to the site, destroying further quantities of bricks that had left whole. A worker picked through the brick pile and tossed good ones into a wheelbarrow, then wheeled it to the point where the bricks were being laid, dumped them on the ground for the mason, and returned for more. This delivery system yielded a loss of some substantial portion of the original load, thereby squandering the country's pollution-rich brown coal resources used to fire the bricks. It wasted the time needed to pick out the good from the pile and required considerable postconstruction cleanup to remove the rubble. Word had it that the shortage of workers required this method. One also noticed a shortage of forklifts to handle pallets. I do not recall seeing any forklifts in East Germany, though there were plenty of multipurpose, self-propelled power shovels manufactured by the Heavy Equipment Conglomerate "Progress" in Weimar that could accept one of several scooping devices dangling from a cable attached to the end of a long beam. Work these pieces of equipment could not handle was often carried out by hand.

In the brick example, every person in the delivery chain was carrying out his or her responsibilities as efficiently as possible. Dumping bricks is faster than stacking them if one has no forklift. Thus, many basic productivity decisions appeared to be made by individual people at their own level of authority. Though the outcome was inefficient, the method did yield desirable statistics at each level showing, to continue my example, large amounts of brown coal delivered to and consumed by the brick industry, high total output of bricks, impressive number of bricks delivered, and so forth. On the one hand, at the large scale everyone would have benefited from increased productivity, but the individual productive units of society, fundamental to Marxist organization, benefited more directly from not increasing output at the smaller scale of their own work environment.

One might recall one's experiences as a soldier in the United States Army, the operation of which shows some similarities. The sergeant in Company A needs a bulldozer to clear some brush. Channels are cumbersome, and a request through channels can bring forth an inquiry questioning the legitimacy of the request. A phone call between units, with reciprocal favors always kept in mind to be in a position where "You owe me one," can deliver the goods immediately and without question. Higher command sees good results, and accountability is avoided as to whether the bulldozer is the most cost-efficient means to do the job. The system gets the job done efficiently, but since accountability is hidden it invites gross waste of somebody else's resources.

Given the centralized authority structure in East Germany, coupled with the nagging shortage of nearly everything and the reluctance to report dysfunctions or unfavorable situations for fear of receiving disadvantage, I observed instances of creative hustling that would fit well into the lore of crafty swindles Americans love about their own past. A hospital nurse told me she needed new bed linen at home, but none was available in the stores. So she took some of her old household linen to the hospital and exchanged it for clean hospital sheets. Her own linen was duly washed by the hospital laundry and returned to her station. She took a look at it and refused it. "There must be some mistake, this is not hospital linen," she said to the hospital quartermaster. "Oh, okay," said the quartermaster, and tossed it out.

"I didn't like doing that," said my acquaintance, "but it was the only way go get decent bed sheets for my home. I knew the linen person wouldn't care because she isn't responsible for the linen either. If somebody paid attention, if I faced a threat of discipline for expropriating 'people's property' (*Volkseigentum*), I wouldn't have done it. But then, if somebody were paying attention, I could buy decent linen in the stores."

Anarchy at the lower levels meant that one could poorly predict the outcome of decisions. Sometimes trying to correct the dysfunctions they caused achieved results that were entirely unanticipated. During the Allende period in Chile, for example, the DDR had a favorable trade agreement with that country. In trade for goods such as East German farm machinery, the DDR received large quantities of copper. At that time the church in the city of Prenzlau, north of Berlin, was scheduled for restoration. The problem was that the walls had been weakened by fire from wartime bombing and could not hold the weight of a normal wooden roof frame covered with clay tiles. So architects designed a lightweight steel roof frame and covered the huge church with cheap Chilean copper. The new roof immediately wiped out television reception all over the city. Television was a must, of course, so the city had to be cabled, at considerable expense, to regain reception. In the end Prenzlau had a more solidly reconstructed church than would normally have been the case, and in fact better television reception than residents had ever imagined. A fortune in copper also sat on the church roof.

Other unintended consequences I learned about did not end so happily. There were many stories. Along Leninallee, a broad avenue in East Berlin leading to the showpiece residential district called Leninplatz, the streetcar lines were laid in concrete without a gravel base in order to finish them faster. Unfortunately a jackhammer effect of the heavy streetcars began to shake apart the new highrise dwellings along the street. The streetcar lines had to be completely ripped out and excavated to a depth of about six feet, bedded in gravel, and relaid.

Some blunders such as this were merely wasteful, missing opportunities to forge the smoothly efficient society envisioned by the country's founders. For example, the KWV, *kommunale Wohnungsverwaltung,* or local housing administration in each city, administered multifamily residential buildings. I say "administered," because the notion of ownership had not much significance in East Germany. Where retail shops occupied the ground floor, following the policy of providing goods and services as close to dwellings as possible, the housing administration would usually lease the space to the retail trade organization, called the "HO," *Handels-organisation*. In Weimar the story was told of a downtown building administered by the housing agency. As with many older buildings, this one had no heating system, and Weimar winters were cold. The agency leased the ground floor to the HO, which proceeded to remodel the space into shops and provide them with a new heating system, but did not extend the heating system to the dwellings above because that was not their territory. The retail organization merely wanted to rehabilitate its commercial area to its standards as quickly as possible at the least cost, while the housing agency wanted to administer its dwellings with as little fuss as possible. In fact, the housing agencies were derided by many East Germans for failing to maintain much of anything, leading to the joke:

"What's the quickest way to demolish a building in East Germany?"

"Let the local housing authority administer it."

The result, of course, was that in wintertime the customers in the shops below were able to buy their goods in toasty comfort, while the people who lived upstairs were freezing. Part of the frustration felt by so many East Germans was that such malfunctions were commonplace and would be easily avoided if somebody were minding the store.

When dealing with the management of complex programs, one may observe some similarities between the East German system and the the the lowest-bidder mentality in the United States, the principal difference being the accountability for failure. The difference between blunders committed by Western decision-makers and similar blunders in communist countries lay not so much in their magnitude—witness Coca-Cola's foray into New Coke. The greatest difference lay in the speed with which they would be recognized and checked. In East Germany the culprit was not lack of skills, for the East Germans were by no means ill-trained or incompetent; the problem was primarily a procedural one. In a society operated by central decision making carried out without opposition, there was no opportunity for users, consumers, or subordinates involved in the implementation mechanism to report that a mistake had been made. The very people who made the original decision, and who therefore had a vested interest in it, were the ones who had to realize that a mistake had been made and order the product or procedure to be altered. Thus the highest-level managers, who had the greatest investment in their decisions, had either to see for themselves or somehow be convinced by highly deferential subordinates that their course was wrong, or they would be allowed to steer it directly, as the East Germans said, into the bucket (*Im Eimer*).

Despite the anarchy at the lower levels, nearly all processes were indeed centrally planned. In East Germany, most materials were accounted for at each stage as they cycled through the process of manufacture, consumption, and disposition. For example every enterprise, and every municipality from the largest city to the smallest village, was required to prepare a plan for the disposal of its waste, and had to comply with its adopted plan. In fact, East Germany was quite proud of its recycling program, where very little was actually discarded, and most materials, from egg cartons to moldy bread, were retrieved and put to good use. The program's effectiveness was indeed admirable; it was one enterprise where East Germany could have exported managerial skills to the West.

Under central planning coupled with democratic centralism, however, the program functioned unofficially in a somewhat different manner than it was supposed to. Not only would the waste be adequately taken care of according to plan, but the correct amount of waste as specified in the plan had to be produced at each level of the system because some other enterprise used this waste as the input for whatever it produced, and it needed to be guaranteed adequate incoming materials to meet its own planning quota. Let us take scrap metal. Each town's waste-management plan specified how much scrap metal would be delivered to the scrap-metal handler. A problem arose, however, if for whatever reason there was less scrap metal than anticipated. An official in one town showed me how he met the scrap-metal quota in times of such stress—he had it manufactured. New, good quality, serviceable metal products were scrapped specifically to meet the scrap-metal quota in cases where the deadline for reporting the latter was more immediate than the deadline for reporting the disposition of the metal goods. Their purported disposition would be reported later, long after their actual demise, and there would be time to develop a story that would not reveal their true fate. The official knew that his report would not be questioned anyway, since nobody at the higher Party levels wished to deal with unfavorable situations. Out of them could come only disadvantage. He said one time he had accurately reported unfavorable plan implementation statistics, but his superiors had returned the report to him for amendments. "You can't say that," they told him.

A further tale by the same official related to the empty-bottle plan he prepared for his town. All beer and soda bottles were recycled in East Germany, and the official had to produce a set amount of empties to be picked up monthly by the bottling plant in the nearby city. Each month the official was required to report to higher authorities that X number of bottles had been delivered for refilling. However, the plant seldom actually sent a truck to his town; the plant did not need the bottles since there was a surplus of empties in East Germany, and the town produced too few to make the trip worthwhile. The official was in a bind. He could not report that the bottler neglected to drive out to the town because that would spell trouble for the bottler, who would probably find a way to put the official at disadvantage. Anyway, it would not be good for the official to become known for getting others into trouble, since others trusted him to handle discreetly their own reporting habits. So the official duly reported each month that his quota had been produced and picked up by the plant. When the bottler showed up, the report was more or less correct; when the bottler failed to appear, the empties went to the dump.

Party functionaries overseeing the fulfillment of plans may have understood power well, but they often seemed not to understand the matters over which they wielded this power. The statistics, irrespective of content, were all-important. One day a dentist for a People's Own Enterprise clinic was complaining to me that he had been accused of laziness on the job. The Party secretary had determined that he had fallen short of the Party-mandated extracted-tooth quota.

"I take very good care of my patients," he said, "and I believe in preventive dentistry. So my people generally have healthy teeth and don't need to have them extracted." He decided to falsify his reports rather than pull good teeth. "The Party doesn't understand that productivity can sometimes be measured by what does not happen, such as not pulling teeth, rather than solely by what does happen."

Sometimes the Party promulgated special programs called "communal actions" (*Gemeinschaftsaktionen*), in which citizens would be expected to participate, in true socialist fashion, to improve the common living standard. Another official told me of one such program called "A Tree for the Fatherland," wherein each citizen was expected to plant a tree. The plan called for trees to be delivered to the city government, which had to see to it that they were planted by a certain date. When he told me the story, the planting deadline was approaching but the trees had still not been delivered. Even so, the official had to make an interim report. He shared his deliberations with me. If he reported that no trees had been delivered, he would risk confrontation with the nursery. If he reported that they had been delivered but not yet planted, he would look bad. So he had decided to lie twice. He would report that the trees had been duly delivered and that X number had been planted, all on schedule.

If and when the trees should actually be delivered he would plant at least one and photograph it, then give the rest away or toss them, since he could not actually cope with a load of trees in the first place. He did not know why the load had not been delivered, but he assumed that some catastrophe had befallen the nursery and that the nurseryman had probably reported it delivered anyway. There was a joke about this kind of situation:

"What the Party decrees shall happen."

"What the Party does not decree won't happen either."

The East Germans had a wonderful protest song, written to the tune of "God Save the King," which summed up many of their attitudes toward advanced socialist society. Its title was "Nothing Will Come of Us." When in private gatherings the evening became late and the beer was flowing, it was sung at full volume. The song was simple, and my unrhyming translation makes it seem simpler, but that made the words easy to remember after all the Pilsator.

> We hold our liquor and don't like to work
> But we are true to the Church.
>
> Refrain: Nothing will come of us.
>   Nothing will come of us once.
>   Nothing will come of us twice.
>   Nothing will come of us thrice.
>   Nothing will come of us.
>
> We have taken it upon ourselves
> To come to nothing.
>
> The occupation forces
> Have brought us our standard of living.
>
> Those who stole our watches
> Are now cosmonauts.
>
> The one who came from the Saarland [Erich Honecker]
> Won't let us travel there.
>
> Whoever knows our economy
> Knows that we take skillful naps.
>
> Fabricate plans
> Report successes.
>
> Perestroika and openness
> Have not gone far here.

The drive to report favorably could have a tragic side as well. The mayor of the village with whom I drank the Pilsator said that in his village one could hear farm animals crying for food. The animals were starving. The production of feed grains, despite plentiful quantities according to reports by the Ministry of Agriculture, had fallen short of the need, so there was not enough to maintain the herds. Feeding the herds discarded white bread had not provided the required nourishment. However, the Party had determined that no feed should be imported because reports showed that feed was available. The Party had also determined that the herds should be maintained at their current levels and that the slaughtering plan should not be amended. Thus the herds were starving. The mayor knew the true story, of course. It was known that there was insufficient feed, but the Party could not approve a reduction in herds through increased slaughter because there was too little cold-storage capacity to handle any additional carcasses. There was insufficient cold-storage capacity because the Party had previously adopted a plan for meat production that coordinated all stages of the process—feed production, breeding, fattening, slaughter, storage, and delivery—and determined that the capacity at all stages was adequate. In Volvograd, said the mayor, there was plenty of fresh meat and no starving animals.

A standard joke held that socialist workers were lazy, as in:

"Who had it harder, Lenin or Gorbachev?"

"Gorbachev had it harder. Lenin had to turn workers into communists, but Gorbachev had to turn communists into workers."

However, I heard frequent complaints that people were prevented by the system from working hard. There were rumors in 1989 that factory workers were sitting at their machines part of the time, collecting salaries, but doing no work because there were no materials for them to work with. Those who did work especially hard, or those who risked creative solutions, often were believed to suffer disadvantage. It was assumed that it was better to work at a common slow pace with fellow workers. However, if each team member consciously avoided working faster than the others, it would set up a dynamic whereby the pace of work became ever slower. This appeared often to be the case in East Germany. Frederick Winslow Taylor had described this situation as "soldiering" in his early-twentieth-century works on scientific management to increase capitalist factory production, but apparently Lenin did not read it.

A cartoon in the satirical East German magazine *Eulenspiegel* in May 1989 showed a worker scooping up dirt from one pile and depositing it on an adjacent pile. When he was finished, he announced, "100 percent!" His boss looked at his work and said, "What, is that all?" Whereupon the worker shoveled the whole mound back into its original place and announced to his beaming boss, "200 percent!"

Some time ago Radio Yerevan, from the capital of Soviet Armenia, began broadcasting a type of political joke. In these jokes somebody would ask a question regarding socialism, usually whether something would be possible. The answer was always, "Yes, in principle, . . ." followed by some absurd condition that negated the possibility and in particular negated socialism. There were many Radio Yerevan jokes in East Germany. One of the favorites was:

"Could Switzerland become socialist?"

"Yes, in principle. But oh, poor, poor Switzerland."

Grenztruppen:
Protecting the Iron Curtain

I TRIED TO escape through Czechoslovakia," said the young man. "I tried through Hungary before they took down the fence," said the second. "I tried to hide on a train," said the third. The three were traveling in my compartment from Weimar through Eisenach, headed into West Germany. Six months earlier they had been caught and imprisoned until the West German government had purchased their freedom, and now they were legally on their way west, holding one-way passports valid only for a single exit from East Germany, along with statements that they had relinquished their citizenship in the German Democratic Republic. The third youth was especially pleased to be riding the train that day because the previous time he had hidden in the superstructure between the roof and the compartment ceilings not knowing that the "ladder man" always came though at the border opening a trap door in the ceiling of each car and peering in with a flashlight.

In fact until the day the Wall was opened in November of 1989 it was difficult for East Germans to get anywhere near the West German border on the train, or by any other means. The transport police regularly rode the trains traveling between Gotha and Eisenach, the last two stops before the West German border, and checked passengers' identification. Young men, the most likely potential escapees, received special attention from the police, with pointed questions about their destination. At other stations near the West German border, such as the end of the line at Salzwedel, the transport police regularly lined up on the platform and detained young men exiting the train to inquire why they would be traveling to that city.

The railroad station at Eisenach looked like an ordinary railroad station, having a waiting room and a tunnel under the tracks to the platforms. When the train to West Germany approached, however, a platoon of transport police would emerge to check the papers of everyone who entered the platform where the outbound train was to stop.

East German authorities had worked out procedures at the border to West Germany with what can only be called admirable precision. When I traveled from West Germany into East on the Frankfurt/Main to Frankfurt/Oder express or one of the other trains plying between the two countries, I exited West Germany through the border town of Bebra. At Bebra the West German border police would sometimes give one's passport a cursory look (*"Ja, ja, alles in Ordnung. Auf Wiedersehen"*), and United States Army troops occasionally examined the passports of Americans intending to enter the Zone. On a typical trip, as the train pulled out of Bebra it wound its way through lush green fields and a few villages—West Germany was very quiet near the Iron Curtain—until suddenly a silver streak like a piece of Christmas tinsel lay strewn across the countryside. It was "The Fence." Suddenly the train sliced through a hole in the fence next to a guard tower, into a sliver of East Germany that projected into the West. The change of state was immediately apparent in the automobiles—tiny, unstylish Trabants instead of Mercedeses—in the poor condition of the buildings and their uniform dirty brown color, in the huge fields of collective farms rather than the small fields of private farmers that characterized the West German countryside. Then the train swept again through the glinting fence and briefly back into the villages of brightly painted houses and neatly clipped roadsides of West Germany, on its way into the Zone for good, at Gerstungen, the East German border stop.

As the train slowed to approach Gerstungen, the most memorable sensation was that of silence. Conversations on the train ceased as it rolled gently through the gray mesh fence that stretched from horizon to horizon at right angles to the railroad track, through a narrow slot lined with more barbed wire and protected by another tall watchtower, and stopped softly in the station at Gerstungen. Silence. There was silence in the fields directly inside the fence, for although hay was mowed there, there were no people, only a few abandoned and sealed old barns. There was silence in the village of Gerstungen, where a handful of cars stood parked on the lifeless streets between the worn brown stucco houses. Border troops in their smartly starched olive green uniforms with the green band bearing the words *Grenztruppen der DDR,* "Border troops of the GDR," on the sleeve marched muzzled German shepherds silently through the still railroad yards of rusting tracks. It seemed that not even birds disrupted the silence at Gerstungen. A single switch engine may have shunted freight cars somewhere in the yards, but all around were barbed wire fences with concrete observation posts, eyes staring silently from within.

The Gerstungen station had all the trappings of a railroad station except for the people. A wall ten feet high, without openings, separated each track to allow the guards on the watch bridge above to have full control over peoples' movements. Baggage carts stood on the platforms, but there was no baggage. The stationmaster announced the arrival of each train, as in every German station, except in Gerstungen he only announced the train number, not its destination, since the border troops checking the passengers were his only customers. In the train the passengers waited, like silent animals before the storm, for the train doors to open and heavy boots of the green-banded uniforms to clomp down the aisle, pairs of eyes peering out from behind green-banded visored caps pulled low. Each compartment became an elevator cab, the passengers staring at some corner of the ceiling or at the heating control, intently minding their own business as the eyes looked in.

Passports and ancillary papers were anxiously held in plain view to avoid reprimand from the guard. The first pass down the corridor would be the foreign-visitor control. Non-German passengers will please present their passports for a check of the correct visas. All please continue to keep your passports at the ready, for the border officers to follow.

The next clomping wave brought officers in pairs. All officials checking the passengers worked in pairs, and all were officers; such was the importance of the passport-stamping tasks for the border troops. Unfortunately the term "border troops" in English is too soft. To convey the ominous aura surrounding the green-banded uniforms it must be said in German: *Grenztruppen.* Eventually an officer appeared exactly at the threshold of the compartment, never stepping in. He snapped open his chest briefcase to form a working tray and inspected the passports clockwise through the compartment by a system that a procedural manual must have spelled out in minute detail, since every officer had exactly the same position, motions, and sequence. One could tell by their actions—which often resulted in humiliation—the first-time travelers in the compartment.

For example, a mother attempted to hand the officer both her passport and her daughter's at once, or someone out of the clockwise order tried to offer the officer his passport for inspection. One did not repeat this sort of act.

Occupations that depend on mistake-free, repetitive actions seem to develop a certain style accomplished with a precision that exudes an air of effortless mastery over all situations. The radio talk of a fire department dispatcher, the hands of a pizza chef, the effortless movements of a croupier. For the East German border troops it must have been the perusal of the passport. Standing erect just outside the compartment—the officer could take one step into the compartment to reach for a passport but had to withdraw to the corridor to carry out his work—he held the passport erect and slightly to one side, affording a simultaneous view of the photograph and the inspectee's face, then with a magnificent flip of the fingers riffled through every page of the passport until the correct place for his work was reached. This hand movement was carried out with such flair it must have been the subject of training sessions at the officer's school in Suhl. He then reached for his self-inking stamp and flipped it like a nightstick onto the passport and crumped it down to saturate the page with so much brown and blue ink from his two-tone stamp that the ink seeped through to the other side. These were possibly the most consistently over-inked stamps that I had ever seen, each one carrying the date, place, number of the inspecting officer, and an arrow indicating whether one was entering or exiting the country.

Each stamp had to be in its exact order in the passport. None of the open-the-passport-and-stamp-it-someplace attitude that many border officials practice. The opening page of the DDR section of the passport (one indeed had to have an entire section if one entered frequently) contained the visa, and upon the first entry into the DDR the officer smashed down an overinked stamp onto the visa itself. Each successive stamp at exit or reentry was placed directly after the previous stamp, so that if one ran out of room at the back of a passport, one was presumably out of luck. Subsequent visas or extensions had to be placed after earlier ones, so the passport revealed an exact chronological record of when and where the person had entered and left the country.

The border troops' inspection was met with apprehension, but if one had the exact papers in the exact order, the task was carried out without incident. More dreaded were the customs officials who followed. Dressed in gray uniforms, they sauntered through the train with an air of capricious power, knowing all were expecting the worst from them and finding some primordial human satisfaction in striking their victims at random. They appeared to seek in particular two types of contraband: forbidden goods and forbidden information. On trains entering the country I saw them carry television sets, portable oil-filled electric radiators (a particularly sought-after product from West Germany), and popular magazines (anything with social, political, or sexual content) into the station at Gerstungen. Other oil radiators would pass through unhindered, though the apprehension level on the train was something to behold. On one trip my compartment stopped right next to the door of the customs office, and my East German traveling companions whispered among themselves, "Look at that, would you. He probably needed a new TV." "They probably haven't read that issue yet." "Shame, sha-a-a-me on them." Once the customs people had passed and taken whatever they decided to take, the passengers slowly became animated once again. Whatever time had elapsed for the various inspections, the train would remain in the station for the rest of its forty-five-minute stop. It always stopped forty-five minutes, even if it was nearly empty and late.

The portion of East Germany from the West German border inward for a distance of three miles was an unusual European countryside. This was *Sperrgebiet,* the "prohibited zone," which one could not enter without a special pass. No gates or police check points marked the entry, merely a little sign that announced the prohibited area as one approached the border. Woe unto those who passed from the interior of the country without permission, however. The prohibited zone was primarily forested as the train left Gerstungen, seemingly for years untouched by human hands, though the people said it was full of listening devices. The road maps of East Germany showed few villages in the prohibited zone, but East Germans knew that the maps were falsified. Should one find oneself in a town within the prohibited zone, one would not be able to find one's way to the fence by looking at the map.

One day as I was sitting around an acquaintance's living room, the conversation turned to the prohibited zone. One person told a story of his family's being forcibly evicted from their village as the prohibited zone was being established. It happened when he was a child in the 1950s; his family was given about two hours' notice, took with them whatever they could carry, and were transported to an inland city. A student in the group told her story of the prohibited zone that she had experienced a couple of years previously. She and friends were driving around looking at historic sites, and the guidebook mentioned a certain abandoned monastery of particular architectural beauty. They went, toured the monastery, and began driving back to town when they were arrested by border troops and interrogated for six hours about their reasons for making this particular trip. Their papers were checked, their backgrounds investigated, their bodies searched, and only after exhaustive questioning were they released with a strong admonition never, ever to enter the prohibited zone again. Unfortunately they had not known they were in the prohibited zone at all, since it was indicated neither on the guidebook nor on maps. "You should know these things," said the officer.

During my sojourn I was actually scheduled to visit the village of Schleid in the prohibited zone, as the guest of another faculty member advising a student preparing a thesis project to redesign its marketplace. Schleid was shown on the maps as a safe distance in from the West German border but actually lay within easy view of the fence, I was told, and I was eager to see the Iron Curtain from the inside. Before the trip, however, the police instructed the faculty member to take a "smaller vehicle," in which there was no room for me, so I was out of luck. Since foreigners were generally excluded from the prohibited zone anyway, I was more surprised by the initial invitation than by its eventual withdrawal.

Other areas of the country were considered to be prohibited zones for nonmilitary purposes. One of my acquaintances had a summer cabin in a village on the Baltic Sea and applied to invite me there for a weekend. The village was designated as a prohibited zone because it was the site of a "competitive sports training area" (*Leistungssportgebiet*), some facility for training Olympic athletes. His application was denied.

Leaving East Germany on the train was similar to entering, with two additional activities of note. At the Gerstungen station, border troop officers repeated their precise passport-checking procedure, but before leaving each compartment the officer placed his hand on top of his military cap with its bright green hatband, announced to be pardoned but he must take a peek under the seat, and squatted down to search for "border provocations." The three young men I met on the train after their having been free-purchased had ended their original escape attempt by being classed as border provocations. Once the officer had left, the ladder man presented himself, opened the trap doors to the space above the ceilings, and peered in with a flashlight in case any provocations should be lurking there. Others scoured the underside of the trains in search of exterior provocations. Occasionally they did the same in inbound trains, servicing the myth that the Iron Curtain was intended to keep class-enemy intruders out, but now they usually did not bother. Nobody else believed that the guard-dog security at the borders was intended to keep out Western provocateurs, and I cannot imagine the border troops believed it either.

Customs inspectors on the way out tended to look for a different kind of product and information. Items such as expensive Meissen porcelain made in East Germany but exported to the West could not be taken out. Of course, no Meissen porcelain was to be found in East German stores anyway, so there was not much to worry about. Also sought was any information that could be used to criticize East Germany. This writing is based on notes I made while there, and since I anticipated that the customs authorities might take an interest in them when carrying them out of the country, I concocted a scheme. First, concerned lest my notes would be problematic to transport from the country, I had written them all by hand with a handwriting so sloppy nobody else could easily decipher them, and when leaving I mixed them in with plenty of newspaper clippings about East German work in preserving historic buildings. Second, I relied on my previous observations that customs officials at the border generally seemed to bank on random terrorization of selected passengers to maximize their sense of power, but were not used to dealing with serious contraband since beyond baby clothes there was almost nothing to smuggle. I calculated that I would give them a chance to annoy me, thereby hoping they would leave my actual contraband alone. On the train I laid beside me an innocuous East German book about socialist art and then answered the question on the customs declaration form regarding objects purchased in East Germany with "none." The customs official may not look at me at all, I thought, but if he did I needed something between him and the notes in my suitcases. He came.

"Is that your book?"

"Yes."

"It is from the DDR, is it not?"

"Yes."

"You say on your declaration form that you are bringing no objects out of the DDR. But you do have a book."

"Well, yes, that is true."

"The form clearly states, 'Gifts received or articles purchased in the DDR.' That includes books. You must write 'book' in that space on the declaration form."

"Oh, yes, of course, I did not think of this book. Next time I shall be sure to include a book."

By that time he had to move on, since he had to pass through the entire train within his allotted time before the forty-five minutes expired. At any rate my suitcases remained untouched.

My belongings were searched only once leaving East Germany, and it was because of carelessness. Of course, an American traveling in and out of East Germany was not that common in the first place, and among the papers that I had to show at the border was a letter from the Ministry of Higher Education explaining my purpose there. I always placed this letter in my passport on top of various documents, and it seemed to satisfy any curiosity. A couple of weeks before the end of my stay I had to arrange my return flight to the United States from Frankfurt, West Germany, which required a five-minute phone conversation. That is, from anywhere in West Germany it required a five-minute phone conversation. From East Germany it meant going to the post office, or perhaps to the home of a friend who had a telephone, which in private residences were few. One had to give the number to the post office clerk or to the operator and wait two hours, six hours, ten hours. The waiting time was never known, and the chance of success of eventually making a connection at all was never known. If one were successful but should be cut off in mid-conversation, which happened frequently, one would have to start over.

I decided it would be less of a hassle to get on the train, ride four hours to Kassel in West Germany, make my phone call, buy bananas for my friends, eat some salad, and mail home a box of architecture slides I had taken with me to East Germany plus photocopies of East German magazine articles on historic buildings. I had no luggage since I would be returning the same day and had only that box. Being preoccupied with making plans to leave, I neglected at the border to have my letter from the ministry at the ready and forgot to fill out the customs declaration slip. An American with no luggage, no particular reason for being there, unprepared for the customs inspection, having none of the standard equipment expected of tourists would probably have something pretty interesting in that box. The inspector cleared everyone else out of the compartment, certain she had caught some big fish, and made me paw through my box of photocopies and Kodak slides all the way down to the bottom of the box. It was actually illegal to transport photographs out of East Germany, and here I had a few thousand of them, no matter that they were of American architecture. I envisioned what the interrogation unit in the train station must look like. In the meantime I showed her my letter from the ministry, of course, but once having made the decision to inspect she had to follow through. In the end she was not interested in my copies or slides, thanks presumably to my letter, and left me with a "What a jerk this guy is" look, as if I had wasted her time.

I made it to Kassel with my box, ate my salad, called the airline, and got back on the train. On the return trip the border troop officer stared at my passport a good long time since the exit stamp had been issued just that morning. *Nobody* who was allowed to leave East Germany stayed only a half day, but he could not determine any reason to question me so he merely flipped the passport back to me and wished me a curt good day. In retrospect I realized that the inspections themselves were never so bad as the dread that preceded them, an anxiety that began to churn one's stomach as soon as one boarded the train.

The border troops were an interesting lot. They were interesting not only because of their officers' Prussian precision, but because many in the lower ranks were draftees, similar to soldiers in the National People's Army, though specially picked. Party members were apparently preferred, since membership in itself was somewhat a test of loyalty. One former border troop draftee told me that inductees were asked the key question, "Would you shoot people?" If the answer were no, they would be disqualified and shunted to one of the regular armed services. Since the East German border troops had regularly shot their citizens attempting to flee across the Iron Curtain to West Germany, I was curious as to how this behavior was instilled into the guards.

Every society certainly produces a small number of people who gain their greatest pleasure from shooting people swimming in a river, but I also think there is a less macabre explanation. One often finds exhilaration in participating in activities forbidden to others, such as patrolling right next to that fence in the prohibited zone, of knowing intimately things which others may not know, and surely for some, the sense of power that goes with having vital decisions over such things as border provocations. The border troops were also given loaded weapons, which for most young East Germans offered the only opportunity they had ever had to be near actual ammunition. The former border trooper told me how thrilling that feeling was, to carry a gun with live ammunition.

In observing off-duty border troop draftees riding the trains home for furlough, however, I came to suspect that such exhilaration was not the only reason young East German men willingly served in the *Grenztruppen*. Part of the answer probably lay in the regimentation of their activities, thus relieving them of most responsibility for their decisions. One ex-border trooper confidant reported to me that the assignment on the border was very simply to prevent any of those border provocations. A provocation was defined as any irregularity disturbing the silence in the prohibited zone. Any unauthorized person, meaning any person not a resident of the prohibited zone and not carrying proper identification, moving through this district in either direction would be a provocation. An automobile entering the prohibited zone along the border would be a provocation, as would a person without the proper papers on a train approaching the border, and so forth. Thus the troops were not asked to distinguish the content or intent of actions. Any aberration was a border provocation that the troops had specific instructions on how to handle in a coolly objective, precise manner.

The troops' operations manuals must have covered the exact words they used when approaching an alleged perpetrator, thus leaving very little to individual discretion. When one sighted a provocation, the order was to yell "Stop!" If the provocation did not stop, the trooper was to yell "Stop or I'll shoot!" If the provocation still did not stop the trooper was to shoot. Of course, said my acquaintance, one could, in the end, decide not to shoot.

The paired operation of troops further removed individual discretion. One member of a two-man border troop team who attempted to jump the fence became a provocation to be handled by the other. The members of a pair continually revolved so that one's partner was usually unknown. At no time would the opportunity arise for an individual to alter this rigid operations procedure, thus the organization had remained quite stable and dependable in uncertain situations.

Border troops guarded the Polish and Czech borders as well, but things there were much more relaxed. In the first place there was no prohibited zone; one could walk right up to the Oder River, which separated the country from Poland. In the second place, there had not been many provocations traveling in that direction.

12

The People's Police

WHEREAS THE border troops were charged with preventing border provocations, other security forces in the country appeared to be actively preventing border provocations before they reached the frontier, as I noted about the transport police at Salzwedel. These blue-suited officers, ubiquitous in railroad stations throughout the country, were distinguishable from the blue-suited railroad workers primarily because the uniforms of the latter were often disheveled, ill-fitting, and threadbare, while the blue uniforms of the former were fresh, clean, neatly tailored, and always impeccably arranged with their leather shoulder bags hanging down below the jackets to about knee level. To exercise the generally unpleasant function of checking people's identity as they traveled, the transport police were awarded what appeared to be an amazing degree of legitimacy. Publicity posters in railroad station display cases spoke of the transport police's protective role, showing friendly officers courteously checking the identity papers of smiling train passengers sitting comfortably in immaculate surroundings, a scene reminiscent of the fatherly bus drivers chatting with contented passengers in the old "Leave the driving to us" Greyhound bus commercials.

The transport police also inspected goods traversing the rails, but their visible role was almost entirely concerned with checking identity papers of the traveling public. Otherwise they would stand around and observe. They would watch, watch, and watch. The "blues" were pointed out to me early on: watch them, I was told. Watch them stand around when people need help and do nothing, and then watch them get into action when somebody looked a little suspicious. Or, as the East Germans said of their police in general, watch them "peep, eavesdrop, and grab" (*Guck, horch, und greif*). The transport police also rode the trains that plied between West Berlin and West Germany, passing through East Germany without stopping. In these trains they also just watched, after having commandeered one of the train compartments where they could sit in comfort without being bothered by the passengers.

Police stations the world over exude a similar atmosphere, I think. It is an atmosphere laden with a suspicion of perpetrators, where conversations are hushed and procedures are exact, where one feels accused of some crime merely by being there. East German police stations were different only in some greater intensity of these feelings, though most citizens in the station during my visits had nothing to do with perpetration but with hope. Hope to travel, hope to invite a foreign guest, hope to register one who had arrived, which had to be done within twenty-four hours. On the one hand, the procedures for taking care of all these things were rigid, and the great fear was having filled out papers incorrectly. On the other hand, much discretion was left up to local police officials, and one hoped through the old positive attitude routine that the police agent would decide in one's favor. This individual discretion of the police, plus the inability of citizens to appeal their decisions or to scrutinize them, led to an inevitable arrogance and unconcern.

On one of my trips to the Weimar police station, in this case to try to obtain permission for my mother to visit, I was instructed by the guard at the entrance to report to Room 113. I proceeded down the long, dimly lit hall flanked by heavy wooden, windowless doors sealed each night with sealing wax. A person was never quite sure how to act in the police station. The doors were always closed, and one faced a dilemma: to knock or not? If one knocked, often one heard nothing through the thick door. Then out may come the police agent and growl, "I said come in. What are you, deaf?" If one merely opened the door to find the police agent already occupied, one would receive a most impolite order to wait until called and could expect curt treatment when one's turn finally came. If one did neither, but merely waited, one did not know if the coast were clear, or if anybody were in the room at all. When I joined the line outside Room 113 that day, the decision was clear because voices could be heard coming from inside. The group before me stood there in silence without knocking, waiting for the hapless citizen in the office to emerge.

Five minutes went by, then ten, then twenty. We still heard voices. This poor guy must be having a terrible time, we thought. Then suddenly the voices stopped, the door opened, and a surprised-looking police agent appeared. "Why didn't somebody knock on the door? We were just drinking coffee. If nobody knocks we can't know if anybody is out there."

Green-uniformed city policemen walked beats in all but the smallest cities. Always in groups of two and armed only with a walkie-talkie, they sauntered through the pedestrian streets in the city centers, also just to watch. Operating rules for beat policemen in America often hold that active engagement with the community can best serve the interest of law and order. Getting to know the shopkeepers and the regulars on the street is a part of the assignment. East German foot patrols on the other hand usually strolled at the edge of activity, spoke with nobody, curtly answered a question if asked (but one did not ask a policeman for directions or information, for example; one asked almost anybody else first), and seemed to watch for any signs of a pace, noise, activity that stood out from the normal daily life of people going quietly about their business. When a youth club was having a potentially raucous party, the police tended to be present in larger numbers, with dogs, positioned just far enough away so the youth were clearly aware of their presence. It must have been exhilarating for a teenager to know that the police were watching him with dogs.

If they did not walk, the police found another way to observe the town in an unobtrusive but obviously present way. In Aschersleben, for example, all the windows on the ground floor of an unmarked building (though everyone knew what it was) at the north end of the market square were shuttered except for one, behind which a policeman sat with a view of all activities in the square. Hours on end someone sat there, silently watching, unobtrusive, disengaged, but his face was visible to anyone in the square who wished to peer into the darkened window.

People had to apply to the police for permission to hold a party in a restaurant, and such permission was apparently often denied for those believed to hold politically problematic views, since the police viewed their parties as potential opportunities for antisocialist expression. The police denied a jazz-musician acquaintance of mine the permission to hold his birthday party in a restaurant, for example, so he had to have it at home where he could fit fewer people. No reason had to be given by the police for a denial, but in this instance the reason was clear to the musician and his friends. The police were probably correct.

American police probably taught the world about speed traps, but the East Germans had learned well. Near Weimar, the Eisenach-Dresden Autobahn dipped low between two large hills to cross a small river. Topographically the hills were somewhat bulbous in shape, so that the bridge at the bottom of the hill was visible for only a short distance before one reached it. Next to the bridge, in a small turnout, the police would wait with radar. The location was particularly fruitful for nabbing drivers who exceeded the rigid 100 kilometer per hour speed limit because Trabant drivers who were busy coaxing their cars up to the speed limit in the first place avoided braking down such a hill because they needed a running start to make it up the other side. Braking also wore out brake shoes, and new brake shoes were hard to come by. So on the way down the Trabants would edge up to 105 or 110 kilometers per hour, and a policeman standing in the middle of the autobahn at the bottom and would regularly wave them down. To make it easy for themselves, the police had built a little hut at the bottom of the hill, behind the trees, where they parked their police car when off duty.

Drivers were indeed not allowed to exceed the 100 kilometer per hour speed limit by even a few kilometers, nor could there be even a trace of alcohol in the blood when driving. Eating a rum chocolate before getting behind the wheel was an arrestable offense. When on the road, one could be arrested for flashing one's headlights to warn oncoming drivers that police were ahead. Radar detectors were illegal, and CB radios unheard of. Nearly everywhere, one seemed to be faced with stringent illegalities imposed by the police. I mentioned to a group a students that at Christmastime the taxi drivers in Bozeman, Montana, decorated their taxis with Christmas lights. "Oh, no, the police would never let us do that here. They have enough problems letting us have driving lights."

Beyond direct contact with the police, their presence was often felt in indirect ways. People needed to show their identification papers when mailing an overseas package at the post office, and the number was always written down. A visitor's identity card number was written down by the door guard if one wished to see a staff member at a museum. Even if the number were not recorded, the identity card was a vital document to present. People could not merely enter a city hall, for example, they had to show their identification and state their business, usually meaning an appointment with an official, who would be notified that the guest had arrived. Signs at the guard booths at the entrances of city halls and other public buildings admonished the visitor, "Show your identity card without having to be asked."

It appeared to me that, in a nation built upon the commanding ideals of socialism, police abuse should long ago have been expunged from society. Even if one could assume that rigid controls over the people were justified in building a better society, there was no room for arbitrary and capricious police power. The Party should have known this, I thought. Indeed, perhaps the Party did, but by 1989 there was hardly anything left of a believable utopia in East Germany. People tended to take abuse of police power for granted. Larger cities had paddy wagons, called by the locals "cashiers' cars" (*Kassenwagen*) because if one were picked up, one could expect to fork over one's money immediately, the amount apparently determined by how much one had on hand.

One acquaintance, an independent craftsman who had turned the garage of his home into a studio, had a problem for which he needed police permission. He could seldom park his truck in front of his studio because other cars normally occupied the parking spaces for the entire day. As a person with a shop, however, he was entitled to a loading zone on the street, so he went to the police to apply for one.

"Who are you?" said the police agent at the station.

"I'm a woodworker."

"Very good. I need a piece of furniture repaired."

"I shall be happy to repair your furniture, but first I need my loading zone."

The next day he had his loading-zone signs, and the policeman soon had his furniture repaired. For free. He apparently liked the repair job, however, because later the policeman told my acquaintance, "By the way, if you every get any traffic violation stamps on your driver's license, just come see me and I'll take care of them."

The relationship between the people of East Germany with the authorities in general, and the police in particular, stemmed largely from a different notion of the role of law in society than has been the case in Western democracies. Generally in the West one is free to do something unless there is a law prohibiting it. In East Germany an activity was prohibited unless a law permitted it. Thus in making applications for various things with the police, the agent would determine whether a law was on the books that would allow the activity. If not, police had the authority to deny the request. Needless to say, this situation was well known to my East Ger-

man acquaintances, and whatever their attitudes toward theoretical socialism, the situation did not particularly help them identify with the role of
either the state or the police.

The requirement to adopt a law allowing something to happen made
it difficult, for example, for the Church to publish materials. The five political parties published newspapers; the various religious denominations
were not allowed to do so. Nor could the Church officially publish books,
pamphlets, or anything else for public consumption. Though one could
find no such prohibition written into any East German law, there was simply no law authorizing Church publications, except for documents for use
by and within the Church itself.

In fact the churches did publish many things, as the limits to "by and
within the Church" seemed to be eagerly tested. In Weimar, for example,
the Catholic and Protestant student fellowships published a quarterly bro-
chure listing the lectures and other events they sponsored. The lectures
often approached the bounds of dared dissent at the time. The fellowships
also published an annual pocket calendar, a mimeographed booklet sta-
pled together by hand, that contained much information having to do with
environmental problems. These things could in fact be published because
prominently printed on the back were the words "Only for inner-church
use!" One could pass such documents from hand to hand, and if one did so
discreetly enough one could even do it outside the Church proper without
risking arrest.

Every society seems to select a group to use as the butt of jokes. Seen
as stupid and loutish, members of this group need three people to change
a light bulb, so to speak. Americans long had their Polish jokes, the
French told Belgian jokes, and West Germans told East Frieslander jokes
about those who lived in a remote rural region of the country. To their
credit, the East Germans did not tell ethnic jokes. For them the three people needed to change a light bulb were policemen:

"Santa Claus, the Easter Bunny, a smart policeman, and a dumb policeman were walking down the street and suddenly found a fifty-mark
bill lying on the sidewalk. Who picked it up?"

"The dumb policeman, of course. The other three don't exist in reality."

13

World's Largest Zoo: East Germans View the World

"What was Erich Honecker's favorite sport?"
"Bobsledding. There's a wall on the left, a wall on the right, and it's downhill all the way."

A PARTY MEMBER acquaintance and I were engaging in East Germany's primary conversation topic of 1989: how the society was not working. Since he had just picked me up at the Hotel Stadt Suhl, the city's "Interhotel" where I had spent the night, this gave him his lead. New, highrise Interhotels, the first-class hotels built primarily for Western foreigners, occupied dominant sites in most major cities, and they represented a decidedly nonegalitarian tradition that reminded one of dual economies in third world countries. A single room in Suhl's Interhotel, for example, cost seventy dollars in Western currency per night in 1989, though with a residency permit I would pay only thirty-five dollars per night in East German currency. Most East Germans could not stay in the Interhotels at all, since the spaces were reserved for persons who could pay in Western currency. Even if they could check in, the price was five to ten times as much as a normal, modest, East German hotel, of which there were very few.

My acquaintance, a dedicated communist, was disturbed by the Interhotel system that excluded most of the people in whose interest the country was founded, and whether or not his perception of the hotel business was true, he likened the situation to that of a zoo. Whereas almost everybody in East Germany had to make do with a modest life, he said the Interhotel bureaucracy dressed Western, bought Western, drove Western cars, traveled to Western countries, all with the intent of drawing Western tourism. Most DDR residents could not do or have those things. The Interhotel people had constructed an elaborate mechanism to lure people into East Germany to see the sights as if inviting people to a zoo in order to view the animals kept in cages. "It's a wonderful system that benefits everyone except the animals in the cages being viewed. That's us." Indeed, that sentiment may have had something to do with the Weimar director for culture's general lack of enthusiasm about tourism during my exchange with him mentioned in chapter 4.

In all the hours I spent listening to people complain about the "shit-state" and "shit-communism," two of East Germany's favorite expressions at the time, the most frequent and intense theme was probably that they could not travel. Though the East German constitution of 1974 established the right of every citizen to travel freely throughout the German Democratic Republic (it was not always so), this republic was quite small. Its total size was about 41,750 square miles, about equal to the combined size of Virginia and Washington, DC, though its sixteen million people gave it nearly three times the population of the Virginia-Washington comparison.

The feeling by many East Germans that they were a caged population derived not from the absolute size of their land. It was, after all, "the biggest East Germany in the world," as the joke went. The feeling derived much more from the prohibition against leaving the country that had been imposed on most of them. If one lives in a small country, or a large one, for that matter, and is prohibited from leaving, one has little opportunity to discover the larger world, to judge for oneself the qualities that are good and bad about life and about his or her own country. Beyond the practical disadvantage, it grated heavily on the soul merely to know that there was a world out there one was not allowed to see. The professors of English at the architecture school in Weimar, who conducted foreign language courses for the students, had never been allowed to travel to England to practice their English. The school's architectural historian, who taught the courses in Greek and Roman antiquity, had to copy pictures from books for his lectures since he had never been allowed to visit the places of which he spoke.

Government statistics proudly pointed to the number of foreign trips made by DDR citizens, and officials cited them to show that foreign travel was no problem for East Germans. The DDR's 1988 statistical yearbook stated that over one million border crossings by East German citizens were recorded in 1987, half of which were vacation trips. However, East Germans knew that many East German retirees who lived in East Berlin traveled daily to work as domestics in West Berlin. If two thousand retirees worked in West Berlin three hundred days per year, that made 600,000 border crossings, nearly two-thirds of the 1987 total for the entire country, and nobody had actually yet "traveled."

Despite the statistics, it was extremely difficult for nearly anyone other than pensioners and high-ranking officials to venture beyond the borders, and many people with whom I talked were incensed at their plight. The largest group of travelers was certainly the retired population. Since retirees no longer contributed their labor to the development of advanced socialist society, they were free to travel when and where they wished. If they decided not to return, they would free up a dwelling unit for someone on the waiting list for an apartment. For others, travel rules changed frequently and the possibilities were generally low.

A few privileged (i.e., Party member) people, even young people, were allowed to travel occasionally in groups to West Germany. Before doing so one had to undergo a kind of travel initiation rite by obtaining the less stringent clearance to travel in socialist countries and have made about five such trips without presenting problems. When one finally made it to West Germany with a group, one's movements were quite restricted. A young Party member who had visited Munich on a youth-group tour told me that they were required to leave behind all their identification. If someone chose to defect in Munich, he or she would be unable to prove East German citizenship, or any citizenship at all for that matter. Without papers, an important matter in West Germany as well as East, there could be no granting of sanctuary. The students were forbidden to walk alone through the streets of Munich, always required to be in groups, and all were responsible to see that the others returned. In other words, if one member of the group defected, all others could expect disadvantage. They were given no money and not allowed to obtain the DM 100 "welcome money" that West Germany offered first-time visitors from East Germany, so they could buy nothing. The tour leaders were quite anxious during the trip as well, reported my acquaintance, surely because they too would receive disadvantage if one of their wards were to "take off" (*abhauen*), as the term went.

The right to travel, especially to the West, was a scarce resource because it represented an economic drain and political risk to the state, which stood to lose an important member of the labor force, in itself a scarce commodity in East Germany, if the person chose not to return. Societies always manage to regulate limited resources by one means or another, and the DDR had perfected a device for regulating this scarce resource of travel. It was a means that carried tremendous emotional appeal, was hardly corruptible, and easy to administer. The device was the birthday. Just as anniversaries of historical figures and events provided justification to allocate resources for housing and other programs, the personal birthday provided justification to seek temporary relief from the normal travel restrictions.

Once tragedy in the division of Germany was certainly the separation of families who were caught on both sides of the fence. For years visits from East to West were hardly allowed, but in the 1980s these restrictions had been eased to allow East Germans to travel to West Germany for special occasions, specifically an important birthday of a "first-degree" relative, for example, mother or brother. The rules had been changed frequently and without prior warning, but in 1988 a husband could travel to his brother's sixtieth birthday (the even-decade birthdays were considered especially important for travel purposes), but his wife could not accompany him, since she was only related by marriage. By early 1989 the couple could travel together, provided of course that the police approved the trip, and the allowable travel occasions were expanded to include confirmations or marriages. Application had to be made several months beforehand, and the decision was normally not received until a few days before the scheduled departure. The police could deny the application without stating a reason, and from this decision there was no appeal. If a person's political records on file with the Ministry for State Security indicated no background of antisocialist activity (nobody then knew but many assumed that these files existed), and if one's position was not deemed security-sensitive (an architect acquaintance who had once worked on the design of a military building was denied travel, for example), one could hope to receive permission to go. A joke was circulated about this situation as well:

"I understand the possession of shovels has been prohibited in East Germany."

"Yes, too many people were caught trying to dig up relatives in West Germany."

Merely to travel to West Germany to see the country, however, was out of the question. The official East German reason for limiting nonbirthday visits to the West was that the country did not have the financial resources to support such travel by its citizens. East German currency was not convertible, meaning that people could not merely withdraw money from their savings account for a trip to the West. The government had to parcel out whatever spending money a person could take along. As it turned out, East Germans were granted a total of only fifteen West German marks for a trip to West Germany—about nine dollars in 1989—and were essentially paupers when they arrived, even given the DM 100 welcome money they received from West German authorities. Even if the person had a large deutsche mark bank account in an East German bank he or she would be allowed to withdraw only fifteen marks per day of travel from the account. Thus, according to the government, for their own protection, East Germans should only travel to relatives who could be expected to care for them.

I asked by what right could the government limit the withdrawal of Western funds so severely, and found on one hand a universal belief that the reason was clear: to provide an excuse for not letting people out. In addition to that, however, there were more complex aspects to the issue than I had anticipated, at least as they came from ordinary citizens with whom I spoke. On the practical level, they believed, if East Germans were allowed to take unlimited amounts of Western marks into West Germany, they could purchase goods such as stereos and resell them at a profit in East Germany for less than the goods could be bought in the Intershops. On the ideological level, such profiteering was quite unacceptable. It was true that some East Germans did have caches of West German funds, some through gifts from relatives. If these people began to live "West," it would quickly set up a dual-class society as had developed in Poland, with those people relying on local currency reduced to an inferior living standard. This duality would threaten to the core the tenets of the socialist state. Such looseness would generate even more looseness, and there was substantial anxiety among even opponents of the system of what would happen when the rigid structure broke down.

Many East Germans regarded the state-run "Intershops" with a combination of envy and resentment. The Intershop, known merely as "*Der Shop*," was the store where West German goods could be purchased. Of course, they had to be purchased with West German marks. Almost nowhere were the contradictions of socialism more directly apparent than in the Intershops. Here one could buy nearly anything from deodorants to auto parts to refrigerators, including delicacies like canned fruits and fine chocolates. Some of the goods were apparently produced in East Germany itself for export to the West, but they were all Western brand-name products found in nearly all West German stores. For East Germans who had access to West German marks, all these goods were available with no problem from the Intershop. For those who had access only to East German currency, on the other hand, they were not available at all. Though the East German unit of currency was also called a "mark," it was differentiated from the West German "deutsche mark" by being called the "mark of the DDR." No German would ever have made the mistake of confusing the two.

The role played by deutsche marks in East Germany was deeply frustrating to many people, who had to spend their lives earning money that could not actually purchase desirable goods of high quality. Although those who had relatives in West Germany were looked upon with some suspicion by the Party, they were looked upon with some envy by many who had no relatives there, because a connection to the West could mean a Christmas gift of deutsche marks, gratefully received and spent in the Intershop.

One of the hottest items in the Intershops was the Japanese-made "boom box" portable stereo, a combination radio and cassette player/recorder with two speakers. East Germany also made a simple boom box, but it cost a month's salary. If West German relatives sent money, an East German could go to The Shop and buy something better.

Nearly every town had at least one Intershop, sometimes in the main railroad station. The windows to the street were invariably painted white or otherwise rendered opaque, reminding me of pornographic bookstores in the United States, but once inside, the shopper was confronted with a plethora of glitzy devices that could make life just that much better, if one had West German marks. The only other problem was that the prices for coveted goods such as stereos were two or three times as much as in West Germany, and the people knew it. When I needed a portable stereo to play music for my lectures, I bought one in The Shop for about $130, and later found a similar model selling for about $70 in West German stores. My East German friends called me an *Esel,* an ass, but they did enjoy the music. I noted that the lessons of monopoly capitalism had not been lost on the Party.

In 1989 an East German attorney and member of the Socialist Unity party elite broke ranks with the Party line to publish, in West Germany, a book entitled "The Guardian State" (*Der vormundschaftliche Staat*). The author, Rolf Henrich, in an interview smuggled to West German television, spoke of a form of "house arrest" (*Wohnhaft*) under which East Germans were held, since under normal circumstances DDR citizens in 1988 could travel to no more than eight countries of the world: the USSR, Poland, Czechoslovakia, Hungary, Romania, Bulgaria, North Korea and Viet Nam. Yet in reality travel even to these countries was difficult. By early 1989 travel to the USSR was becoming increasingly problematic given the fallout from perestroika. Given the conflict over Poles' buying and selling goods excessively, one could go to Poland only by invitation of someone living there. East Germans were restricted from buying nearly anything in Czechoslovakia, making travel there not especially pleasant. Before Hungary removed the Iron Curtain, making travel there in general problematic for East Germans, West German tourists were flooding Hungary with their deutsche marks, and East Germans had to pay with coupons that the Hungarians accepted only disdainfully. Romania was so financially strapped that there was hardly enough food to buy, and anyway people found the country's condition depressing. Travel to Bulgaria was still possible but had become almost prohibitively expensive. A two-week trip to Bulgaria as part of a tour cost 2,800 marks per person in 1989, plus incidental expenses, amounting to about three months' income for an average worker.

East Germans could perhaps travel to North Korea or Viet Nam with a group tour, but there were only a few available spaces, and the itinerary was tightly controlled. Few people demonstrated a great deal of interest in traveling to North Korea for a sunny vacation anyway. One may have believed that East Germans should also have been allowed to visit the socialist states of Nicaragua, Yugoslavia, or Cuba, but there were fine distinctions to be made. Nicaragua was only a "society of socialist orientation," and Yugoslavia was not considered socialist—or, more precisely, "actually existing socialist"—at all. Cuba was an official socialist state, but travel there, as to the other two, was categorized as travel to nonsocialist states, requiring the same security clearance and entangled paperwork for travel to the West. The reason was clear to my acquaintances. These were "plane change" countries. From each it was easy to catch a plane to West Germany.

Despite the shortages at home, East Germany had constructed and staffed an entire hospital in Managua, Nicaragua, the "Carlos Marcos" Hospital. The daughter of an acquaintance was a nurse there, and the mother told me something about her daughter's life. There was the hospital, of course, and the apartment building next to it where the East German staff lived, and a small market square out in front where they could buy food. That was the extent of their allowed travel range. They could not travel around the country, or even through Managua for that matter, without official permission from the hospital supervisors and as part of a group. I asked her why her daughter's travel was so restricted, and she responded with a knowing smile, "Oh, it is quite a dangerous place, you know." After thinking for a minute, she added, "But an opportunity like that is one of the few ways to get out of here at all for a while."

Thus, except for the coveted trip to West Germany for a relative's birthday or, for very exceptional people, to some professional meeting, East Germans were essentially unable to leave their country, and the feelings about the entrapment ran high. As I was leaving the train in Kassel on one of my trips to West Germany, a tearful East German woman asked me to help her with her luggage. "Oh, you are an American, how nice," she cried. "They wouldn't let my daughter come with me. My sister is seventy years old tomorrow. They said that was no excuse."

In trains, at parties, and in restaurants one heard much talk of travel or, perhaps more accurately, nontravel. A casual mention of a visit to West Germany would slowly cause heads to turn and questions eventually would be forthcoming, "Well, how was it over there?" Inevitably the answer was something about a different and dazzling world. I shall probably never forget the account by one East German of eating Chinese food during a trip to the West. It was the first time in her life she had ever had Chinese food, and to her the various stringy ingredients were a kind of marvel. I also remember the time, on my way home from Weimar to Los Angeles for Christmas, when I met one of the students in the Weimar railroad station, she awaiting the train to Leipzig. We chatted and I mentioned that I was catching the train to Frankfurt am Main, then to the Frankfurt airport for a flight to Dallas, where I would change planes for Los Angeles. She gave me a kind of wistful look and said, "You know, it's hard for us to imagine such a trip. First across our border, then flying halfway around the world. . . ."

The sense of being in a zoo came not only from the inability to travel.

It came also from the inability to find out what was happening in the world. Part of this feeling derived from the censored press but, beyond that, access to even the censored press was sometimes restricted. In East Germany one did not merely send a check to a publisher and request a subscription to a magazine or newspaper. All subscriptions were handled through the "Periodicals Distribution Agency" of the post office. To receive anything from a local newspaper to a foreign magazine one had to fill out an order form at the post office. Delivery would commence on the first of the next month, with the subscription fee collected monthly at one's door. Subscriptions were important to obtain because delivery of daily newspapers to the local newsstands, "kiosks" as they were called, was uncertain at best, and in such small quantities that desirable publications were sold out early. *Das Volk,* the local newspaper in Weimar, was regularly gone from the kiosks by 6:30 A.M., and the national *Neues Deutschland* often by 7:30. By 10:00 A.M., one could find only such periodicals as *Stamp Collector's Express* or *Soviet Woman,* in addition to a plentiful supply of foreign newspapers such as *L'Humanité,* the French communist paper, or papers from Viet Nam. *Pravda* and other Soviet newspapers were hardly ever to be found.

When I arrived I immediately subscribed to *Neues Deutschland,* but later I decided to test the subscription system to see where it would lead me. What would happen, I wondered, if someone wanted to subscribe to a newspaper from the West? I decided to try ordering a subscription to the *International Herald Tribune,* published in Paris. Dutifully I went to the local post office, filled out the periodical request form, and handed it to the clerk. She looked at it, then looked at me, and said, "I doubt this is on our list, but we can look it up." She disappeared for a minute and came back with a large three-ring notebook full of pages listing all the periodicals to which one could subscribe. International periodicals were listed by country.

"The only French periodical we list is *L'Humanité,* and the only American periodicals are the weekly edition of *People's Daily World* and *Political Affairs,*" both published by the Communist Party of the USA in New York. "There's no *International Herald Tribune.* But," she was actually quite helpful, "we can send a request to Berlin and see what they say."

I waited. A few weeks later I received a courteous, personal letter from Chief Inspector Harenberg in East Berlin stating, "It is unfortunately not possible for us to deliver the *International Herald Tribune* to you, since this publication is not included in the Postal Periodicals List of the DDR, part II." I presumed I had received such a nice letter because he had checked on me to find that I was a visiting American. I suspect that an East German citizen would not have received a personal letter but would instead have received disadvantage.

Undaunted, I decided to see if I could at least subscribe to *People's Daily World* and *Political Affairs*. Again I went to the post office. Once more the clerk hauled out the notebook, but this time she told me that although these were indeed on the list, they were preceded by an "X," meaning that new subscriptions were not being accepted. I could again see what Berlin had to say, so I filled out an order form, waited a few weeks, and sure enough received a reply. This time it was not a personal letter from Chief Inspector Harenberg, but merely my order form bearing a faint rubber stamp saying, "Your subscription order cannot be accepted because the copies available through the Periodicals Distribution Agency are already spoken for." This was probably the type of response the locals could expect. It meant, however, that I had to do without any publications from the United States. For my English-language reading I had to content myself with occasional copies of *New Age,* the crudely printed newspaper of the Communist Party of India. There was no rush by anyone else to buy it at the kiosks.

One would not have known it by checking the kiosks, but East Germany did publish a number of handsome and useful magazines, though they were hardly to be seen and seldom available for subscription. One could always subscribe to *Neues Deutschland,* to be sure, but *Das Volk* was unavailable to new subscribers for about six months while I was there, ostensibly because of a paper shortage. This chronic paper shortage was often cited as a reason for the lack of printed materials. There were no written syllabi for courses in the architecture school, for example, and it was also cited as the reason why the few available photocopy machines were kept in locked rooms, even pre-*Sputnik*. Everyone seemed to know the real answer, though. As one colleague described it to me, "We don't have a paper shortage so much as a freedom shortage."

One of the most informative of the East German magazines, entitled *Magazine for House and Apartment,* was full of recipes, money-saving household tips, and articles such as how to get the most out of one's WM 600 washing machine. One typical issue in 1989 included the following articles:

- Legal requirements for residents' associations.
- Building interior partition walls.
- New household products: food mixer, vacuum cleaner, room fan, coffee pot.
- How to insulate windows.
- Restoring sgraffito decoration on historic house facades.
- A column called "How Does it Work?" this time on hydraulic door closers.
- Correct use of laundry detergent.
- "People's Own Enterprises Introduce New Products": hammers, doorbell.
- Living together after divorce.
- Tips for do-it-yourselfers.
- How to recognize the traditional farmhouse in the Mecklenburg region.

The magazine, illustrated with numerous color photos and diagrams, represented a major editorial effort. The problem was that the subscription lists had long been full, and one often had to wait years for a subscription. Few people ever saw this magazine, and copies were handed around from friend to friend.

East German bookstores were large and well stocked, with titles covering a range of technical fields, social sciences, and fiction. East Germany did produce a rich tradition of fiction, which was eagerly read. In addition, every bookstore had a large Marxist-Leninist section, but there were also sections on history, sports, and computers. If one entered a bookstore looking for some treatise on contemporary East German society, or a book about the United States, one indeed could find it, though what lay between the covers was not necessarily what might be expected. Books about contemporary East German society were often incredibly wordy Marxist exhortations that nobody seemed to read. Books about the United States tended to fall into two categories: the excoriating and the irrelevant. A required text for a Marxist-Leninist class at the university was called *The Political System of the United States*. It contained around three-hundred pages of nonstop diatribe about the exploitation of human potential, and the misery, homelessness, racial bigotry, and shameless behavior found throughout the course of American history. In fact, one could say that everything in the book was true, and one could find such a book in the United States as well. Yet it portrayed only part of the truth, and the book left an entire other realm of American life unexplored, as if human fulfillment, creativity, tolerance, and integrity were not part of the American consciousness.

On the other hand I was intrigued by a book whose title caught my eye, *Life in America*. This was in fact no diatribe, but the account of a German traveler to the United States a hundred and fifty years ago.

In the end, I realized that what was missing from East German publications was insight into, criticism of, and controversy about the world of today. Without this insight one could not begin to question in any profound sense the values set forth by the ruling power, which promulgated the acceptable way the socialist person should live. East Germans— nearly every one of them, it seems—knew the system was failing, but they had no access to the formal knowledge that would tell them why, or what they could do about it.

Control of information was not only true with books and magazines but also with requesting photocopies in preparation for my class. Since I had assigned my students the project of redesigning the center of an American small town, I requested that the architecture school photocopy department make copies of a street plan from an American book I had brought with me, to serve as an underlay for the the students. No, I am sorry, Professor Gleye, no drawings may be copied from books. I asked around about why that would be so. A copyright issue, it was suggested. But I could copy text from that same book, so copyright was not the issue. The truth, I suspect, was that drawings include maps, and there was great sensitivity to any reproduction of any map showing anything that could be useful to an enemy army, though everyone knew that the military of both sides had detailed satellite maps, and city maps could be purchased in newsstands. That I wanted to copy an American map was, I also suspect, a subtlety the Party overseers may not have understood. Disadvantage lurked.

In addition, one was required to submit requested materials to be copied *four* weeks before needing them. "We have much work and too little staff." I surmised that a four-week delay allowed the authorities an opportunity to review the material before it was copied. Yet perhaps more importantly, I suspected, if the political significance of all material could not accurately be judged and appropriately censored before it was copied, a four-week delay at least reduced the effect of politically oriented materials that may have escaped the censors. If nothing else, it discouraged the process in general because almost nothing was worth the bother of having it copied.

In January 1989 *Neues Deutschland* published a prominent article illustrated with a large photograph of a high barbed-wire fence next to a guard tower. The story was obviously intended to portray the United States in a bad light, but it was equally obvious that the real message had to do with East Germany's fortified borders. The headline: "Between USA and Mexico: A four-meter-wide concrete ditch built next to a barbed-wire fence; Washington confirms it is increasing border security." The article quoted Francis Keating, of the Justice Department: "A country is not a country when it cannot protect its borders." Indeed, the fence looked very much like the Iron Curtain, and Keating's comment echoed the statement repeatedly made by East German authorities that the "antifascist protection wall" between East and West Germany was justified because the DDR had the right to protect its borders.

"Look at that, would you," said an East German friend indignantly when he saw the article. "They only forgot to mention one fact. Your fence is intended to keep people out. Ours is to keep people in."

Keeping the people in the country and keeping them ignorant of what went on outside appeared to be a dominant feature of the tensions I observed in East Germany. Many people assumed that the Upper 10,000 did not understand the crying need to be released from the zoo, either physically or intellectually, because they were sheltered from it, but I eventually perceived that the country's top leaders were not the only ones sheltered through privilege. One evening I was having dinner with an official of moderately high rank, but far from the top. Our conversation centered, as usual, around the topic of problems. A way needed to be found to get the country moving again, he said. He had picked me up in his new Wartburg station wagon, the larger of the two East German automobiles, and on the way home told me that automobiles were a real problem. He had an old Wartburg station wagon that was giving out, so he had spent considerable time cajoling the automobile-distributing authorities into letting him buy a new one. They finally relented, and he had picked up his new car only a few days before.

After dinner a friend of his, an official of similar rank, stopped by the house. The friend and his wife were out for a spin in their new Soviet-made Lada, which they had purchased just that day. The two men, eager to show off their new cars, led us out to the driveway and proceeded to admire the new purchases, looking under each other's hoods, sitting in the driver's seat, checking the location of the controls, and testing the comfort. Upon the general conclusion that the Lada had been better designed, the friends drove off to continue their ride.

The scene was reminiscent of American suburbia; two executives checking out each other's new toys on a Saturday afternoon. However, for most East Germans this scene would have been unimaginable. Hardly anyone could afford a Wartburg station wagon in the first place, and Ladas were seldom available. Even if they could afford one, most people would have had to wait seventeen years between the time a Wartburg was ordered and the time it was delivered.

On another occasion, when I was riding the train from Weimar into West Germany, I noticed two people in my compartment who were different from the usual riders consisting of retired people and the occasional businessman. The man, in his forties, apparently had something to do with the border troops because he understood exactly the procedures followed at the border. He understood the rigid clockwise checking of passports through the compartment; he knew immediately when the customs officer walked by our compartment without stopping that the last inspection had been passed. He was wearing a wedding ring. His companion, in her thirties, was an obvious first-time traveler to West Germany, offering her passport at the wrong time, listening intently as he quietly explained the border process to her. She was also wearing a wedding ring. They sat close to each other, their new-love happy faces divulging that they were probably not married to each other.

Later, a comment by an acquaintance suddenly made me realize what I had been seeing in these episodes. The acquaintance, having reached a position of fairly high responsibility in the Party, was a confirmed Marxist-Leninist. He had dedicated his life to improving conditions in East German cities and maintained a faith in the ultimate goodness of socialism. As the atmosphere of frustration was palpably rising in early 1989, small demonstrations were already taking place in Leipzig, and the mood of the people could be gleaned when eavesdropping on nearly any conversation. The impatience of the people disturbed him deeply, and he found it difficult to grasp. After all, everyone had food and shelter, and despite the rigidity of the Party, conditions of life represented a solid achievement of socialism. Protest was being fueled by propagandistic Western media, he believed, and the street demonstrators were rowdies. "All we want to do is lead an ordinary life," he said, "and continue working to make the country a better place." I think his attitude was firmly grounded in his own life, and I think his view was typical of that held by many people who had risen to responsible positions, though by no means as part of the Upper 10,000.

What he did not realize was that his view of ordinary life included an annual two-week trip to France and occasional trips to England, paid for by the state. These were not junkets, it was not a matter of corruption, for the travel was reciprocal under agreements with comparable organizations in those countries. However, several times a year found him on the train or airplane to Western Europe. One of the banners carried by demonstrators in the fall of 1989 bore the slogan *Visafrei. Von Rostock bis Schanghai!,* which might be loosely translated as "Let us Fly. From Rostock to Shanghai!" The very travel that my acquaintance took for granted as part of his "ordinary life" was the thing being demanded on the streets of his country by other, ordinary people, to whom that was denied. It is so easy to forget the others, I thought, when one could indeed get the new car, have dinner in the Eiffel Tower, or slip one's girlfriend into West Germany on the train for a fling. It is especially easy when it is obvious that the others are deeply envious of these perquisites of position.

During a lecture for one of my classes in Weimar I showed slides of the United States Capitol building, which led to an illuminating exchange about the attitudes toward our respective countries. "Here is our Capitol," I noted casually, "where our senators and representatives meet to pass laws."

A student came up to me afterward. "You used the word 'our,'" he said. "Do Americans really think of that building as 'theirs'?"

"Sure," I responded, not yet understanding his question. "Our elected legislators meet there."

"OK, I just wanted to check. Because most people here would never think of the Palace of the Republic in East Berlin as 'ours'."

14

ALF Orders a Pizza:
The Influence of Capitalist Culture

I WOULD NEVER have considered giving Post-it Notes as a gift until I left some for the school secretary when I was packing to depart. She was intrigued by those little yellow slips that stick to anything you put them on. There was nothing like that in East Germany. She wrote notes to her friends and her boss and posted them all over the office. I also left her a staple remover, which she had never seen, and after I showed her how to use it, she left it on the top of her desk where others would have the opportunity to ask her what the thing was. This kind of a story does not reveal a people of less than average intelligence; it merely reveals the isolation of East Germany from so much innovation. In fact, the secretary's response to the staple remover was quite thoughtful. She admired it for its simple elegance. "The human mind is so wonderfully creative," she said.

Actually I was unprepared for the interest people showed in the fairly ordinary things I brought with me. Nearly every time I pulled out some gadget people seemed to take notice, and eventually it led to a kind of game on my part to see what I could come up with next that would slowly cause heads to turn my way until somebody would ask, "Say, what's that you've got there?" I had a hard suitcase, the kind they run trucks over in the TV ads. "A real money case, *wah*?" said the taxi driver. Absentmindedly I said, "Yup." He suddenly took greater interest. "Hey, do you *really* have money in that thing?"

150

I previewed the slides for my lectures with a little hand-held illuminated slide viewer that made the rounds of the office. "My, my." My down sleeping bag aroused some interest, "Naw, a sleeping bag can't be that small." Then there was the day I brought some peanut butter to coffee break at school and offered it around. The jar was duly sniffed, the color inspected, and knives were hesitantly stuck into the goo and smeared on rolls. Suddenly we had a whole table of grinning people with peanut butter stuck to the roofs of their mouths. I went to a Fasching party, the pre-Lenten bash, dressed in a denim jacket with a necklace of Big Red chewing gum laced together with paper clips. I had dreamed it up as an emergency measure because I had no costume with me. Since the German word for chewing gum, "*Kaugummi,*" is pronounced something like "cow-goomy," the ensemble gave my costume a handy alliterative theme: "Cowboy and *Kaugummi.*" I must say it was quite a hit. People kept coming up to me all evening and striking up conversations. For a while I was most flattered until I realized all they really wanted was a piece of my *Gummi*. East Germany did have chewing gum, of course, but it was bland and the taste short-lived. My chewing gum was Western.

People appreciated receiving a small bottle of American whiskey from me, which is not unusual, but young people asked me for posters of cities, especially of Los Angeles, and people were curious about popcorn, Band-Aids, and hand lotion. A popcorn entrepreneur could have made a fortune in East Germany, and the hand-lotion episode was a caricature of the TV commercial where the housewife, satisfied with her Brand X detergent, does not believe the miracle whitener will get her clothes cleaner until her neighbor convinces her to try it. "Don't put that greasy stuff on my hands!" Then, "Hey, that's pretty good, actually."

I took a copy of *A Day in the Life of America,* the popular book full of warm-toned photographs of everyday life, and nonchalantly left it on my work table at school. People would stroll by and thumb through it as if it were a copy of *Playboy,* pretending that the articles rather than the pictures were the real draw. Now and then it would disappear for a few days, always to return.

It was not only my own objects that fascinated. One staff member at the architecture school received a visit from West German relatives who drove up in their big, fire-red Mercedes. As the staff member walked out the front door and proudly climbed into the car, people were leaning out the windows watching the spectacle.

One of my acquaintances is probably still telling her friends about the heavenly feeling of riding in the front seat of a Volkswagen Passat. A West German friend with this car visited me one weekend, and as we toured the countryside I suggested we drop by acquaintances in Arnstadt. Since few people had telephones, dropping by unexpectedly was perfectly acceptable. We did so, the acquaintances were at home and glad to see us, and they wanted to show us their garden on the edge of town. "No, let's not take your Trabant," I said, "let's take the Volkswagen Passat. It's larger, so we'll all fit in better." I think neither of my acquaintances from Arnstadt had been in a Volkswagen before. The husband, reticent man, said nothing as we approached it in the parking lot, but his wife's eyes were obviously gleaming. "You're the guest of honor," I said, opening the front door for her. Such a grin I have seldom seen. "Oh, yes, of course, this is quite a different sensation, yes, quite, yes . . ." she kept saying as she ran her hands over the leatherette upholstery and luxuriated in the bucket seat.

Of course, anyone who had spent much time riding in an East German Trabant would know the feeling. By the end of my stay I found myself feeling depressed when I realized I had to ride in one. Imagine the combination of rough, poorly maintained streets, an auto with a tiny wheelbase and spongy seats that threw one around on the slightest bump, plus a low ceiling never more than two inches from one's head, coupled with a windshield so small it seemed like riding in a tunnel, all the while accompanied by the shuddering and fairly screaming noise of the two-cycle engine, and you can understand the Trabant. It sold for an average year's salary after a twelve-year wait for delivery. It is no wonder that so many people had a Western fixation, whatever their political beliefs about socialism and capitalism.

Part of the Western fixation had to do with music. American music was still the world's most popular in the 1980s. The performers may have been from anywhere, but the music came from Los Angeles. I met a number of East German fans of American jazz or rock. Their music collections were composed partly of things released in East Germany, like Bruce Springsteen's *Born in the USA* album. The East German record enterprise had released an entire series of traditional American blues recordings that were popular. In addition, records brought in by visitors from West Germany made the rounds of people's cassette recorders, to be recorded on tape. Indeed, the juxtaposition of the suggestive lyrics and wanton drive of Western rock music with the repressed life of East Germany created some surreal moments. I shall never forget cruising through drab, lifeless

East German villages in an ancient, shuddering Trabant with the Doors' "L.A. Woman" blaring from the car's huge Japanese stereo.

As a matter of fact, I came to a major foreign policy conclusion during my stay in East Germany: the United States did indeed have the world's most successful propaganda agency. Despite the good efforts of the United States Information Agency, however, even it could not compete with the world's true propaganda masters: the American film and recording industries. These industries flooded a country like East Germany with images of American lifestyle, the relentless beat of rock music, and the intellectualism of jazz that were impossible to submerge. The image of America they portrayed was not necessarily good, but conveying good images of a country is not what makes people like it. Fascination draws people to a country. Even through images showing a seemingly chaotic environment, which was part of the vision many East Germans had of America, the fascination endured, gleaned from the messages conveyed in American film and music.

One may recall the Nick Nolte film *Teachers,* a wonderful movie about the nightmares we all shared as high school students: the teacher so boring that he dies in class and nobody notices; the teacher who is found to be an escapee from an insane asylum; the injured student who goes to the office and nobody pays any attention to him; the graduate who sues the school because he never learned to read. A dubbed German version was shown in East German theaters. Not only that, schoolteachers in Weimar were *required* to see the film as part of their School of Socialist Work program. It was presented as a documentary of American education, showing the bankruptcy and chaos of education in a capitalist society. Though I do not think many people believed it, the film did generate enormous interest, and several people asked me what it was that they saw. I had to tell them it was a farce, but as in all farces there was a grain of truth to it, and that was what made it so interesting. Yet beyond its chaos, people saw in it a free life of single-family homes on tree-lined streets, and it piqued interest in the United States perhaps more than any real documentary on American education could have done. Despite the fears of propagandists who think that everything said about one's own country should be good, one cannot be an enemy of a country that fascinates. I thought we should send Spike Lee's film *Do the Right Thing* to East Germany.

Television had been another powerful player in the hearts-and-minds battle going on over Germany for the previous forty-five years. East Germans watched a lot of West German television beyond "Dallas" and "Denver"; it was the only mass violator of the Party's attempt to control knowl-edge of the outside. In fact, most people watched *only* West German television. Common knowledge had it that about 2 percent of the popula-tion watched East German, and 70 percent watched West German. I do not know if the figures were correct, but the television I saw people watch-ing in bars and restaurants, as well as in their homes, was almost exclu-sively West German.

Evening news from the second West German channel came on at 7:00 P.M. News from East German television was broadcast at 7:30. I usually watched the seven o'clock news, then switched to the 7:30 East German news to watch at least the brief summaries of the stories that they ran at the beginning of the program. One evening while visiting a friend who held a fairly high position in arts administration in East Berlin, we watched the 7:00 P.M. West German news as was his custom, then I switched to the East German channel to catch the headlines. He left the room. "I don't need to watch that shit. I live it."

I never actually met anybody who admitted to watching "ALF," the American television series about the beloved but mischievous alien crea-ture that appeared in dubbed German on a West German channel, but there must have been many surreptitious "ALF" watchers in the Zone. A young girl in Karl-Marx-Stadt made me take a picture of her in her ALF t-shirt. "ALF greets the rest of the world," it said on the front of the shirt. Of all ALF's shenanigans, perhaps his most enjoyed was his ordering out for a pizza. It was hard to order out for a pizza in East Germany because not many people had a telephone at home, but even so the concept of hot food delivered to one's door was quite foreign to labor-short East Germany. It suggested a very different world from the bratwurst kiosks of the DDR with their eternal lines of hungry customers waiting to be served.

In the early postwar years watching West German television was con-demned as "letting the class enemy into the parlor," and overzealous members of the Free German Youth climbed up on roofs to rotate the an-tennas toward the east. Children were asked in school which clock they saw on the television screen before the evening news, and shown pictures of the West and East German versions. The parents of children who gave the wrong answer could expect disadvantage. West watching was appar-ently not to be stopped, however, as more children learned the difference between what was appropriate to say at home and what was appropriate to say in school, and as many people apparently mounted television anten-nas in their attics, away from public view.

In the meantime a strange phenomenon was observed in Dresden. The area around the city in the far southeast part of the country was the only one in East Germany too remote from West Germany or Westberlin to receive its television programs. That is why it was called the "Valley of the Ignorant," since its people did not have a clue about what was going on. In reality they were not entirely isolated from news, since they could receive West German radio, but the image-rich message of Western life came from television. However, rather than being *more* satisfied with conditions in East Germany because they were not tempted by Western television, they were found to be *less* satisfied. In fact, the highest percentage of applications to emigrate from the country apparently came from this region. Given this insoluble contradiction, the Party eventually granted permission to watch West, and watched it was, with a fervor.

There were even plans underway eventually to bring West German television to Dresden by cable, but in the meantime tall mast TV antennas and an occasional satellite dish jutted above rooftops as people tried to reach up over the mountains to receive Western programming. One acquaintance in Weimar mentioned to me that his in-laws were coming from Dresden to visit. "I hate it when they come. They always stay two weeks and spend the whole time watching West German television."

Of course, East German programs offered little competition with the West German channels even if one desired to watch them. News programs spent ten minutes with a camera panning the honor guard at East Berlin's Schönefeld Airport while Erich Honecker and the visiting prime minister of Mozambique reviewed the troops, or interviewed factory workers at length about how they exceeded production quotas for potash. Other programs featured entertainment such as clumsily lip-synched, supposedly bawdy sailor's songs from a stage-set wharf hangout. The regular program "You and Your House Pet" generated especially enthusiastic reviews. One night I watched an East German movie that was set in World War II Berlin, where the main characters were Germans busy collaborating with the Red Army. The idea was to help the Russians slaughter German troops more rapidly so the Soviet "liberation forces" could sweep across Germany and free it from the scourge of Nazism. Despite the troubled relationship Germans have to their past, I think few Germans could have stomached this one.

So the people "watched West," as they said. East Germans spoke in detail about political affairs in West Germany, sitting around discussing the fate of Chancellor Helmut Kohl as if he were their own head of government. In addition, of course, they watched the commercials. West German commercials flooded East Germany during the evenings in the coveted times before and after the newscasts. These commercials offered twenty-second vignettes of an urbane, carefree life in handsome, impeccably maintained surroundings. West German television commercials purveyed rich coffee, fine champagne, and luxurious chocolates with a cinematic technique that gave everything an upper-class pretension. The material things presented daily in West German television commercials were precisely those goods most scarce or lacking in East Germany, unless one had deutsche marks and could buy them in the Intershop.

A commercial that seemed especially to catch the East German imagination was that for Nescafé coffee. It featured a slender, young, blonde female international business-executive type who emerged from jet planes, drove expensive convertibles, and sat on the terraces of Riviera hotels. "I live so spontaneously; I am so free," went the jingle and, rhyming in German, "Nescafé is part of it." This fantasy image, full of power and confidence, almost made me, who knew perfectly well the difference between television commercials and life, go buy some Nescafé at the local Intershop. One saw "I am so free" stickers in semipublic places like the *insides* of car doors in East Germany, where they were not too visible.

The signals of at least two West German channels flowed over the border, more in East Berlin where the popular Radio in the American Sector inaugurated a television channel in 1988. West German television reported the extremes about its own society, to be sure, discussing unemployment problems, newly arising xenophobia, rapidly escalating rents. Yet all this took place in an atmosphere of prosperity, of clean streets and fine automobiles, of vacations in Italy. One acquaintance had taken the commercials quite to heart. She had received a supply of West German toiletries and had displayed them in her bathroom as hunters display trophy heads. Each plastic bottle of hair conditioner and 4711 eau de cologne was set neatly on her shelves, spaced apart like birds on a telephone wire, the label of each neatly faced to the front. When I visited she insisted on giving me a tour of her family's one-bedroom apartment, making a major stop in the bathroom where she kept me captive until I had tried nearly everything I could, short of taking a shower, and had commented on the excellence of each West German product.

West German programming had an especially strong effect on children, since kids are the same everywhere. They turned the dials and watched the commercials about things like toys and cookies, and then they asked their parents to buy the products. Parents told me how difficult it was for them to explain to their children why they could not have the things they saw on television. No, that's a different country, with different money, and no, you can't go there. I suspect that, of all the factors conspiring to frustrate the building of a socialist state in East Germany, in the long run West German television had been the most effective.

Children in East Germany fell into the same pattern of attempting to show one another up as could be found anywhere else. The neighbor child who had West German candy or a new West German bicycle or real Lego toys became the envied one. The East German version of the brightly colored Lego toys, called "Lege," was crudely fashioned of softer plastic and dull colors. The intensity of colors in Western toys made them easily recognizable. In some circles it was fairly gauche to have to play with East German Leges.

Partly through the contradictions made evident in television, children at an early age seemed to pick up an acute awareness of the East-West German relationship as it applied to their world. First- and second-grade children tended to know the black market exchange rate for West German marks because kids would nag their parents for West German change to buy candy and ice cream in the Intershop. "West marks are to our kids what drugs are to yours," said one parent to me. "They are the key to happiness." "Over there," meaning West Germany, took on a magical aura partly because of the life for children portrayed in its television programs and commercials.

East German television suffered from a problem beyond boring programming that intensified the strange vacuum in which so many people found themselves. While much of what was seen on Western television was not available, what was seen on East German programs was not necessarily available either. I watched a geography program where the narrator climbed into a handy Interflug plane waiting on the runway to fly him up and observe the countryside from the sky, as if such an activity were a normal thing to do. In reality the average *Osti* (East German) would never be able to do that unless dispatched by an official agency, as the narrator was. Or a science program where the host radioed the pilot of an Interflug flight over Africa to ask the weather conditions. He and the pilot chatted about the weather over Zimbabwe for the benefit of the youthful television audience as though it were no big deal to fly over Africa, a place where most East Germans would never be allowed to go. Thus East German television itself became part of a deception, this one however not a deception of a fantasy life but a deception of what in the West would be a normal life if one wished to do such things.

I had many discussions about the West in general and the United States in particular, partly trying to help people discern reality from fantasy in the latest American film. Yet when Oz topples, it falls hard, and perhaps the most difficult time for me was the week after the *Exxon Valdez* hit the rocks in Alaska. The great Americans, and a giant firm in our free-enterprise system, suddenly let a ship dump its cargo of oil on the American coastline. The government had relied on the company to handle mishaps, and the company acted with what seemed a callous indifference. Of course had I been allowed that subscription to the *International Herald Tribune,* I would have had better answers, but it was difficult for me to explain the American system in this instance. "How can the United States claim to speak with moral authority in the world when it lets something like this happen?" someone asked me. I did not have a good response.

Other concerns about Western life arose often in conversations as well. As I was sitting around at coffee break one morning, somebody reported receiving a letter from a former East German then living in West Germany and working in a microchip factory, where he wrote of rumors that part of the work force would be laid off. The specter of "unemployment" visibly passed through the group's faces. Perhaps the most successfully inculcated fear in East Germany that had kept the West at bay was that of unemployment. *Neues Deutschland* reported almost daily on unemployment figures in some Western country, and by 1989 often in other East Bloc countries, with the subtle suggestion that an 8 percent unemployment rate meant that the same 8 percent of the workforce was eternally unemployed, living in hunger and misery. West Germany was "the two-thirds society" according to East German dogma, adopting with fervor the West German self-critical slogan. Two-thirds of the people lived well, but one-third lived in humiliation and misery. Of course the message was that it would happen in East Germany if the system were disrupted. "Look at the unemployment figures already coming out of Hungary. . . ."

One of the most frequent comments made to me regarded unemployment. "You know, we may not have much here, but at least we all have work. It may be true that the unemployed in West Germany actually live better financially than those with jobs in East Germany, but that does not take into account the terrible humiliation of *not having a job.*" Of course, a fundamental tenet of East German socialism had been to declare work a "human right." That assumed something false—that everyone would rather work than not work, regardless of the quality of the job. Yet this feeling that a job was, without question, a part of the desirable human condition seemed to have become a central feature of the East German psyche.

The East German media spoke of Western society not only as a "two-thirds society" but also as an "elbow society," where one had to elbow one's neighbor out of the way to get ahead. Thus the vision of the West was often truly confusing. On the one hand, there were the visions of freedom, but on the other, concern about how one coped in an elbow society. In the States, I responded, much depended on one's own sense of self-responsibility. No political party or government told us how we should live or what we should say. When East Germans asked me what it was like to live in "America, the Land of Unlimited Opportunity," I reminded them that we Americans had only the opportunity to try, to decide for ourselves what direction our lives should take. There was no guarantee that our dreams would be fulfilled, however, and the inevitable problem was that some people fell through the cracks, made wrong decisions, or sought to avoid the responsibility for one's life that accompanied the opportunity. That was a price we paid for the good things our society offered us. East Germans often spoke of the "browbeating" (*Bevormundung*) attitude of the Party, and my comment about having responsibility for one's own life seemed to be one of the most effective things I said about America. Heads would nod in approval, and there was even occasional spontaneous applause from an audience. Many of my listeners seemed eager for the opportunity to test their elbows a bit, though I sensed that many only dreamed of success and did not well understand the responsibility part.

Despite the specter of unemployment and homelessness that complicated the thinking about the West, I also found an uncanny insight on the part of some people. One person said to me, for example, "We have no unemployment and no homelessness, but we also have no creativity. Perhaps the astounding level of creativity that emanates from American society would be destroyed if you built up the same level of social security that we have under socialism." A few people were not convinced, however. One devout socialist said to me, "What good does your freedom do you if it leads you to unemployment and poverty?"

However confused the attitudes toward the West may have been, and however uncertain the notion of "freedom" on the part of those who had never experienced it, a Western orientation, especially to West Germany, was intense among many. One person in Weimar told me his wife was away visiting relatives in Hamburg, her first trip to the West.

"Have you ever been there?" I asked.

"No, I have never been to Germany."

Rather shocked by his answer, I leaned over to him and said, "You're in Germany now."

"Yeah, sort of."

15

Russians

E AST GERMANS not only looked to the West with a complex set of attitudes but also looked East with many questions. One of the salient differences between the two postwar German peoples had been their respective attitudes toward the Second World War and the rise of Nazism. During the 1980s many West Germans had engaged in profound personal soul-searching over that dark period. I recall numerous conversations with younger-generation West Germans when the discussion would eventually gravitate to their country's past, with the question raised and pondered of how the Nazi era could have possibly happened. Attempting to come to terms with that past has certainly been part of the West German Greens' and other liberal groups' attitudes toward an appropriate German society in the late twentieth century, and it may partly explain the rise of that country's arch-conservative *Republikaner* party in 1989, which proclaimed a policy of reasserted German national greatness. In that year West German media engaged in lengthy analyses of Nazism and the world situation in the 1930s to mark the fiftieth anniversary of the war's beginning.

In socialist East Germany that past had been handled differently, partly given the legacy of brutal treatment of communists by the Nazis. "Hitlerfascism" (*Hitlerfaschismus*), as it was called, had been viewed purely as a result of the capitalist society so detested by the country's founders and many who followed. Thus the Party viewed the Nazis as an

161

alien force driven by capitalist exploitation that descended on the people, and the Soviet Liberation Forces as the saviors who rescued German society from their grasp. This attitude was continually inculcated through education, literature, and the media, and was easily discerned in passing references to the past that one found in East German books. The tourist guide to the city of Bautzen, for example, noted that, "In the heavy fighting for the liberation of Bautzen by the Soviet Army, the old square was totally destroyed."

The old administration building at Buchenwald concentration camp near Weimar had become a museum documenting the atrocities committed there. Many days one would see schoolchildren being taken through the museum, its exhibits presented to them in detail. Museums and galleries throughout the country mounted frequent exhibits, some of which came from West Germany, documenting Nazism. The Party's slogan emblazoned on banners, "My workplace—My place of struggle for peace and socialism!" related to its frequent assertion that the socialist German state was dedicated to maintaining that a war would never again emanate from German soil. The way to find liberation from the past was to work toward the socialist future.

Thus while many West German young people had continued to bear a sense of responsibility for their past, I found that many young East Germans felt themselves freed from it. Whether or not they were committed to socialism, East Germans had more easily put the past aside.

Soviet liberation of a part of Germany from Hitlerfascism had established a set of attitudes toward the Soviet Union with a somewhat different foundation than those held by other Eastern European communist parties since the war. It helps to explain, I believe, the East German leadership's protracted resistance, until the bitter end, to perestroika in the Soviet Union and to the dismantling of communism in Poland and Hungary. It helps to explain the long-standing slogan of the East German Party, "To learn from the Soviet Union is to learn triumph," "*Von der Sowjetunion lernen heißt Siegen lernen.*" For the country's leaders the Soviet Union, at least in its pre-perestroika formulation, offered a model on which to base a nonexploitative and peaceful society. The stage for a political crisis in East Germany was in fact set when this slogan had to be withdrawn because perestroika rendered the Soviet Union no longer worthy as a model. People could then ask, "If we can no longer learn triumph from the Soviet Union, from whom can we learn it?"

Once perestroika had begun to forge a different Soviet Union, *Neues*

Deutschland could publish an article like "43 Million Soviet Citizens Under Poverty Line." This article, hidden in the inside pages of a January 1989 issue, was the primary topic of conversation that day at coffee break. Not that anybody was surprised about the figure, but that it was reported.

The aura of the Soviet Union as benevolent guardian had been fostered as well by ubiquitous references to German-Soviet friendship. This aura was maintained partly by sloganeering, in the frequent banners proclaiming such things as "Forever allied with the Soviet Union," and in streets named "German-Soviet Friendship" (*Straße der deutsch-sowjetischen Freundschaft*). Many towns had such a street, usually a broad thoroughfare leading into the center. "DSF Street," as each was called since the name was much too long to say, often served as the government protocol street, the one with the nicely maintained facades because Party officials were driven down it on their way to official functions.

Friendship with the Soviet Union had also long been fostered through the country's largest societal organization, the Society for German-Soviet Friendship, or *Gesellschaft für deutsch-sowjetische Freundschaft*. Also called the DSF, the organization established "houses of culture" in many East German cities, each with a theater intended for lectures and programs on Soviet society and a restaurant serving Russian dishes. In recent years membership was probably so large because East Germans were expected to belong to such organizations as part of their demonstration of societal engagement. Dues were a few marks a month, for which one received credit for belonging whether or not one participated. Yet the organization may have served its original purpose well. Given the intense hatred between Germans and Russians by the end of the war, the programs offered by the DSF served to show that the people who had liberated the Germans from Hitlerfascism had a rich history and culture, and were a people with whom one could indeed live in peace after the brutal slaughter.

There lingered as well, however, a more populist attitude toward the Russians, by which name as in the United States one tended to refer to all the Soviets. This attitude was shaped partly by the Soviet military's still exerting a strong presence in East Germany and partly, in Weimar at least, by memories of the two armies that occupied that region of East Germany in 1945.

"I remember your American soldiers who occupied this area right after the war. They came in their jeeps, throwing chewing gum to the children. Then they left and the Russians came, on foot, barefoot in fact, with primitive wagons pulled by exhausted horses. The first thing they did was

steal our watches, and people said, '*This* army conquered *us*?'" The famous watch-stealing habits of the Russian soldiers had by no means been
forgotten, and a recalling of this made its rounds in a joke regarding the
street clocks installed on street corners around East Berlin in the 1980s.
"At least the Russians can't steal them."

American soldiers in West Germany certainly grated on the West German soul. Even though they were there as part of the NATO forces defending Western Europe from attack by the East, many West Germans
tended to consider them as remnants of the postwar occupation armies.
Questions probing the extent to which West Germany was a sovereign
nation were tested anew in the late 1980s, primarily in debates about low-
level flights following the crashes of military aircraft at Ramstein Air Base
and in the town of Remscheid. Yet I easily noted a difference in attitudes
toward the respective foreign military presences. Soviet troops in East
Germany by the 1980s were surrounded by a substantially different aura
then were the Americans in the West.

First, for good or ill, the Americans tended to populate the bars and
restaurants, easy to spot in their American clothes and with their accents.
Russian soldiers were never in the East German bars. In fact, they hardly
left their casernes except in closely supervised groups, and always in their
spiffy, elegantly tailored wool uniforms with fur hats and red trim. Americans fraternized with the locals; at railroad stations on Sunday evenings
there were tearful leave-takings of American soldiers from their German
girlfriends. Russian soldiers were to be seen in East German train stations,
but usually in fatigues and full battle gear on their way to or from some
training exercise, filling platforms and cars with their rank odor and greasy
boots. Soviet officers, of course, were with benefit of family, some living
in specified buildings "on the economy," as the Americans would say,
intermingled with the natives. Russian officers' wives had a twofold repu-
tation. Some were pictured as buying up all the good clothes and household objects in the stores, since they had plenty of time on their hands.
Others had less time on their hands because they worked in East German
factories. It was illegal for them to work, of course, but people said they
made good assembly line workers for 3.50 marks an hour, paid in cash
with no paper trail.

Russian children lived with their officer-fathered families, and they
played with each other outside the building. What did they play? One day
at coffee break my associates were discussing the Russian children in their

neighborhood. Among other games, they said, the children played Red Army vs. Nazis.

An article in 1989 in the West German weekly *Die Zeit* on the fiftieth anniversary of the beginning of the Second World War noted that one of the important transformations of West German society since the war had been the total removal of off-duty uniformed soldiers from the streets. Neither West German soldiers nor the allied troops were ever seen off duty in uniform in public, said the newspaper, changing the long-standing German tradition requiring soldiers always to be in uniform. In East Germany the old tradition remained. There were many uniforms on the street. East German and Soviet soldiers and sailors, as well as East German border troops, on and off duty, in trains and restaurants, were always required to be in uniform.

Given the siege mentality held by the Party, the military that protected it had taken on a kind of independent existence outside the scrutiny of the civilian state. The Soviet military in East Germany appeared as a sovereign and often ominous presence to be avoided. One of the faculty members in the architecture school was driving on an icy highway in winter. As he rounded a curve he braked to avoid a car halfway in a ditch, skidded, and was hit in the rear by a car driven by a Russian soldier. The Police came, inquired, and determined that the faculty member was at fault.

"Why am I at fault? I didn't hit anybody and he hit me from behind," he complained.

"Perhaps," said the police officer, "but if he is at fault, we'll have to wait all afternoon for the Russian military police, and there will be no end of explanations we will have to go through. In the end you'll be at fault anyway."

The machines from the Soviet military helicopter school near Weimar circled over the city daily, although the residents had protested. Their training flight path in fact took them a few hundred feet directly over my apartment building. Their spindly form, guns bristling from both sides, appeared as huge mosquitoes lying in wait for the American to dare step out on his balcony. Sometime before my arrival, people told me, one of them crashed in a field near town. The area was cordonned off and the scene was completely cleared within about three hours, with no trace of the accident. In the unfathomable way that such information became general knowledge, although it was never publicly reported, people had an exact picture of the event, one that did not vary among the tellers. Photographs of such a military mishap would be cause for arrest, since such events were considered military secrets. It was a matter of prestige that the military organization protecting the socialist state be flawless, and it was not the public's business when it was not.

Then there was the day a few years ago, also generally known, but not reported, when a Soviet tank tried to cross an East German railroad track, became stuck between the rails, and was hit by a speeding express train. The soldiers in the tank apparently emerged unhurt. The passengers in the train were not so lucky.

Black Volga limousines chauffeuring Russian officers roared through the countryside blowing the walking locals off the streets with their horns. Tour buses carrying Russians were accompanied by military police who would stop traffic and rush the buses through town. When I observed these things I thought of armored princes hurtling through towns in medieval Europe. These events seemed to exert a more powerful influence on East German attitudes toward the liberation army than did the nattily dressed, shy Soviet troops walking around in their officer-escorted groups with their guidebooks discussing historic towns.

A Soviet military convoy was pointed out to me as a kind of comic spectacle. Soviet army vehicles were always spanking clean, freshly washed ("They don't have anything to do but wash their trucks"), but when convoys lumbered down the road they seemed to drop malfunctioning vehicles like a dog's having a litter on the run. One knew when a convoy had passed because there were trucks alongside the road with hoods up and a couple of soldiers' feet sticking out of the engine compartment. ("These guys couldn't fight a war if they had to.")

Officially, East German culture oriented itself to Eastern Europe, and to some extent this orientation was freely shared by many people in the country. Russian authors were popular, for example, not merely because they offered acceptable reading, but because they offered insight into the socialist way, which many East Germans thought was fundamentally right, irrespective of the Party's abuses. Most of this literature, however, was read in German translation rather than the original Russian. As part of the policy of friendship with the Soviet Union, all students were required to take several years of Russian language in school, yet almost none of them seemed to have emerged knowing how to speak it. One woman's disdainful comment to me, "The kids, they all have to learn this Russian," probably sums up the feeling.

In the end, I realized, the East Germans' Western orientation resulted from fundamental cultural links in that direction more than from West German television. The language barrier between Germany and its eastern neighbors Poland and Czechoslovakia to the east was much more difficult to breach than the language barrier with France or the Netherlands to the west, for example, and Switzerland and Austria to the south were German-speaking countries. Despite all the Russian restaurants in the DSF houses, the only dish that had worked its way into the East German kitchen was a delicious, spicy sausage soup called Soljanka—and that was Ukranian, not Russian. Since it was based on sausage, Soljanka was close to the German culinary tradition anyway. Such things as borscht were never seen. Even after forty years of government with a political overlay of Russian administrative forms and the constant barrage of pro-Russian propaganda, in nearly every respect East Germany had remained a Western country.

Attitudes toward East Germans' links with the East were revealed in a joke having to do with COMECON, the "Council of Mutual Economic Assistance," or the trade organization of East Bloc countries. Marxist literature often talked of various communal social structures that made up the "pillars of socialism." East Germans talked of the five pillars of COMECON: German hospitality, Russian high-quality work, Polish reliability, Mongolian microelectronics, and the Hungarian language.

16

The Five Rules of Shopping

THE EAST GERMAN state enterprise in charge of retail shops and restaurants, the "HO," or *Handelsorganisation,* had a slogan. Emblazoned on plaques and banners in the stores were the words "High achievement to your advantage" (*Hochleistungen zu Ihrem Vorteil*). Westerners have sometimes thought of communist countries as lands where people lined up for hours in front of some shop waiting for shoddy goods to be dished out by a rude and slovenly salesperson. Part of the image East Germans had of the West was that our salesclerks were fawning and obsequious. When I went to East Germany I braced myself for haughty treatment in the stores, but indeed I found generally the opposite to be true. Though the entire shopping experience was somewhat different from that in the West, once I learned the ropes I concluded that the East Germans believed in that "high achievement" slogan and had nurtured some admirable shopkeeper-customer relationships.

Often I found a true sense of helpfulness by salesclerks that made their American counterparts look mediocre. There was general suspicion in East Germany about the poor quality of goods produced there, and this distrust was shared by many of the clerks. Perhaps an advantage of the state as employer was that salesclerks were salaried, did not operate on commission, and had no stake in making big sales. If I perceived a primary motivation of East German clerks, it was probably to avoid hassles, and one hassle was having to accept returns of defective goods. In the glass and porcelain shop, therefore, the salesperson unwrapped each piece of purchased dinnerware and tapped it with her fingernail to test for cracks, then rewrapped it for the customer. The clerk at the record store removed each record from its sleeve and checked for warps and obvious defects. Signs hung in many stores, stating something to the effect, "We are dedicated to quality service to our customers in the name of socialist society," over the manager's name, and each store had a "customer book" hanging within easy reach, in which any customer could write a complaint or suggestion. Of course, given the shortage of people and materials, store managers often could do little about the suggestions, but the problems at least were spelled out quite handily.

Other unexpected services seemed to be taken for granted. Guarantee slips were carefully filled out by store clerks for nearly every purchase. Clerks were usually careful to describe exactly what was covered in the warranty and what to do if something went wrong. I bought a quartz alarm clock for fifty marks—a DDR product, about twice as expensive as a comparable clock in West Germany—that ran five minutes fast per day. When I returned it to the store after a week, the clerk gave me a new clock with no hesitation. I came to believe that the East Germans had learned an important lesson about business. Given their penchant to downplay consumerism, they tended to view a sales transaction as selling not the product but rather customer satisfaction.

A film-developing store in Weimar set up a new procedure for processing film. On a table they placed envelopes with detailed instructions on how to fill them out so one could complete the form and hand over the film without delay. One also filled out a self-addressed card to be sent by the store when the film was ready. Further, the store presented a choice of two film-processing labs on a trial basis, to see which gave better service. All this was quite efficient and carefully thought through for the benefit of the client. Of course, once the film was out of their hands the efficiency was reduced somewhat. It took four weeks for slides to be developed. Hence the need for the postcard, otherwise one might have completely forgotten to pick up the film. I was nevertheless impressed by the store's attempt to make the best of a sluggish system.

It was most refreshing, and relaxing, to know that a package of zwieback always cost 85 pfennigs in any store, anywhere in the country. There were no loss leaders, no discount pricing, no warehouse outlets, no exhorbitant prices for watery spaghetti in places like railroad station cafeterias. The spaghetti may have been watery, but it was cheap. An item always cost the same in any store, and the retail price (*Einzelhandelverkaufs-preis*), or EVP, was always clearly marked. Of course East Germany had no sales tax, so the 85-pfennig zwieback actually cost 85 pfennigs. In fact, central planning had allowed East Germany to calculate exactly what an item should cost and charge accordingly. A bottle of soda water cost 12 pfennigs, plus deposit, and apple juice 67 pfennigs, for example, so the final bill for a purchase might amount to an uneven figure like 2.68 marks. Unfortunately, stores often did not have change and the lightweight aluminum coins were hard to count without having them spill out of your hand, so people tended to round up to the nearest 10 pfennigs, establishing a tipping tradition seldom found in the West.

City maps published by Tourist-Verlag indicated the locations of restaurants, cafés, theaters, gas stations, and other services for the traveler. These services shown on the maps were especially helpful because there were not many of them to be found, and given the socialist abolition of competition there were no large signs blaring out "EAT!" Finding a restaurant in an East German city could be a problem, but with the city maps I found my way easily. On the other hand, and there was always an other hand in East Germany, the maps themselves were not that easy to find. Printed once a year in many cases, they were soon sold out and would not appear until the next year's edition. Yet if one had a map, the way was considerably smoothed.

Problems did arise, however, because some goods were in short supply, and one had to learn to act quickly. One day I went into the photo shop on Schiller Street, the pedestrian street in the center of Weimar. Standing on a shelf behind the counter were stacks of slide mounts with glass, exactly what I was looking for in preparing my lectures. I bought a couple of boxes. A few days later, realizing I needed more, I returned to the store. None were visible on the shelves. Greenhorn that I was, I foolishly asked if they had any more of those mounts I saw on the shelf a few days ago. The clerk looked at me as one looks at an annoying child. "Listen, do you see any slide mounts on those shelves?" Shopping rule number one I learned early on. If the store had something, they displayed it in the window. If it was not in the window, one could go in to see if it was displayed prominently on a shelf. If it was not, one knew not to bother asking for it because they would not have it. Not only that, they would have no idea when they would receive more. Some craftier shopper than I had seen the slide mounts and had bought them all.

For the next couple of weeks in my travels I glanced in every photo shop window I passed, looking for slide mounts. None here, none there. Suddenly I passed a shop with slide mounts in the window. I went in and bought enough mounts to last me for years. That was rule number two. The word among the East Germans was that one did not go shopping to buy certain things, one went shopping to see what there was. If something looked good, one bought it. Something could look good for two reasons: First, if one needed the item oneself; and second, if it was tradable. "Buy and trade" was rule number three. Buy something that looks marketable, then trade it for something you want.

Yes, there were lines. There were lines at the baker, the butcher, and the checkout counter at the supermarket. A line often formed waiting to get *in* to the supermarket. These were ordinary lines, with too few sales-people handling too many customers, and I soon learned to calculate them into my shopping time and not to worry. One frequent complaint of East Germans was that shopping took so much time that it kept one from getting much of anything else done, and the frustration, as usual, brought forth a joke:

"Why are bus fares ten times cheaper in the DDR than in West Germany?"

"It takes ten trips to accomplish the same thing."

When the line extended out into the street, however, one would know something was up. These lines had their own ritual, which one also learned quickly in East Germany. When one would see a line, the first thing to do was stand in it. That was rule number four. Then ask the person in front, "What is it today?" If the line went into a grocery store and the answer was "bananas" (they arrived occasionally from Colombia), one probably decided one needed some bananas. My neighborhood store had bananas once during my stay, and although the line was exceptional, the clerk knew how to handle the situation. Assuming that everyone wanted bananas, she parceled them out to each customer according to family size (known by the clerk of almost all customers), or how many she thought they needed. Since the bananas were pretty ripe, I assume that people in my neighborhood ate a lot of bananas that night.

Indeed, bananas were taken as a common symbol for the fresh fruits and vegetables seldom found in East Germany. Lettuce was stacked to the ceiling at harvest time, but otherwise not seen. One could buy cherries and strawberries at harvest time, and apples much of the year, but there were almost no peaches, plums, melons, or olives. The subject of olives came up at coffee break one day. "Ah, yes, olives. We used to be able to buy them, but, gosh, I haven't thought about olives in years." Especially, there were no bananas. As the joke went:

"Why are there no apes in East Germany?"

"Apes can't live for ten years without bananas."

Then there was the day cornflakes showed up at the grocery store near the architecture school. I happened in just as the stock clerk was carrying out carton after carton of bags of cornflakes from the back of the store. People grabbed them up as fast as she could open them—four, eight, ten bags at a time, all one could carry in one's arms. "Oh, we see them so seldom." "They're for the children, you know." "How do you eat them anyway?" "This is really made from corn?" The corn flakes, packed in plastic bags by the People's Own Foodstuff Works in the city of Wurzen (hence the name "Wurzener Corn Flakes"), carried a note to the "Esteemed Customer" (*Werter Kunde*): "Made of high-grade corn according to the most modern procedures." I bought as many bags as I could carry, hustled them back to school, and spread the word, "Cornflakes," though by the time the others arrived they were gone. Nevertheless, later I traded some for a couple of bottles of ketchup someone had stashed away. At first the cornflakes tasted rather bland because they were made from nothing but corn. No malt, no salt, just pure corn, mashed and roasted into flakes. When I had become used to them they were quite good.

Many of the country's food stores were small, neighborhood establishments where one normally bought enough food for that day only. East Germany also had large supermarkets, called "buying halls" (*Kaufhalle*), similar in layout to those in the United States, where one wheeled around a shopping cart. Each buying hall was equipped with a large milk and cheese department, plus a meat department stocked with plenty of freshly ground sausage and sometimes true cuts of meat like pork chops. One was never quite sure what would be on the shelves that day, so rule number five was to be resourceful, as in plan your menu while you shop.

One aisle of a typical supermarket was devoted to wines and liquor, the former coming primarily from Bulgaria and Hungary, another aisle for various powders: potato, gelatin, and gravy, for example. A bin dispensed rolls through a slot in the bottom like a gigantic bird feeder, beside which huge loaves of bread were stacked on wooden racks. As in American supermarkets, specials were featured in displays at the ends of the aisles. Here might be piles of East German flags in preparation for May Day, or stacks of candles for Christmas. Those returnable bottles of Pilsator were piled in plastic cases on the floor, along with apple juice, milk, soda water (in East Germany called *Party-Soda*), and occasional specials such as currant juice. Since some bottles would emerge from the bottler without labels, a sign often hung nearby, "Please take only bottles with labels." Otherwise the checkout clerk would not know how much to charge.

The shopper wheeled a cart through the aisles of the supermarket, past the food, then through the housewares like bread slicers, and on to the checkout stand, where the clerk would pick up each item from the cart and toss it into a waiting empty cart as she rang it up. Then one wheeled the newly filled cart to a table near the exit, to unload the goods into the shopping bag one had brought along. A smart shopper carefully placed the heavy goods on top in the cart when shopping, otherwise they would be thrown on top of the eggs and bread at the checkout counter.

The popular nylon shopping bags (*Einkaufsbeutel*) that shoppers brought along to the store were made of some of the most colorful fabric I have ever seen and added color to the street on shopping days. One would see black bags with purple and green polka dots, bags covered with red and orange blotches, and bags with blue and brown swirls.

East Germans were great ice-cream fans, and their real ice cream was quite good. A big dish of ice cream covered with whipped cream and chocolate bits was one of the country's true pleasures. On the other hand, their soft ice cream, made from powder, was hardly worth waiting in line for except that it was incredibly cold. No matter, rumors were circulating in early 1989 to expect a shortage of ice-cream powder by summer's end anyway. The only question was what to do when there was not enough ice cream to go around. Ice cream availability varied considerably from city to city, for reasons I could not figure out, and the city of Aschersleben was particularly poorly supplied. Every city center and large dwelling complex had an ice-cream parlor, always crowded, and Aschersleben was no exception. However, the downtown parlor was closed on Friday and Saturday, without doubt the major ice-cream days of the week.

Figuring out the store hours in fact contributed to the fun of shopping. In Weimar, for example, most stores were open from nine to one and three to six, Monday through Friday, except for grocery stores which were open from nine to one and two to five, except Mondays when the downtown stores were open only from one to six, except for the downtown record store, which maintained regular hours every day, except for some liquor stores that opened at noon and remained open until eight in the evening. Large department stores and some grocery stores were also open on Saturday mornings from nine until noon, unless they were open from eight to eleven. Everything remained closed on Sundays except for a few of the odd-hour liquor stores and kiosks in the railroad station where one could buy the necessities: cigarettes, coffee, candy, and liquor. One of the interesting local specialties was California Lemon Liquor (*Kalifornia Zitronenlikör*), pale yellow-green in color and syrupy sweet, of which I never had any in California.

I found shopping to be one of the exciting adventures in visiting cities. A certain satisfaction went with learning the rules and using them deftly. Here is where the East Germans had their own elbow society. East Germans, among their other talents, were gifted shoppers.

Where salesclerks are constantly confronted by a never-diminishing line of harried shoppers elbowing their way in before the goods are gone, the pressure can cause anyone to become crabby. In East Germany, to understand the hassled existence of many clerks was to treat them kindly and with respect and thus to receive the same treatment in return. Of all the workers in East Germany, probably none worked so hard as the sales clerks. Not only did they have to face a relentless, never-ceasing line of customers trying to buy something, but when the delivery truck arrived they had to close the shop, put on gloves and unload the truck. When a truck pulled up in front of a stationery store in Eisenhüttenstadt, I observed saleswomen dressed in flowered nylon aprons hang out the "Temporarily closed for merchandise stocking" sign, don canvas gloves, form a human chain from truck to front door, and toss boxes from one to another until everything was inside the door. Then they took off their gloves, unpacked the boxes, removed the sign from the window, and opened back up to face an even longer line of waiting customers. The line was indeed longer because people had noticed the store being stocked up.

I did suffer, however, one case of classic communist salesclerk treatment. Upstairs in the Berlin-Lichtenberg railroad station was a pleasant restaurant. Given the crowds usually thronging through East Berlin's busiest train station, those who were tempted to carry luggage into the restaurant were admonished by a sign outside the door, "Please do not bring luggage into the restaurant." Being so tempted, I asked the woman at the cloakroom if I could leave my overnight bag with her.

"No."

"Well, where is the best place for me to leave it while I am in the restaurant?"

With caustic disdain she replied, "I frankly couldn't care less what you do with it." The solution, of course, was the lock boxes downstairs, which would have been as easy to direct me to as to chalk one up for communist salesclerk stereotypes. On the one hand, people must have asked her the question a hundred times a day. On the other, she could have put up a sign.

The DDR produced everything, from harmonicas to beach chairs, railroad cars to excavating machinery. Almost nothing I saw in the stores was imported. In some cases the products were of excellent quality, such as phonograph records, though East Germans knew all about compact discs and complained that they were not available. Many other products were not quite up to par, but the people generally knew how to deal with them. I tried Orwo film, from the People's Own Enterprise Film Factory in Wolfen, and found the colors to be rather bland and pasty. Somebody gave me advice about it. Buy ten rolls with the same production number, then shoot one roll and have it developed before trying the rest. If the colors are off or the quality is otherwise unsatisfactory, return the remaining nine to the store and try another batch.

Consumer life at times took on the aura of the unreal partly because the ideals of socialist society seemed to have become confused. Socialism was supposed to draw human nature away from the blind consumerist mania characterizing Western society. Though billboards urged East Germans to achieve "More productivity for peace and socialism," one knew that a long-standing complaint among residents in Eastern Europe was the scarcity of consumer goods. The Party had taken action to rectify this situation. It was not that products had been improved so much as the people were encouraged to buy more. East Germans were bombarded with consumerist exhortations in the best free-market tradition: shopping bags were imprinted with "Joy in Shopping" slogans, department store entrances lured customers in with jazzy music, store windows sported cardboard signs saying "See Select Buy," and the pre-show music from behind the movie theater screen was interrupted by reminders to "Shop at your local record store, where one can find fine records on the Amiga and Eterna labels to suit all tastes." Of course, Amiga for popular music and Eterna for classical were the only two East German record labels that existed. All record stores stocked the same records at the same prices, and everyone knew where the record stores were. Indeed, if one had connections, one could snap up the choice records before they ever hit the shelves.

I prowled the record stores myself and bought many records to bring home. Generally I had no trouble finding the records I wanted, since I was looking for things many people passed up, namely East German rock and jazz music. In Halle one day I bought a stack of records I had not seen elsewhere, and when the saleswoman saw my cache she obviously thought my joy in shopping should be rewarded. From under the counter she pulled out two records and said, "How about these? I only have a few left, and they're both from 'over there' [*drüben*]." One was a record by a West German rock band, the other an ancient Willy Nelson release, recorded before he learned how to sing.

East Germany had indeed removed the competitive market condition that called for advertising in the first place, a basic goal of socialism, yet the Party had reinstalled it. Ah, but it was curious. Even if the advertisements were superfluous, they added life to a fairly dull existence. Advertisements seemed to reassure people that the natural desire to possess was indeed all right, and it provided soothing voices that made people feel good about consuming. The voices had the same effect as the matchmaker in traditional societies. "Yes, listen and you shall be made happy." I had always taken advertising to be a minor annoyance of capitalist life, but when it was absent, as in East German villages, I felt a certain societal loneliness, as if the outside world were passing me by. I gained in East Germany a new appreciation for advertising, and reluctantly admit I was glad to see it when I returned to America. Since East German products did not need to be advertised, however, messages took the form of "apparent advertising." Huge neon signs, for example, adorned the rooftops of many tall buildings in the centers of cities. Though most advertised things that people either could not have or could not use—like the East German airline Interflug, or earthmoving equipment from Bulgaria—they added life to an otherwise dreary nighttime city.

Apparently there was a need to be spoken to, cajoled, and impressed even in socialist society, where it was not supposed to happen. I was particularly struck by how well the East Germans had learned to mimic the trappings of "real" advertising one day when I passed by the Centrum department store in Magdeburg. A salient achievement of East German city planning had been to place a large department store in the center of most larger cities, often sheathed in an aluminum sunscreen glinting brightly on sunny days. The department stores were based directly on the Western model, with similar kinds of goods and similar attempts to display them. There were also similar attempts to pitch the wares. Loudspeakers aimed at the sidewalk in front of the Centrum store in Magdeburg incessantly repeated a taped message that translates something like, "Chop-n-Eat. Fast and Complete. A kitchen appliance you should have."

"Apparent participation" and "apparent advertising" worked quite well together. Not to be outdone by the big flea markets in West Berlin, there was indeed a flea market in East Berlin as well, twice a week. Yet there was not all that much in East Germany to sell at a flea market. A friend of mine who made craft objects of wood explained how it worked. He was *required* to set up a booth a certain number of times a year, to display his wares—of which he actually had none because he did only custom work. He was required to attend, he says, because it had to look like East Germans had things to buy and sell. "Nobody buys from me because I have nothing to sell; it merely gives an appearance of things happening, when nothing is happening, and it keeps me from my own work."

17

Just Keep Talking: Coping with Shortages

THE WARTBURG AUTOMOBILE, the larger of the two DDR cars, was designed in 1964 and produced until 1988 with only minor alterations, the entire time being equipped with a two-cycle engine that not only provided a loud and vibrating ride but also emitted a continuous plume of blue exhaust. In 1988 the Wartburg, named for a castle near the city of Eisenach where it was manufactured, was newly equipped with a Volkswagen Rabbit four-cycle engine, but the car's design remained unaltered except for a new grille and taillight design to distinguish it from the older models. The cost was 36,000 marks, or about $21,500 at the official exchange rate. East Germans were aware of automobile technology in West Germany and Japan, given tourists and television commercials, and this new Wartburg was not exactly heralded as a triumph: "A mummy with a pacemaker," it was called. Or:

"The Wartburg won second place in a wind tunnel contest."

"Yeah, first place was won by a chest of drawers." Besides, there was a seventeen-year waiting period from the time the car was ordered it until it was delivered, unless one had connections.

East Germany's other automobile was the Trabant, the "Trabbi." One had to wait twelve or so years for delivery of a new Trabant, except that in 1989 the factory in Zwickau was delivering only eight months of orders in a calendar year, so the wait was becoming longer. It cost about twelve thousand marks by the time one added on extras like windshield wipers and a spare tire. East Germans had an interesting attitude toward this incredibly long waiting period for a new car. It was frustrating to be sure, but people expressed to me that if everyone had a car, there would be no room for them in the cities. For those who were so lucky as to have a car, streets were relatively empty and one could nearly always find a parking place. Though the day of reckoning would surely come, in the meantime the low auto ownership rate made the planning of housing districts easier. My new apartment building in Weimar had twenty-four dwellings but only eight parking spaces.

One had to make application to be placed on the list for a new car, and upon receipt of an ordered vehicle, one's first action was often to make application for the next one. The date of one's application also made for good cocktail party conversation, as people compared their status on the list. I noted that the system appeared to operate in a fairly orderly fashion, and people were good-natured about their wait. Of course one had to be careful not to do something that would bring disadvantage, which could bump one from the list, and it was well known that Party higher-ups and those with connections to the state security police did not have to wait at all. The long wait did cause some aberrations in the marketplace. One could take delivery of a new car and immediately sell it for substantially more than one paid for it. This situation had not caused widespread black marketing of new cars for two reasons, first being that if one bought a new car and sold it, one would be carless. The next new car was at least twelve years away. Second was the problem of what to do with twenty- or thirty-thousand marks given the limited number of things one could buy with the money.

Relatively speaking, the used-car market was a going concern, limited only by the small number of cars available. Local newspapers carried classified ads for autos. The following advertisements appeared in the Weimar paper one day in January 1989:

'79 Wartburg, good condition, 18,000 marks.
'63 Trabant, 2,000 marks.
'74 Wartburg, 15,000 marks.
'74 Trabant, 8,000 marks.
'88 Trabant, 11,000 marks.

A year-old Trabant for a little less than the price of a new one? One wondered who would wait twelve years if one could buy that car right away. Ah, but these were the authorized prices. In the West one could hope to buy a used car for a little less than the asking price, but in the DDR it was the opposite. The selling price would be much higher than the price quoted in the paper, the car probably going to the highest bidder. In fact, a ten-year-old car could fetch about the same price as a new one; a recent model at hand might bring twice the price.

East Germans certainly had a love-hate relationship with the Trabants most of them drove. Trabant jokes were of course numerous, like the one about the American who ordered one:

> The salesman duly delivered the vehicle and said to the American, "How do you like it?"
>
> "You East Germans certainly have a wonderful system," said the American. "No American car maker would present a toy model for the customer's approval before delivering the real thing!"

> Sign on a Trabant: "Never again a Porsche!"

> "How do you double the value of a Trabant?"
> "Fill the tank with gas."

The long wait for automobiles suggests much about the economic health of East German society in 1989—nearly all goods were in short supply—and about the way people coped with the situation. The five rules of shopping helped people to plan strategy when buying goods. Living with continued shortages lent a certain zest to life, since shortages of products and people to handle them sometimes required crafty thinking. East Germans gave me some advice on how to cope: "You have to keep talking."

"I see by your sign that you aren't taking any empty beer bottles today, but I lugged twenty here and I would really appreciate it if you could make an exception and take them." One pitied the poor clerk, because the reason for taking no bottles was that the bottle truck had not arrived, and the storeroom was overflowing with empty bottles out into the driveway. I was surprised that I never saw anyone pick up a few cases of empties from the driveway and carry them into the store for a deposit refund, but the society was much too orderly for such shenanigans. Or, "I see that all your tables are reserved, but would it be possible to find two places so we may eat?" One already knew that a "reserved" sign on a restaurant table often did not mean reservations at all but that insufficient personnel were available to serve the tables.

One was not always successful, but often as not the employee could make that "very large exception" and take the bottles or find a space at a reserved table. Neighborhood storekeepers might be able to find a few extra links of sausage behind the counter or a loaf of bread when the shelf was empty, since they tended to put a few away for regular customers. One developed a fine sense of negotiation. Sometimes my being an American would make the exception more readily forthcoming, but primarily the means to squeeze the last capacity out of a trade establishment was polite, unrelenting assertiveness, a trait honed to delicate sharpness by many East Germans.

One had to remember to eat lunch right at noon for the day's big meal, since by one o'clock some restaurants stopped serving. With a little discipline one could manage fairly well. Many restaurants that stayed open all day, some of which serving only beer and coffee in the afternoons, banned smoking from eleven until two. The policy was a welcome courtesy for nonsmokers (many public areas such as railroad stations, even the platforms, were designated as nonsmoking areas, one of East Germany's truly enlightened policies), but I suspect that the noontime smoking ban in restaurants had not only to do with public welfare. Smokers tend to dawdle, and prohibiting smoking assured a faster turnover, thus increasing the number of people who could eat and thereby decrease the lines.

In other realms, private entrepreneurs, officially illegal, tended to compensate for shortages with their own capital and labor. For example, in the mid 1980s the government had authorized private taxis as supplements to the overburdened official taxis. People could use their own four-door autos as supplemental taxis if properly registered as such. Despite the effort, however, there was still a shortage of taxis, since many people could not take advantage of the opportunity. Registration procedures were cumbersome and the fares one could charge were restricted, thus providing limited return on all those extra miles driven. But the main problem was that most people had Trabants. Since Trabants had only two doors, they were ineligible for use as supplemental taxis. The obvious solution was the "black taxi," whereby a person would use his Trabant or any other auto illegally, without authorization, as a taxicab. The system in fact worked quite well.

Since black taxis were illegal, anyone could immediately become a taxi driver if one avoided the authorities. The entrepreneur would drive somebody to the railroad station, or perhaps merely cruise by, park across the street, and wait for a while. The more aggressive of the two, potential passenger or driver, made the first eye contact, but the first step would be to size each other up. A person standing in line at the taxi stand might saunter up to a waiting driver, or the driver might scan those waiting for taxis and eventually sidle over to a likely fare.

"Where you headed?"

"Weimar North."

"Say, I'm going that way, I'll give you a ride."

At the destination, the passenger could possibly say "Thanks" and hop out, but everyone knew the score. "How much can I give you," asked the passenger. "Oh, I suppose you could give me five marks for gas." After the first few trips, of course, regular passengers knew that five marks was the going rate in Weimar, about double that of metered taxis, and the formalities were dropped. It was a system that worked well partly because one had to be subtle about it, not flaunt it. Passengers arrived home faster, automobile owners made extra money in their spare time, and regular taxi drivers who were usually overworked appreciated the relief. There was still always a line at the taxi stand at the Weimar railroad station; it was merely shorter because of the entrepreneurial help. Some East German acquaintances were reluctant to use black taxis since the notion that everything must be authorized and regulated had become quite ingrained, particularly in the older population, and there was a reluctance to traffic for fear of bringing on disadvantage. Yet for me, once I learned the rules, they were my regular ride. The only problem was that people who sat in their cars legitimately waiting for someone to emerge from the station were hounded by requests for trips home.

A few private enterprises had survived in East Germany, such as small restaurants, retail stores selling books or toys, and local bakers. Life for the private bakers was not especially easy because, given the shortage of bakers' supplies, state-owned bakeries were given first priority and the private bakers were often left to fend for themselves. The case of Christmas Stollen illustrates the problem and the ingenuity with which East Germans had learned to overcome problems of insufficient goods.

The making of Stollen, the traditional German fruitcake, was hampered in East Germany because there were no almonds from which to make marzipan, the rich, grainy confection made of ground almonds and sugar. Marzipan could be found in every West German candy store, formed into little bears and a thousand other shapes, often smothered in chocolate. In the Zone, however, it was only to be found in the Intershop and not at all in wholesale distribution for bakers. Undeterred, since Christmas is not Christmas without Stollen, East German bakers had developed a substitute made of pea meal and spices. It had a rather greenish tint, but if one ate it fast the substitution was hardly noticeable.

Raisins form the other essential ingredient of Stollen, and one would expect a baker to buy his raisins wholesale. Unfortunately there were not enough raisins to go around, so all wholesale raisins were distributed to the state bakeries. Though the private baker may not have had a raisin allotment, he did have connections. Retail grocers from time to time received large shipments of raisins, often from Afghanistan, harvested and shipped even during the war years. The clerks were expected to bag them in retail portions and set them out for sale, but this took time that the harried store clerks did not have. Thus when the baker showed up and offered to purchase the retailer's entire shipment of raisins for cash, it solved a problem for both of them. The retailer could show the same income on the ledger book for reporting purposes while avoiding having to bag the raisins and handle each package at the checkout stand, and the baker received his raisins for Stollen. On the other hand, it meant there were no raisins for anybody else.

Being a private baker was a tough business. A student who worked part-time in his father's small-town bakery invited me home one weekend. Since the Christmas rush was on, I had to help make gingerbread houses.

Given the nagging labor shortage in East Germany, questions such as who stoked the furnace at the architecture school had to be dealt with, since no stationary engineers were available to do so as part of their daily work. As it turned out, the faculty members stoked the furnace. Secretaries cleaned the floors. Students took turns running the guard booth at the entrance to the dormitory. Taking care of these maintenance functions had become a regular socialist tradition literally called "standby service," *Bereitschaftsdienst,* or translated more colloquially, to be on duty. The school basement had a little room furnished with a bed and desk, and every night one or another faculty member, except the department heads, slept there and kept an eye on the furnace. Since such institutions as *Bereitschaftsdienst* had long been part of East German society, they were taken in stride as part of one's participation. Anyway it was quiet in the basement, and one had plenty of time to catch up on one's work when on duty.

"You can tell a lot about East German society by counting the trailer hitches," somebody said to me soon after I arrived. Nearly every car, even an asthmatic, thirty-year-old rusting Trabant, seemed to have a trailer hitch on the back. The DDR manufactured a small, two-wheeled trailer that one saw parked along the streets in residential neighborhoods, and cars often pulled their trailers through the streets of a town carrying all imaginable kinds of goods, from refrigerators to manure.

"What do trailer hitches have to do with anything?" responded the newcomer.

"Well, there is absolutely nobody around to deliver anything, so when you buy something you have to shlep it around yourself." Americans get the word "shlep" from Yiddish, but actually it is the German *schleppen,* meaning to drag.

Not only was there nobody to deliver pizzas, there seemed to be nobody to deliver washing machines or furniture. When one ordered coal for the winter, the truck dumped it out in the middle of the sidewalk in front, and the resident had to spend a couple of afternoons shoveling the brown briquettes into the coal chute. This image of elderly men and women dressed in dirty blue smocks, their heads wrapped in cloths to keep the coal dust out, wearily shoveling coal briquettes from the pile on the sidewalk into a coal chute, was one of the caricatures of communist society that was a regular scene in East German towns. Brown coal as the country's motive power in fact brought back childhood memories I had not thought of for years: the smell of coal in the basement and the dank darkness of the coal bin were relics of Old Germany that helped give much of the country a prewar aura.

The telephone network suggested the quality of services in the DDR. It is not that the service was so bad, but the need for it far outstripped its capacity. Making long-distance calls during business hours required extreme patience, as one would dial again and again, only to get a busy signal because the lines were full. Especially, reaching a number in East Berlin from outlying cities could require twenty minutes or a half hour of continuous dialing, interspersed by swearing. If a connection was finally made, there was always the danger of being cut off, and one returned to square one. Comments about telephones were another litany of complaints. For some reason I often found myself in somebody's office when he or she had to make a phone call, perhaps to arrange something for me. Before picking up the phone, the caller would invariably prepare me for the event. "You already know, of course, about our phone system . . .?"

Pay phones were scarce, though their locations were helpfully indicated on city maps. My apartment stood in an area of about three hundred dwellings, and one pay phone out on the street served them all. No phone lines for private dwellings had been laid in that part of town. Yet when one finally made a connection, handy lights on the front of the phone indicated how much money to feed into the slot, so calling was a pay as you go proposition, easy to master even if one did not speak German. It was also cheap, at least within the country. A couple of marks sufficed to talk from one end of East Germany to the other. Calling outside the country was nearly impossible, so it did not matter if is was expensive or not.

People had become used to not having a phone, so most people carried a pocket calendar. When one met somebody and made an appointment for two months ahead of time, duly writing it in the calendar, all parties would show up two months later at the appointed time without worrying about confirmation calls. I found an orderliness to life in this way that universal ownership of telephones does not allow to happen. At the same time, many people of course wanted telephones installed in their homes. Without being a Party member or otherwise having connections, that was difficult to achieve. One of the faculty members in Weimar, supportive of socialism but proud that he had never joined the Party, had applied for a telephone in 1963 and was still waiting for its installation. In 1989 he decided that twenty-six years was long enough to wait for a phone, so he convinced the local committee of the Free German Trade Union, in which he was active, to put him up as a candidate for the local elected body in the March election. As a candidate he was elected, of course, and soon thereafter had his telephone.

Another enduring shortage-related problem in East Germany was that of photocopies. The ability to make photocopies has revolutionized the workplace, of course, and continuing reliance on carbon paper and mimeograph machines made the East German attempt to develop a high-technology society look a little awkward. East Germany actually produced a line of copy machines, but they presented a problem that was partly political and partly economic—which in the end, of course, was a political problem as well. The political problem lay in the potential danger of photocopying, discernible in the *Sputnik* affair. Yet at the architecture school there would have to be at least a semblance of normality in such things if it proclaimed itself to a be an institution of higher learning, so while I was there the school library decided to set up a photocopy center: two machines and an operator. No self-service, of course, because only pages of books and magazines in the library holdings could be copied. No manuscripts, for example, or recipes, since their content could not be monitored.

However, in setting up the copy room, the economic problem came into play. The machines broke down fairly regularly, and it often took a week or two to get them fixed. To make things worse, there was that shortage of paper. Whether planned or not, there was, in fact, insufficient paper for the copy machines, and the soft, rough East German paper tended to jam as it went through. I brought back a couple of reams of good copy paper from one of my trips to West Germany. My contribution was only a drop in the bucket in the big picture of paper shortage, though the administrators and secretaries were quite thankful to have it.

The library set up a trial photocopying system for three months. The photocopy room would be open only during limited hours, and the price per copy would be thirty pfennigs. That price was relatively high (a little over fifteen cents a copy, officially) though not outrageous by Western standards. By East German standards the price was prohibitive. Hardly any student, and almost no faculty member who was doing serious research, could afford to use the service in more than an incidental way. The only people who could afford to make large numbers of copies were foreigners who had access to other money sources.

It cost substantially less than thirty pfennigs a copy to buy paper, pay the attendant, and amortize the machines. The price was set primarily as a use disincentive. Too much use would wear out the machines, and there were no replacements. Too much use would deplete the paper, and more was not readily available. Here, as so often in East Germany, I heard people say that money was not the problem; there was plenty of money. There was money to buy replacement parts and more paper, but no amount of DDR marks could buy these things since they were not produced in sufficient quantities to be purchased.

I discussed the photocopy policy with the library director who said the only way he could deal with the issue was to regulate use by price. The fact that it was actually priced beyond the means of the average student or faculty member seemed akin to the bus line that regularly plies its route but does not stop to pick up any passengers because that would get the inside of the bus dirty. One often heard in East Germany that the inefficient economy was the basis of the country's political problems, of the Berlin Wall, and so forth. Were the economy productive there would be no need for police-state repression, and the country would be attractive as a place to live. Yes, indeed, that is true. Shortages breed discontent. Discontent breeds lackadaisical work. Lackadaisical work breeds shortages.

I gave a lecture in Bautzen at the "House of the Sorbs," the cultural center built in the 1950s for the Sorbic community, East Germany's official minority group. On the wall of the lecture room hung a huge painting in a sort of Pre-Raphaelite style. It portrayed Wilhelm Pieck, the first president of East Germany, in office from 1949 to 1960, appearing as a saint entering the city and moving among the adulatory crowds, blessing the beaming-faced Sorbic children gathered about him. People waiting for my lecture began to discuss the painting and its Socialist Realism style of the 1950s. "You know," I overheard one member of the audience say to another, "In those days the people probably *were* enthusiastic like that."

Uncertainty about what things might be available at any given time resulted in an impressive level of creativity. What food would be on the market shelves that day was always a matter of some conjecture, for example, so people who had shopped according to rule number five often demonstrated an accomplished culinary resourcefulness. Pizzas were coming into style in restaurants, but there was often no choice of toppings, and after I ordered one without asking what was on it I vowed to be more careful. A sauerkraut and tripe pizza. At home one would often have to make do, though generally I noticed one did fine. It was like car camping when a meal must be made from whatever you find in the kitchen box, and weird combinations are scarfed with relish. So the East Germans were handy at making things out of simple ingredients. Butter cookies dipped in chocolate and spread with jelly were heavenly. Or take a dish of rice sprinkled with chopped green peppers to give it some color and flavor. Except that hardly a green pepper had shown its face in East Germany for years. How about rice cooked with cucumbers, then? It's a little slimy, but it adds a bit of green to the rice if you don't peel the cucumbers.

As usual, there was a joke about shortages. An East German goes into a greengrocer's shop and says, "Do you have any bananas?"

"No bananas," says the greengrocer, "but we have cucumbers."

"How about tomatoes?"

"Sorry, no tomatoes, but we do have cucumbers."

"Well, do you have any lettuce?

"No. How about some cucumbers?"

"Well," says the customer, "I'll take some cucumbers."

After the customer leaves, the greengrocer turns to his comrade and says, "That customer, he sure has a terrific memory."

In the preceding chapters I have documented my experiences with those features of East German society that functioned poorly. There were many such features, indeed. The production and distribution systems functioned only viscously, democratic centralism precluded serious discussion of issues, and the threatening presence of the Ministry for State Security held change in check in the same way an invisible nylon thread might hold together a fine carpet. By 1989 I encountered very few people who would defend the system in private conversation as well as in public. State socialism was universally regarded as a failure, merely waiting for the top leaders to die. Of course, as it turned out barely four months after I left, the state died. But this future was not even imagined a few months previously.

Americans had long been enculturated into the evils of the communist system, and the restrictions on thought and action I have reported may certainly corroborate that view. It was clear that the Socialist Unity party in the end abused the East German people in whose name it governed, in its pursuit of humanitarian goals which had been lost along the way. The ends seemed to have escaped from view, leaving only the harsh means as a goal in themselves.

I am left with one unanswered question in the narrative that I present in this volume. Could some kind of a balance sheet be drawn between the failures of East German communism and its successes? Did the society, restrictive as it was, achieve some level of social progress from which the West might learn? Were there in reality, as there were in East German slogans, discernible "fruits of the socialist revolution"? The answer, I believe, must to some extent be in the affirmative. I came to believe that, despite the repressive political state, certain humanitarian achievements in East German socialism could offer lessons for Americans seeking the "kinder, gentler nation" of which George Bush so eloquently spoke during his acceptance speech at the Republican party convention in 1988. I shall attempt to portray them in the next chapter.

18

Basement Potatoes:
The Fruits of the Socialist Revolution

FOUNDERS OF THE East German socialist state as a workers' paradise were driven by a magnificent vision beyond a dwelling, job, and food for every family. According to this vision, the working class in the mature socialist society would actually not have to work very much. The goal was to organize the productive forces into large-scale, automated processes that would be directed, indeed for the most part largely observed, by a few skilled and committed workers. The few technicians in charge of massive technology would release the population from toil, and most residents of the socialist state would spend most of their lives enjoying free time. Cynics said that East Germany had already achieved its goal, but knowing the intended ideal state is helpful in understanding why a note was tacked on the door of each dwelling in the fall announcing the delivery of "basement-delivered potatoes" in hundred-kilogram lots. The People's Own Enterprise for Wholesale Fruit, Vegetables and Eating Potatoes would deliver one's choice of Class A or Class B potatoes, containing 2 or 3 percent rotten tubers. "Please support the swift completion of the basement potato delivery action by keeping your money and basement key at the ready," said the note. Potatoes came with a two-month guarantee if protected from dampness, heat, frost, and light. With a single delivery, therefore, one could load one's basement with as many pounds of potatoes as needed for the year. In the fall, basements of many houses tended to be neatly full of potatoes and brown coal in preparation for winter.

In every modern nation, the state of the society can be measured largely by by the quality of its housing. East Germany was no exception, of course. Though it is easy to excoriate the poor quality and social insensitivity of its mass-produced housing, other characteristics of the East German housing program make for a worthy lesson in civics. A house or apartment in East Germany was not an item for financial speculation. That firmly established socialist policy resulted from the belief that real-property ownership was one of the most heinous aspects of capitalism. Those with property were seen to exploit directly those without property by setting rent levels as high as possible. If one owned a home in East Germany one could sell it, to be sure, but there would be no profit. Dwelling prices were set by the government at low levels from which a seller could not vary. Thus there was no opportunity for investment, but there was also no risk of losing that investment if the market dropped.

The low price levels, a few thousand marks, had in fact removed the real-estate market from the society. It was an extraordinary event when a person actually sold a house. If one wished to transfer to a job in another city, one traded dwellings with someone intending a reverse move. If the children had grown up and one child wished to move into a smaller apartment of his or her own, the parents often advertised to trade their large dwelling for two smaller ones. Another couple, perhaps recently married, might wish to trade their two individual apartments for a single, larger dwelling. Local newspapers carried numerous classified advertisements for dwelling trades: "Seek single-family house in Kranichfeld or vicinity. Offer two-room apartment, central heating, in new housing complex in Rudolstadt." Of course, certain dwellings had advantages. A new unit in an industrialized housing complex might not be large or have a private garden, but it probably had central heating so one need not shovel coal or stoke the furnace. In a sense a real-estate market existed, but it flowed on a mutual satisfaction of desires rather than on cash.

Here is revealed a fundamental difference between the socialist, state-enterprise vision of the good society and the capitalist, private-enterprise vision: the differing value placed on the need for money in order to reap the benefits of the society. Marxist idealism proudly proclaimed that inhabitants of the socialist state should be free from want, and that the necessities of life should be accessible to all at insignificant cost so that the burden of paying for food and shelter would be lifted. In fact, this goal had been accomplished in East Germany. All the necessities of life were universally provided, heavily subsidized, and never denied. Of course it is true that better housing was allocated to favored people such as Party functionaries, and much older housing was still in poor condition, but these represented abuses of the system rather than necessary outcomes. Most significantly, there was absolutely no homelessness in East Germany. Every person was to be provided—indeed guaranteed as a right of citizenship—a decent place to live.

The rent for a typical new one- or two-bedroom apartment in a housing complex, utilities paid, was perhaps eighty marks a month—less than fifty dollars at the official rate. The price varied little by size, which was assigned according to need. Apartments in West Germany cost twenty times as much. Hot water was available in unlimited quantities as part of the rent, whereas in West Germany hot water cost a small fortune and people treated it very gingerly. Although I did not test it out, I learned it would be possible to refrain from paying one's rent without being evicted. The "elbow-society" tendency to evict people for not paying rent was foreign to East Germans, but something those who fled to the West had to learn. Training sessions in West German reception centers for newly arrived East German refugees apparently had to stress that one's foremost duty was to pay the rent on time.

East German society was largely based on a socialist ideal that each person should work for the good of the whole, thus rendering unnecessary the private accumulation of money with which to pay other people or the state for things purchased. This ideal in action could be observed in the "interest associations" voluntarily organized by interested citizens and supported by the state. As a voluntary effort, members of such associations could from time to time create order out of some chaos. One architect told me he and a group of friends had formed such an *Interessengemeinschaft* to address the problem of abandoned buildings. Buildings vacated for renovation tended to stand vacant for such a long time before renovation began that they were stripped and trashed by antisocials, the *Asis*, to the point where they had to be demolished. In their spare time the architect's group kept an eye on the buildings, reported break-ins, and made sure the doors were locked. Otherwise the buildings would be lost before the centrally planned renovation program could begin. Despite all the problems in East Germany, I thought, here was an instance where Americans could learn something about caring for our cities.

The ideal of individual enterprise directed to improving the good of the whole could be seen especially in the government policy of subsidizing basic foodstuffs. A subsidy totaling thirty-two billion marks in 1988 was reported by *Neues Deutschland*. For years the small *Brötchen* roll had cost five pfennigs. In West Germany a roll cost ten times as much. Meat and potatoes were subsidized; brown coal was sold to the people for perhaps a third of its cost. Workers' clothing could be purchased for less than it cost to make.

In fact, bread was so cheap it was tossed out in copious quantities, though as was nearly everything else in East Germany it was recycled. Outside each building, next to the garbage dumpsters, sat a "pig pail" (*Schweineeimer*), into which one tossed old bread, vegetables, or whatever else farmers could use for feed. Bread was so highly subsidized that farmers regularly fed their animals with bread, since the baked product could be purchased for less than the raw wheat that went into it. Even grass was sometimes recycled. In a large housing complex in Chemnitz (which East Germany had renamed Karl-Marx-Stadt), I saw a group of farmers, with their Trabant and trailer, mowing the grass and forking the clippings into their trailer for use as feed. They complained to me, however, that the housing administration was going to make them start paying for the grass.

For about ten marks one could buy a bag of groceries containing a pound of sausage, a large loaf of bread, a liter of milk, plus cheese, cabbage and beer to feed a family of four for a day. In addition, most places of employment provided employee cafeterias where the noon meal, the main meal for most East Germans, could be had for about one mark, or fifty-six cents in 1989. The fare was solid but uneventful: a piece of beef or pork with the ubiquitous boiled potatoes and red cabbage, smothered in what the locals called "universal sauce" (*Einheitssoße*), a bullion cube gravy that was not quite compatible with anything but was palatable with everything.

Local bus fares cost twenty pfennigs per ride, one tenth of the typical fare in West Germany and certainly less than it cost to print and distribute the bus tickets, let alone contribute to operating costs. One paid about the same to mail a letter to anyone in another socialist country. It cost twice as much to send the letter "over there" to West Germany.

To quote prices, however, is of little use alone. Relative costs are meaningful only within the entire constellation of earnings, taxation, and prices of basic necessities and luxuries. First, one must determine what a DDR mark was worth. It is difficult because the currency was nonconvertible; one could not legally take it in or out of the country, or exchange it for West German marks. Though the "mark of the DDR" was officially equal in value to the deutsche mark, or slightly more than fifty American cents in 1989, West German banks were selling nine DDR marks for each deutsche mark, or about six cents each. This nine to one ratio actually undervalued East German marks, however, because one had to smuggle them across the border at high risk, and the price certainly took this risk into account. So what was the DDR mark really worth? One commonly heard the suggestion in East Germany that the rate of true value in 1989 was about four DDR marks per West German mark, making the DDR mark equal to about thirteen American cents.

The mark may be assessed in another way by comparing salaries and prices between East and West Germany. Housing in West Germany may have cost twenty times as much as in East, and food ten times as much, but salaries in West Germany were, on the average, about four times that of typical salaries in East Germany, mark for mark. Let us assume a typical East German husband and wife both worked, together bringing home 1,800 marks a month. They might pay 100 marks for rent, 300 marks for food, and perhaps another 200 marks for clothing and other necessities per month. That left the family with 1,200 marks a month of disposable income. A typical West German with a salary of 4,000 DM per month had by no means that much disposable income.

It is a seeming contradiction but nevertheless true that East Germans had to pay income taxes, and the taxes were lower for hourly wage earners than for monthly salary earners, again reflecting the ideology of the workers' state. A typical hourly wage earner earned about 950 marks per month in 1989, and after taxes brought home about 890. Many salaried workers such as administrators and professionals also earned about 950 marks per month, but after taxes they brought home about 695. This being a socialist state where the working class nominally controlled power for its own benefit, positions such as custodians and garbage collectors were rewarded with high salaries. The high salaries may also have reflected the undesirability of these jobs; many such positions were difficult to fill and remained empty.

Top managers and holders of prestigious positions such as university professors could earn double or triple the amount for average workers. However, it must be said that the spread between the highest earners, with gross monthly incomes of about 2,500 marks, and the lowest wage earners, at about 400 marks per month, was still a much narrower spread than the differences between the upper and lower classes in Western societies. Only a few people such as the Upper 10,000 or movie directors who traveled in international circles lived beyond this norm.

A truly socialist aspect of this fairly uniform level of wealth, coupled with the frequent assignment of housing by one's workplace rather than by purchase, was that people of nominally different classes lived in close proximity to one another. The four apartments off a stairwell might be inhabited by a physician, a truck driver, a teacher and a factory worker. All of them might earn comparable amounts of money.

East German housing prices were low because the state subsidized them, as a major statement of the socialist way of life. The annual subsidy for dwellings amounted to about sixty billion marks. Thus the total state subsidy for what it regarded as basic needs amounted to about one hundred billion marks per year, as *Neues Deutschland* reported. This level of subsidy amounted to about six thousand marks per person annually, or about a half year's salary for many. Such subsidies of course had to come from someplace, and they came partly from artificially high prices for nonnecessities, as well as from the "public profit" of state-owned enterprises— since there was no "private profit" to tax. A chocolate bar like that available in West Germany for ninety pfennigs cost four marks. A stereo tape player similar to one costing 150 deutsche marks in West Germany, cost ten times as much in East Germany, while a twenty-six-inch color television cost 6,900 marks. At the official rate this amounted to $3,670, and represented a typical worker's total gross earnings for a period of five to eight months. The Wartburg automobile, with its Volkswagen Rabbit engine and simple construction might be comparable to a car costing 8,000 DM, but cost 36,000 marks—after the seventeen-year wait.

Yet the average amount of excess cash available to the East German family resulting from subsidized basic needs helps explain why nearly every family of my acquaintance had a television set and washing machine, most had an automobile, and nearly everyone was comfortably and attractively dressed. One of the things that would quickly disappear were East German society altered, it was widely believed, would be the subsidies for basic necessities, a major socialist goal. That indeed happened.

East German society was also organized around the notion that workers should be able to take the necessary time off to recover from illness, should have ample vacation time—often four weeks, in fact—and time for their children. Sick leave was generous; one received up to six weeks at 90 percent of salary, then up to six months at 70 percent. Indeed, sometimes it appeared that sickness was part of the planned economy. On February 21st, one might see a sign in a shop window, on an official form authorized by the city: "Will remain closed from February 20 to March 3 due to illness." Women tended to take more days off than men because they were expected to care for sick children and received a monthly "housekeeping day" (*Haushaltstag*), a paid day off to run errands or clean their house. In the end, women worked on average only about thirty-two weeks per year, with twenty weeks off, while men tended to work thirty-nine weeks.

It appeared from my observations that the role of men and women in East German society was very similar to that in the United States. Emphasis was still placed on the role of woman as the primary child rearer, though the East German state supported this role with the extended sick leave and housekeeping day allotments. Most secretaries were women, but one frequently saw female professionals as well. About half the students in the urban design section of the architecture school in Weimar, where I was assigned, were women. Male dominance did obviously prevail in the Party, however.

Financial support for families was central to East German life. A woman with her first and second child received one year off work for each, with pay, and her job was guaranteed when she returned. A woman with her third child received eighteen months off, with pay, and a woman with her fourth child received two years off. In addition, newly married couples received a loan of 7,000 marks to buy goods needed for the marriage. With their first child they had to pay back only 6,000 of this money. With the second child the sum was reduced to 4,500 marks. If a third child were born, they would be considered "child-rich" (*kinderreich*) and needed pay none of it back. Children also received free food at school. As a further support for families, married couples were placed higher on the waiting list for dwellings than were single persons. I should say single men, since single women had a particularly low priority for dwellings. Hence there was a high marriage rate, and also a very high divorce rate.

I cite these figures because I came to view them as essential in understanding the fabric of East German society. Politically the country was founded on Marxist-Leninist principles; but beyond them is where one found the fundamental *socialism*, the society taking care of its people, around which daily life turned. The difficulty with such subsidies was to determine the source of the monies needed to pay for them. For this reason televisions and automobiles were extremely expensive. Through all of this the East German government prided itself on balancing its budget every year.

In the nature of contradictions, many retired people whose labor was instrumental in building the East German state were not subsidized so generously and had to live on quite small pensions, some as low as three hundred marks per month. The elderly population, composed of those joining the work force in the late 1940s and retiring in the 1980s, had devoted their entire working lives to building up the country and realized few of the benefits of the society they helped create. They were often not able to travel and many never owned a car. As they retired they would receive a modest pension and could leave for West Germany if they wished, though if they did so they went as paupers. The state no longer took a great interest in them, and concern over their plight was often expressed to me. Those who had not yet made a major contribution to the workers' society were treated lavishly, it was said, while those who had made their contribution saw little reward for their life's effort.

In general, however, I had to conclude that the Marxist visionaries of East Germany had achieved a substantial degree of success in organizing their society, a society that clashed to the core with the economic foundations of Western society by removing wealth as the basis for social differentiation and access to the things society had to offer.

Given the shortages with which one was so often confronted, coupled with the absolute power of the Party over the allocation of goods and services, one would expect to see a rich culture of corruption. Yet a remarkable characteristic of East Germany was the near total lack of money corruption and personal crime in everyday life. I think these achievements can largely be traced to the limited role money played in providing for the good life. I did not once have a suspicion of corruption in dealings that affected me, nor did I observe it with others, Out of curiosity I began to ask acquaintances whether my observation was correct. Yes, indeed, it was so.

To be sure, one had to expect a fair amount of petty corruption. One often coaxed manual laborers, such as plumbers, to the job with a bottle of something, and workers tended to be more willing to moonlight when paid in West German marks. For example, a friend wanted to build a room on his house to use as a studio. He called his studio a "children's room," even though he was not planning to have more children, since the state would grant loans for children's room additions but not for rooms intended for use by adults. That was not yet corruption, merely a gambit in the best American, as well as East German, tradition. Once the loan had been received and construction begun, however, he had to find some windows for the exterior walls. He first tried contacting a window supplier in a straightforward way and was told that there would be a five-year wait for windows. Undeterred, and expecting such a response, he contacted an independent craftsman, gave him a hundred West German marks a relative had given him as a gift, and had the windows within two weeks.

In contrast to countries where money corruption was a part of everyday life, East Germany seemingly had few high rollers taking advantage of their positions to amass personal fortunes. Even with connections (the lack of which for ten years, according to the joke, being the country's stiffest sentence), one usually gained only what one needed. Other than gifts for manual workers, most corruption seemed to be limited to Party functionaries. The Upper 10,000 were widely known to live lavishly, but even so it was a modest lavishness compared with that of Third-World dictators. It was also generally believed that these people were provided with West German products for East German marks and had such things as fruits and vegetables delivered to their opulent homes in Volvograd. Such abuses were indeed revealed after the fall of the communist government, but among all the country's problems they were not considered major. When, on the other hand, at the end of 1989 East Germans learned of the private hunting reserves of the top leaders, they were incensed. I, on the other hand, could not but reflect on the tameness of such excesses.

Lesser party functionaries were believed to use their positions for personal gain, since they received priority for goods and services, but in the big picture these also were quite limited in extent. In a generally dilapidated neighborhood of Weimar one suddenly came across a new concrete street leading to a few houses in a vacant grassy area. A local Party functionary, as it turned out, was building a new house at the end of the street.

Indeed, there was resentment about such privilege. At coffee break one day the story went around of an incident in the nearby city of Erfurt. A group of high-school students had brought bananas to school and were promptly beaten up by other students. Bananas were then only available at the special shops for use by Party functionaries. If one received bananas from a visiting West German relative, one had best eat them at home.

If one wonders at the lingering Third-World admiration for communism, one reason can perhaps be found in the absence of large-scale money corruption that was found in a country like East Germany. In the eyes of the Third-World students studying in Weimar with whom I spoke, a society without rampant corruption offered a powerfully positive societal model that they believed the West, with all its talk about participatory democracy, had been poorly able to match. Thus while many East Germans saw their system as bankrupt, the Third-World students still tended to see it as a model.

Even if one were somehow to come into a great deal of money—East German money, at any rate—one would live largely within the comfortable but modest standard of East German living. It would of course be possible to buy a good used car but not a fancy dwelling. One could build a house in the countryside, but the limitation on doing so was not the amount of money one had as much as the limitation on the available materials. Prices were set for building materials, and their distribution allocated through the Party rather than by by market mechanisms. It would be possible to travel, but to exotic places such as Viet Nam it was necessary to apply for a position on a tour, just like anybody else. Having a lot of money would not have opened the possibility for independent travel to a country like North Korea, let alone France or Italy. Other trappings of wealth such as a yacht would be out of the question; there were no yachts to be had. So in the end having a lot of money would not buy one much more than having a modest amount of money did. Needless to say, medical care was free for everyone. Moving up to the high ranks of the Party certainly delivered more privilege than did more money alone, and the role of political privilege certainly helped maintain the system for some time against rising discontent. However, the truth remains that the need to hustle after ever more money was effectively removed from East German society. Indeed, once I had become used to that way of life, it engendered a certain culture shock when I returned to the West and confronted the outstretched hands that surrounded me. From the perspective of a staid, secure, comfortable but modest life for every person in the society, the East Germans had achieved what must be determined a success.

One may not wish to trade the Western plethora of goods for the East German dearth, I concluded, but something could be learned from the East German experience. People managed to accumulate things like handsome china, but because it took time they felt a deep appreciation for what they had and shared things readily. Many women dressed well, often having made their own clothing from an assortment of fabrics available in shops, and were careful about their appearance. Shopping was like a roller coaster ride, to be sure, and one had to be careful what one said in public, but through this I gleaned the emergence of a set of values difficult to maintain in Western society. When people share a modest life, where pizzas are not to be had for a telephone call, there is time to devote to friends and family. The closeness of friendships was indeed a matter of pride among many people I met. People often commented that the quality of private togetherness would certainly be lost if East Germany were to change. People knew former East Germans who had fled to the west, and somehow these people had become different. My acquaintances who had traveled to visit relatives in the West commented that certain aspects of West German life, for all its bounty, left something to be desired. The struggle for wealth and security, absent in the DDR, meant that personal relationships suffered. People became harried, more distant, more isolated from those around them.

The balance sheet between the East German model of socialist society, at least until its demise in late 1989, and Western democratic pluralism is a very complex one to draw, and it depends on one's own values. East Germans had lived under a police state, their lives and their freedom of expression closely regulated, but they also had lived in an environment where there was no unemployment, no homelessness, no strife, no hunger, no poverty, no disease, and no significant crime. Indeed, the DDR took seriously the right to work, the right to a dwelling, and the right to food, calling them "basic human rights," even though these are in fact not human rights but privileges of membership in the society. Americans choose nighttime fear over a police state, but this is a choice many East Germans would have had a difficult time imagining, despite their hopes for "freedom." Which is worse, I was asked, to fear the police, with whom one knows the bounds and the risks, or to fear whoever might be walking down the street?

The dissatisfaction that drove so many people to the streets by the end of 1989 had not to do with the material or personal level of existence as much as with the spiritual, the intellectual, the creative. A lack of consumer goods was often cited in Western media as a primary dissatisfaction, but in the end I came to believe the deeper yearning was in those other realms, and the mad buying of bananas once the Wall was opened represented only a superficial manifestation of the problems created by "actually existing socialism." To understand why many people wanted to remain in their country despite the Wall and the frustrations, hoping to wend a slow and frustrating path toward a more open society, one must understand East Germany's truly socialist accomplishments. These accomplishments would be overwhelmed by the rush to instant prosperity when the possibility of unification with West Germany was offered, but through the tumultuousness many people realized that much of the life they cherished would be discarded along with the life they disparaged. There still remained, among many East Germans of my acquaintance, an idealism about the human condition, a deeply felt belief that the society should care for all its people, and a sincere commitment that the bounty created by human action should be distributed equitably to all with nobody left to want.

19

Epilogue

B Y THE TIME I left East Germany in July of 1989, my notes bristled with conjecture about the question, Whither East Germany? Not two months after my departure, the people took to the streets and the whithering of the society began in earnest. Conclusions from my year were quickly wrested from the realm of speculation and turned into action by the East Germans themselves.

A recurring theme in my notes had to do with the nearly unfathomable complexity of attempting to maintain what the Party called the "fruits of the revolution," the good things about socialist society, while forging a nation in which the people could feel a sense of fulfillment. Short of a revolution that would bring forth another *Stunde Null,* the "Zero Hour" when the Old Order had been totally wiped away in 1945, the path through the maze would be arduous, and it would be very risky for all. By the end of the year that revolution, though peaceful, would begin to unfold.

Thus I write here an epilogue, leaving the conclusions to history. As in the rest of my narrative, I should like to report what people were thinking before the Wall was opened, because the concerns expressed in East Germany before *Die Wende,* the "turning point" of late 1989, may be important for the historical record. A structure had developed over forty years that determined the lives of sixteen million people, and many of the problems could not easily be solved. These concerns were shared by many East Germans before the Marxist-Leninist order was disrupted, though time would quickly intervene to end that East Germany of forty years. My acquaintances understood the risky future well, though they had few suggestions for its management when it arrived, even as they knew it would.

First, many expressed the belief in 1989 that the real issue on the agenda was not the future of socialism. Whether one viewed socialism as a failed experiment or the ultimate societal organization, the economic organization of the country could find its own path. The real issue was democracy or, as they said, "freedom." The challenge was to discover a means by which the people could take charge of their own destiny, away from the paternalism of the Party. Second, assuming an eventual response to the forces calling for democracy, the worried question on the minds of many was what this democratization would bring. The dilemma lay in the message of the discredited slogan "To learn from the Soviet Union is to learn triumph." If the Soviet Union no longer offered a model, what would replace it? If the opening to political opposition would lead to a continuing crisis as in Poland, if the opening to a market economy would lead to worsening economic conditions for the majority as in Hungary, if West Germany offered an unacceptable model of a "two-thirds society," the matter of deciding which future path the country should take became extremely difficult.

When I was there, right before the Wall came down, three possible scenarios were envisioned, none with pleasure. I should note that these scenarios were discussed by East Germans resolved to remain in their country, since those who had decided to leave were already pretending they were in West Germany. The first scenario was that of Romania before the fall of the Ceausescu government. When the Party conferred East Germany's highest honor, the Karl Marx Order (known locally as the Carnival Order) on Nicolae Ceausescu in 1988, the joke went around that Russian would no longer be the required foreign language in schools. All students would have to begin studying Romanian since to learn from Ceausescu's Romania was to learn triumph. Many believed one possibility to be lip service granted to reform groups until the point where those who still held the elements of physical force—the state security agents, the transport and local police, and military officers, none of whom had anything to gain from a democratic order—saw themselves seriously enough threatened to regroup and force a retrenchment into a patriarchal state on the then-existing Romanian model, even more repressive than had been the previous case in East Germany. Over the long run such a condition could not last, but the country could be destroyed before the long run arrived.

The second scenario was that of Hungary. Poland did not loom as a model, because my acquaintances uniformly believed that such chaos, at least as they viewed it, would never come to pass in Germany. In Poland one had always been allowed to walk on the grass. Hungary, on the other hand, caused worry. It had in fact already become problematic during my tenure. Despite each eagerly awaited piece of news about newfound democracy in Hungary, East Germans easily saw themselves in the picture. Their place in the picture was that of the people left behind.

The Party, when it still held exclusive political power, was most displeased by the events in Hungary. Article after article on the Hungarian situation appeared in *Neues Deutschland,* most purveying the message that Hungary's path meant a decrease in standard of living and social security. Articles in January 1989 proclaimed "The population of Hungary throughout the country reacted strongly against the planned price increases. . . ." or "The developments of 1988 were accompanied by major sacrifices by the people of Hungary. . . . On the one hand it was possible to fulfill governmental programs, but on the other the results were not sufficiently successful to support long-term development." The message was clear: the Hungarian model would lead to a high degree of instability and uncertainty with proven economic sacrifice.

Many East Germans had seen Hungary for themselves, of course, and as I noted many felt themselves to be second-class citizens unable to enjoy what the country had to offer. They went as paupers and watched the West Germans throw around their deutsche marks with the Hungarians scrambling for them like pigeons after popcorn. One person said to me, "The first thing that will happen if the system changes is that our money will be worth absolutely zip." Many feared that the comfortable economic standard that they had so long worked for would disappear in the ravages of a new "elbow society" that few knew how to handle. Numerous of my East German acquaintances, set as they were on democratization of the country, were not so certain that the Hungarian solution was worth the sacrifice. I sensed that many eyes gleamed more readily in response to my pictures of America when the people felt sheltered from actually having to live its reality.

The third scenario had to do with West Germany. For years the presence of West Germany, prosperous, free, democratic, exciting, had dominated the East German consciousness. Yet in a way the fence and prohibited zone separating the two countries, along with the "antifascist protection wall" in Berlin, served the very purpose claimed for them by the Party. They protected East Germans from West Germany. Whereas thousands of East Germans demonstrated for reunification, others viewed the new possibilities with concern. Of course, it was not known what a future East-West German association might look like. There was vague talk of some form of confederation, but what loomed most visibly was the idea of the big fish swallowing the little.

The Party had long been concerned about the specter of West Germany. One member of the Politburo rejected discussions with opposition groups in early 1989 that would consider nonsocialist alternatives for the country, with the admonition: "Consider the situation of a free-market East Germany next to a free-market West Germany. What reason would there be for East Germany to remain a separate state? There would be none." On the other hand, even some of my acquaintances who followed the technical data of the latest model Volkswagen or the political discussions in Bonn as if they were their own, viewed the possibility of some opening up to West Germany with concern. The feeling may be best explained by returning to my zoo metaphor. West Germany was seen as so dominant, so successful in all its dealings with the world that a West German involvement in East Germany might equate to a form of invasion. There was little excitement about giving up their status as zoo animals for Western tourists if it were only to become zoo animals for Western investors. With their wealth and competitive skills the West Germans would quickly take over the management of the zoo. Even if released from their cages, as it were, East Germans would become the cage cleaners. They would tend to fill the lesser positions of society, becoming second-class citizens in their own country. East German acquaintances who visited Hungary in 1989 and witnessed the wrenching effects of West German currency flooding into that country could see it coming.

In short, despite the intense discussions about the future of the country, I sensed a deep-seated concern among the people with whom I associated, people out in the provinces away from Berlin, that none of the possible scenarios provided a vision of the future one could believe in. In addition, they had little clear idea of how to achieve whatever future was in store for the country. Yet one could certainly not believe in the present either; one could no longer live with the status quo.

When the first workers' and farmers' state on German soil unraveled in late 1989, the adrenalin of power to the people overwhelmed these concerns and replaced them with hundreds of thousands of feet and voices proclaiming that the unknown future must be realized, that the socialist order must go. As I observed the demonstrations from my haven in Montana, I could at least rest assured that none of the three scenarios would probably come to pass. The only law of history one can count on is that it never turns out the way one anticipates, and the hastily organized unification with West Germany in 1990 would end differently than anyone could foresee.

Students in Weimar sometimes asked me about American "freedom." What was, they wanted to know, this elusive quality that Americans wished to transport around the world, and how did it differ from chaos? I responded with the analogy of the fist and the nose. Freedom, I said, is the right to swing your fist around any way you want to, until it meets my nose. At that point your freedom abruptly stops. For all its imperfections, American society is characterized by continuing discussions about where one's fist ends and where another's nose begins, whether it be the right to have an abortion or the right to bear arms. When the students asked me what I thought of East Germany, I reminded them of their good nature. For all the problems and oppression they had suffered, East Germans kept smiling, never turning on each other in the violence that political frustrations often cause. I expressed my deep admiration for their personal openness and willingness to help one another. I also reminded them of their country's achievements in caring for all the people, helping those who might otherwise fall through the cracks to enjoy the bounties of the society as well, and told them they should never leave these things behind. East German life had not been orchestrated by some supernatural influence, I suggested, but by people who had succumbed to an all-too-human trait to believe in a single, all-powerful truth that one should impose on others. The instruments of this imposition were clear: the oppression of the thoughts and actions of those who believed otherwise. Society is at its best when we are all able to swing our arms around until we almost, but not quite, hit someone else's nose. For this to happen in East Germany, I told them, everyone must actively participate in the discussions of where fists end and noses begin, without the burden of pre-chewed values or governing ideology, and everyone must have the opportunity to discover how all the East German fists and noses might live to the fullest. History does not hold the answer, I said. You do.

Paul Gleye is an associate professor in the School of Architecture, Montana State University. His articles have appeared in United States, Canadian, and German journals, and his book *The Architecture of Los Angeles* was published in 1981. In 1988–89 he lived in East Germany under a Fulbright teaching grant.